S0-DUU-419

Aboriginal Sites, Right and Resource Development

Academy of the Social Sciences in Australia

FIFTH ACADEMY SYMPOSIUM
11 November, 1981
Proceedings

Aboriginal Sites, Rights and Resource Development

Edited by

RONALD M. BERNDT

Published for the
Academy of the Social Sciences in Australia
by
University of Western Australia Press
Perth, 1982

First published in 1982
for the
Academy of the Social Sciences in Australia
by
The University of Western Australia Press
Nedlands, Western Australia

Agents: Eastern States of Australia, New Zealand, Papua New Guinea: Melbourne University Press, Carlton South, Vic. 3053; U.K., Europe, Africa, Middle East: Peter Moore, P.O. Box 66, 200a Perne Road, Cambridge CB1 3PD, England; U.S.A., Canada, the Caribbean: International Scholarly Book Services Inc., P.O. Box 1632, Beaverton, Oregon 97075 U.S.A.

Wholly produced in Western Australia

Photosetting and origination by University of Western Australia Press.
Printed by Frank Daniels Pty Ltd and bound by Printers Trade Services.

This book is copyright. Apart from any fair dealing for the purposes of private study, research, criticism or review, as permitted under the Copyright Act, no part may be reproduced by any process without written permission. Enquiries should be made to the publisher.

© Academy of the Social Sciences in Australia 1982

National Library of Australia Cataloguing-in-Publication data

Academy of the Social Sciences in Australia.
Symposium. (5th: 1981: Canberra, A.C.T.)
  Aboriginal sites, rights and resource development.

  Includes bibliographies.
  ISBN 0 85564 221 1.

  [1]. Aborigines, Australian—Land tenure—
  Congresses. 2. Mineral industries—Australia—
  Congresses. 3. Mines and mineral resources—
  Australia—Congresses. I. Berndt, Ronald M.
  (Ronald Murray), 1916- . II. Title.

332.2'0994

Organizing Committee
for the Symposium on
**ABORIGINAL SITES AND RIGHTS, AND THE
IMPACT OF RESOURCE DEVELOPMENT**

Professor R. M. Berndt (Convenor)
Professor R. T. Appleyard   Professor G. C. Bolton
Professor Fay Gale   Professor C. D. Rowley
Dr L. R. Hiatt

General Note

Neither the editor nor the Fellows of the Academy of the Social Sciences in Australia are responsible for individual opinions expressed by the contributors to this volume.

Contents

Preface

Each year at the occasion of its Annual General Meeting, the Academy of the Social Sciences in Australia holds a symposium on a topic felt to be of current national significance. The first four such symposia were:

Social Science and Public Policy (1976)
Youth Unemployment (1977) (proceedings published)
Trade Unions and the Law (1979)
Refugees: The Challenge of the Future (1980) (proceedings published)

The fifth symposium, held in 1981, was entitled *Aboriginal Sites and Rights, and the Impact of Resource Development*. This topic was chosen because it involved issues which are now, and which are likely to remain, of national significance for those concerned both with the preservation of Aboriginal culture and the welfare of Aboriginal society and with reasonable economic development of the nation's resources. The symposium brought together those who had studied closely all aspects of these problems and aimed to find the consensus between traditional concepts and practices and developmental objectives.

The Academy expresses its appreciation of the work of the Organizing Committee, the Speakers and Discussants; and particularly to Professor Ron Berndt, Convenor of the Committee, who also accepted the task of editing the contributed papers and discussion for publication.

Academy of the Social Sciences in Australia
Canberra

K. J. HANCOCK
President

Contributors

The Hon. Mr Peter Baume: then Federal Minister for Aboriginal Affairs.

*Dr Catherine H. Berndt: Department of Anthropology, the University of Western Australia.

*Emeritus Professor Ronald M. Berndt: Honorary Research Fellow in Anthropology, the University of Western Australia.

*Professor Geoffrey C. Bolton: School of Social Inquiry, Murdoch University, Western Australia.

*Dr H. C. Coombs: Centre for Resource and Environmental Studies, Australian National University, Canberra.

Mrs Priscilla Girrabul: Gunbalanya Community, Oenpelli, western Arnhem Land, Northern Territory.

*Dr L. R. Hiatt: then Chairman of the Australian Institute of Aboriginal Studies; Department of Anthropology, University of Sydney.

Ms Sue Kesteven: Social Impact of Uranium Mining (N.T.), Australian Institute of Aboriginal Studies.

Mr Wesley Lanhupuy: Manager, Bureau of the Northern Land Council, Northern Territory.

Mr H. M. Morgan: President, Mining Industry of Australia.

Mr Charles Perkins: Chairman, Aboriginal Development Commission, Canberra.

Professor B. L. Sansom: Department of Anthropology, the University of Western Australia.

Professor Colin Tatz: Chair of Politics, Macquarie University, North Ryde, New South Wales.

Dr John von Sturmer: Director, Social Impact of Uranium Mining (N.T.), Australian Institute of Aboriginal Studies.

* FELLOWS OF THE ACADEMY

Foreword

The chapters of this book were presented in their summarized form at a symposium entitled *Aboriginal sites and rights, and the impact of resource development*. This symposium, arranged by an organizing committee appointed by the Academy of the Social Sciences in Australia, was held in the Coombs Lecture Theatre, Australian National University on 11 November 1981, as one of the functions of the Academy's annual general meeting.

The symposium was opened by the then President of the Academy (Professor A. G. L. Shaw) and divided into four panels, each under a chairperson. Panel 1, on Contemporary-traditional Aboriginal perspectives of the land and its resources, was chaired by Professor C. D. Rowley; panel 2, on the Impact of resource development on Aborigines, by Professor W. R. Geddes; panel 3, on Economic and socio-political perspectives, by Professor G. C. Bolton; and panel 4, on an Overview, by Professor Fay Gale. For the purpose of this book, the panel titles have been dropped, and the order in which the contributions were given has been changed. The full versions of the papers presented at the symposium are given here. Some have been revised in part by the authors, and all have been edited to conform to the overall concept of the book. Professor B. L. Sansom, who was unable to be present at the symposium, has been able to have his paper included here. However, Dr N. Peterson of the Australian National University, who spoke at the symposium, was unable to complete his paper for inclusion. Ms Sue Kesteven, although she did not speak at the symposium, was kind enough to help Mrs Priscilla Girrabul to complete her contribution, and has added a commentary of her own. It seemed appropriate also to have a final overview which pinpoints some of the problems relevant to the topic of this book, and focuses on Western Australia in order to explore these; this has been added by the editor. The whole symposium was recorded on tape; however, it has not been possible to reproduce the opening remarks of the Academy's President, and of the Panel chairpersons, and the discussion which followed each paper from the body of the audience.

This book concerns one of the most insistent challenges in today's Australian scene: the need to understand what land means to Aborigines—land as a concept, and land as an empirical part of ordinary living. The protection of Aboriginal sites of significance, and recognition of Aboriginal rights to and in land, pose difficulties in the face of conflicting views and interests. These stem not so much from what Aborigines themselves have said about such matters, but primarily from European attitudes toward economic growth and the use of environmental resources. Both Aborigines and other Australians are, of necessity, concerned with economic survival. Aborigines, however, see other elements as equally relevant. Issues of social and personal welfare go beyond economic well-being in the narrow sense in which that phrase is often used. That is not sufficiently appreciated by people who, because of their other commitments, are removed from the more severe and traumatic impact of intrusion into areas still regarded by Aborigines as their own.

Difficulties are compounded by the lack of uniformity in state and federal governmental policies, and lack of common agreement on procedures in regions where, for instance, mining is planned or is taking place. They came to a head only a little over a decade ago. Since then they have loomed large in the minds of all Australians—but particularly of Aborigines. As our Australian economy is shifting quite markedly toward a resource-based, technologically more complex industrial orientation, and Aborigines are well within the front line of these developments, the need to resolve differing ideas and expectations is of fundamental concern to us all.

In this book the various contributors outline some of the facts, from anthropological, social historical, economic, political and legal perspectives, and, not least, the implications for the future.

I take this opportunity to thank the then President of the Academy (Professor A. G. L. Shaw) and the Executive Director (Professor W. D. Borrie), and Mrs Erica Harriss (Secretary) for the considerable help they gave before and during the actual symposium. I also wish to thank members of the organizing committee (Professors R. T. Appleyard, G. C. Bolton, C. D. Rowley and Dr L. R. Hiatt, and particularly Professor Fay Gale) and all the contributors who so readily prepared and in several cases revised their material. Mrs Harriss retyped some of the articles and arranged others to ensure uniformity of format; and Miss M. Tomkins (of the Department of Anthropology, University of Western Australia) undertook the original task of typing this series. Mr J. E. Stanton (Curator, Anthropology Museum, University of Western Australia) organized the preparation of the maps and chart which appear in Senator Baume's paper: these were originally colour transparencies. Mr Stanton also helped with the technical tasks involved in preparing the manuscript for press production. Especially, I should note the help of my wife, Dr Catherine Berndt, in the final editing of this volume. However, I must take full responsibility for editing all the contributions.

RONALD M. BERNDT

TRADITIONAL CONCEPTS OF ABORIGINAL LAND

RONALD M. BERNDT

Aborigines occupied without challenge virtually every part of the Australian continent and its adjacent islands for a still not finally estimated period, but one that is well in excess of 40,000 years. Now, in a short span of less than 200 years, that picture has changed almost beyond recognition. The pervasive settlement of Australia by a different population, mainly from Europe, destroyed many socio-cultural systems and affected all the survivors in one way or another, some quite drastically. For others, the full impact of that contact came later. We can, therefore, speak of some present-day Aboriginal groups as being traditionally-oriented -- oriented toward their own, Aboriginal traditions -- because an appreciable amount of that life continues.

Because of this past history, which involved a reversal of their independent status, as well as displacement from their territories, land-occupational patterns have changed. Despite that, the fact of Aboriginal occupation of their land is not a main issue: that is too well documented to need further discussion here. Rather, what concerns us is how Aborigines occupied their land, the relationships they constructed vis-à-vis specific stretches of land, and the organization they developed to cope with it and with getting a living from it.

Since I am focusing mostly on existing traditionally-oriented Aboriginal societies, it is necessary to add that I am not saying that such societies have come down into the present encapsulated, unchanged, in their traditional mantle. Aboriginal societies in the past were subject to internal change: but such change was probably limited by two major factors -- religion, and natural environment. Social organization revolved around these two aspects.

Land as a resource for living:

Life came from and through the land, and was manifested in the land.
The land was not an inanimate 'thing': it was, and is, 'alive'. Stanner
wrote (1965a:217) about Aboriginal religion being 'vibrant with life'. The
precious essence we call 'life' came out of the Dreaming, mediated through
deities and spirit beings, and sustained in its material form by what the land
had to offer. Physical birth in itself was a ritual, though mostly without
embellishments. Death was a ritual celebration of the transformation of life
back into the Dreaming, for eventual return. The process was comparable with
the coming and going of the seasons, like environmental renewal of resources
for living. Men and women and children were among those resources, intimately
bound up with the land. Land was thus pivotal to Aboriginal existence.

Aboriginal religion was, and is, essentially land-minded and land-centred.
Deities as mythic beings are specifically linked with land, with particular
places and sites. Their adventures as told in song and myth, and as danced
out in ritual, covered all aspects of the land over which they travelled,
shaping, naming and humanizing what there is within that land today; and in
the course of this they left part of their own spiritual substance at certain
places. But more than this, in their shape-changing capacity, they are
responsible for and manifested through natural species, including human beings.

Aboriginal social systems traditionally included, and include, a three-
dimensional model that provides a blue-print for living. It hinges on relationships between people and land, between people and deities, and between people
-- enmeshed in an interactory frame which, ideally, stipulates interdependence
within and between each set of relationships. Because of that, in all
traditional Aboriginal societies we can distinguish a hard core of basic
assumptions, or imperatives, which have retained their significance in varying
degrees, through all the vicissitudes of alien contact. It is this continuing
firmness or 'hardness', almost uncompromising as it were, that seemed to
provide justification for outsiders categorizing Aborigines as being

conservative and not amenable to change. That interpretation is only partially true. There is plenty of evidence of innovation, of readiness to accept 'new' things and ideas -- within an established framework, but to some extent serving to modify that framework. (See R. Berndt 1980: 281-96; 1982.)

The general position:

Returning to the essential ingredient of land. Aborigines were utterly dependent on the land and on all it could provide. To cope with this circumstance, they developed a kind of social organization that would enable them to use their natural environment successfully so that their expectations could be sustained in relation to it. In their case, this meant the harnessing of the supernatural (or 'spiritual', a term which seems to be increasingly used in this connection) to the material. The less in the way of technical equipment people can draw on for utilizing their environmental resources, and screening or cushioning the processes involved in doing so, the greater the opportunities for religious growth, and the more dependent they are on the non-empirical. Concomitantly, there is more obvious need for a social milieu which will ensure maximal cooperation. Aborigines managed to achieve this by having structured in their social systems two complementary kinds of units, or groups, each with differing criteria of membership and differing spheres of responsibility. One is the territorial unit, the other the socio-economic unit.

The territorial unit:

The territorial unit may well be referred to by other terms such as a local descent group, or a clan. Membership, both male and female, of such a unit is recruited through a charter of descent, in a primary sense -- most commonly through patrilineal descent; in some other cases, more rarely through matrilineal descent. Recognized genealogical linkage between such persons is significant in determining membership of this kind of unit. (See R. and C. Berndt 1981: 135-43.)

The basic reference is to a specifically designated stretch of land (Stanner 1965b: 1-26, called it an estate) to which its members are linked spiritually; the boundaries of such a unit are not necessarily firm. That land contains places associated with mythic beings, or deities, who in the Dreaming left part of themselves there when they passed through it, or ended their journey within it. Special topographic features, therefore, are located within that territory. They indicate that, through the metamorphosis or some other action or transformation of a deity, part of an essential life-giving substance remains embedded or attached to the material representation and, what is important, is accessible to members of that unit. This unit is, therefore, based on a religious understanding and has religious responsibilities. Its members hold in company particular mythological knowledge and are responsible for carrying out relevant ritual, part of which is focused on species-renewal -- the perpetuation of species associated with the particular mythic beings linked with that territory.

A varying number of similarly constituted land-holding units made up a wider constellation -- one that has sometimes been called a 'tribe'; but these days it is perhaps more appropriately referred to as a language unit, provided dialectal variations are taken into account. Cooperation between members of these contiguous units was a prerequisite for the performance of ritual, where the issue of ownership is paramount. In other words, members of each such unit were responsible for attending, ritually, to the species mythically associated with their own land. It was on this basis that the ideal of land ownership, and ownership of what the land contained, was defined and vested in the living representatives of particular mythic beings. The land was not viewed as a commodity, but as a religious and spiritual as well as an economic resource. It was inalienable and non-transferable, held in trust for the mythic beings, and for human beings: for the dead as well as for the living, and for future generations.

Personal rights:

With this in mind, it will be recalled that I spoke of 'the ideal of land ownership'. The traditional picture seems to have approximated closely to that.   However, it also provided for what I call 'secondary rights'. In the consideration of land-rights submissions in the Northern Territory, emphasis has been placed on the first. But, as far as I can gather, there has also been, both directly and indirectly, recognition of other, 'multi-affiliatory' rights. (See R. Berndt 1981: 12, but particularly Note 4.) To understand this more clearly it is necessary to focus on kin relationships on one hand, and sites on the other. In doing so, I do not think we detract from the hard fact of what constitutes an owned 'parcel' of land. I think it is quite appropriate to speak of a 'parcel' of land, which is an estate of a local territorial descent unit. The major issue here is how resources within that land were disposed of -- the degree of sharing by others who were not recognized as members of that estate. I will take this matter up a little later.

Rights to land, in traditional terms, are stipulated as being relevant to a number of persons who are related primarily in patrilineal terms and in a charter of descent. There are cases of adoption where, for various reasons, a person originally belonging to a unit other than the one in which he/she is accepted is recognized as a full member with proprietory rights. In my experience, however, such instances have been rare. In general terms, it is land possessed by a group of people who not only share it but collectively hold it in trust. The ranks of membership are virtually closed, except in special circumstances. These circumstances usually involve limited rights on a personal basis. They may be substantiated, for instance, through a person's mother and mother's brother, or a mother's mother's brother whose estate would be different from that of a mother's brother. In some cases the tie between grandchildren and matri-grandparents is especially strong, and concerned with particular religious commitments. A person's stake in the land of such close kin, while not usually regarded as primary, is certainly important, and something that must be taken into account.

Or, to take another example. Such a problem is raised -- most notably in the Western Desert, but also elsewhere -- in connection with spiritual 'conception' resulting from some act on the part of a mythic being, or by an agent of that mythic being, in relation to a pregnant woman. An event of this kind, which can take many different forms, is believed to be responsible for animating the foetus in a potential mother -- bringing life, which comes from the Dreaming. In many cases, but not necessarily in all, the mythic being responsible resides spiritually at a particular site, or his or her agent is locally identified. Because of the semi-nomadic nature of traditional Aboriginal living, there was always the likelihood of foetal 'animation' occurring outside the territory of the land-owning group to which the father belonged -- however desirable it might be, in particular cases, for that event to take place within it. A special and personal relationship exists between the child who is eventually born, and his/her animator and its relevant site or area. Aboriginal words designate that relationship, which has been called conception or birth 'totemism'. A further implication is that the person involved in that relationship has also a personal stake, not only in regard to the appropriate site, but in the group territory in which that site is located.

The pivotal significance of sites:

Such sites of mythic significance are always important in determining the religious affiliations of persons associated with them, even if the sites are located outside the territory of their fathers' estates. Claims on this kind of personal basis were, and are, traditionally recognized.

Traditionally, and in all cases over the years where questions of land ownership have been discussed, sites are considered to be pivotal features in defining specific areas of land and, in so doing, indicating by their mythic associations the kinds of persons who should primarily belong to that land.

Ownership, therefore, is not ratified simply by making a claim to land, even though substantiating genealogical information may be available. A major issue is _knowing_ that particular land -- knowing about the sites, their songs and rituals. Knowledge of such sites and territory traditionally constituted the basis of an Aboriginal's primary identity. Further, there is the question of tending that land, of 'looking after it'. The land is a living thing, the source of all life, and the mythic deities who symbolize that land and its inherent life-giving properties need to be nurtured. The implications of this view are far-reaching in the present-day situation, where cultural knowledge has been considerably modified.

However, in so far as sites are concerned, it must be remembered that not all of them are sacred, except in so far as the _whole_ land has a sacred quality. They are in many cases graded according to their mytho-ritual importance. They range, for instance, from secret-sacred (with limited access) to open-sacred. Some are of direct ritual concern; others may not be. Moreover, the concept of 'secret-sacred' is not an absolute one with regard to ritual matters and gradations of knowledge. And there are other categories of site -- for instance, places of danger, places of historical relevance, ritual grounds, and so forth. One thing, however, is clear. Religious sites cannot just be 'made up' willynilly. They are embedded in the matrix of mytho-ritual patterning and, traditionally, a wealth of knowledge was associated with each of them. Their importance cannot be over-estimated.

The concept of 'country':

I said before that members of a territorial unit, a local descent group, are concerned, among other things, with sustaining and spiritually renewing those species manifested through the mythic characters within their own territory. This task is not undertaken solely for themselves, but also for others. Each local descent group possessed some sites -- at least one -- that contained the nuclei of the life essence of particular species. When such power is released by a ritual act, this ensures the procreation and distribution of particular creatures etc. over the land. More or less similar ritual acts are carried out by members of other territorial groups, in relation to the same or different species. Thus there is a cooperative network between a limited number of similarly structured groups.

On the other hand, we come back to the second kind of unit or group that I mentioned. Members from several of these local descent units would combine to form small land-utilizing groups. They hunted and collected food over one another's territories; their movements and the size of the group depended on seasonal fluctuation. This wider area over which they moved, and which all of them knew intimately -- both topographically and resource-wise, including water, as well as in its mythological associations -- provides a concept of 'country' in an expanded sense, as a broader facet of identification in socio-personal terms. This was 'country' over which, in addition to the territory of their local descent groups, they had resource rights. In expressing this in a generalized way as 'my country', Aborigines were emphasizing the matter of social interaction and cooperation, because all persons traditionally involved in such an economic group would be related to one another; and that, in turn, would involve a network of responsibilities. It would not have been possible, under the conditions of semi-nomadic living, for members of a local descent group to obtain sustenance simply from the resources of its own territory. Apart from that, there is the question of local descent group exogamy: although wives shared with their husbands, they did not relinquish their rights in their own local descent groups.

While there were restrictions on access to particular sites, people would normally move fairly freely over the territories of their own and other local descent groups, within a certain range, and use the resources available, with some exceptions. Traditionally, resources are for sharing, in an assortment of ways, including gift exchange and trading relationships; but they are also owned, in a mythic and religious sense, by members of local descent groups responsible for their spiritual procreation and growth or presence in the land. This is in no way contradictory when we take into account cooperation as the accepted basis of social interaction. So, the idea of 'country' expresses socio-economic commitment. An Aboriginal is as much a part of it as he or she is a part of his or her own religiously defined territory.

Conclusion:

To summarize, then. Traditionally, from an Aboriginal standpoint, all land was, and is, sacred -- sacred because the deities shaped it, humanized it and put within it the resources it now contains. Moreover, the presence of deities in the land is symbolized by the sites: sites which are spiritually alive, a constant source of protection and reassurance for the future -- no matter how difficult the present may appear to be. They represent a spiritual resource. It is that land which Aborigines held in trust for the deities and for future generations. They did this by spreading responsibility for it among people who are attached to specific territories, bound to them by strong ties of descent, and in many cases regarded as living representatives of the deities.

Thus members of such a group hold the land collectively or are in possession of it and are responsible for caring for it. In our terms, they are the primary owners. Nevertheless, others, by virtue of a particular relationship to one of these owners, or through the accident of birth or reported conception at a particular place, also have a personal stake in that land and in its religious associations. While this did not constitute 'ownership' in the primary sense, it did mean that some rights were involved. But it is not a bond which is transferable: it is specifically personal and cannot be handed on to any other person.

However, people were and still are dependent on others for resources, of which some are owned by members of local descent groups but are shared with others as a recognized right and obligation, and in the spirit of cooperation; and those resources are obtained from a fairly large area which is _also_ regarded as 'their country'. This means in effect, two dimensions of ownership, which are based on religious and economic factors.

The first concerns, without doubt, land which is now subject most consistently to land rights claims. Such claims are usually exclusive, framed in mytho-ritual terms by persons related to that land in defined ways. The other concerns the economic aspect. This refers more particularly to the issue of resource sharing, or the sharing of rights in and to such resources -- which did not and do not imply simply food resources. The religious and the economic were always, traditionally, complementary; but they have also been conceptualized in terms of what could be called exclusive as contrasted with inclusive rights. In 'inclusive' rights, that are spread more widely, more people are involved -- all those persons who regard themselves and who are recognized by others as belonging to 'one country'. This is the largest area over which, if not the people now living, then their parents and grandparents, hunted and collected food as an inalienable right. One implication, therefore, relates to the present scene of resource development. While royalties, as in the Northern Territory, may be paid to members of a territorial unit from whose land minerals, for instance, have been extracted, there is no real recognition in this respect of other persons who would traditionally have shared in those resources, equally with the more specific or primary land-owners.

My concern here has been with the traditional Aboriginal picture. While much has changed, much also remains, the traditional past continuing on into the present. Even in areas where rights to land in the terms I have discussed can no longer be demonstrated, what still can be, mostly, recognized is the idea of 'my country' and what that implies: the wider constellation of 'belonging', including rights in and to the land and its resources. That is, an emphasis is placed quite rightly on the economic side of such a claim -- which may perhaps be more directly relevant these days than is the religious dimension.

REFERENCES

Berndt, R.M.   1980 Looking back into the present: a changing panorama in eastern Arnhem Land, Anthropological Forum, Vol. IV, Nos. 3-4.

Berndt, R.M.   1981 A long view: some personal comments on land rights, Australian Institute of Aboriginal Studies Newsletter, No.16.

Berndt, R.M.   1982 Looking ahead through the past. The Wentworth Lecture, Australian Institute of Aboriginal Studies, Canberra. (Forthcoming.)

Berndt, R.M. and C.H.   1981   The World of the First Australians. Lansdowne Press, Sydney.

Stanner, W.E.H.   1965 a Religion, Totemism, and Symbolism. In Aboriginal Man in Australia. (R.M. and C.H. Berndt eds). Angus and Robertson, Sydney.

Stanner, W.E.H.   1965 b Aboriginal territorial organization: estate, range, domain and regime, Oceania, Vol. XXXVI, No. 1.

TRADITIONAL ATTITUDES TO LAND RESOURCES

L.R. HIATT

In considering 'land resources' I include in my discussion resources of
the sea and waterways. To omit them would be to ignore a vitally important
component in the subsistence economy of coastal and riverine Aborigines around
the continent. Furthermore, exploitation of marine resources by European
fishermen in northern waters has become increasingly vexatious to Aborigines
and looms as a political issue of some importance. By resources, therefore,
I mean those naturally-occurring things that Aborigines traditionally valued
and sought. In the most general terms, they comprised organic species and
inorganic materials judged to be edible, potable, useful, or otherwise
desirable.

The question in what degree access to resources depended upon ownership of
the land on which they occurred has proved to be one of the most controversial
matters in Australian ethnography. Without implying that the issue has been
finally settled, it could be said that whereas earlier writers tended to
represent land and resources as a single territorial package, recent ethnograph-
ers have dwelt on the distinctive principles and attitudes to which they are
respectively subject.

With regard to the ownership of land, three questions arise: (1) Who are
the acknowledged owners? (2) What are they said to own? (3) What is the
nature of their title? The standard short answers are: (1) Patrilineal
descent groups; (2) Sacred sites; (3) Mystical charter. Amplifications
and qualifications are required in each case.

First, it has become increasingly apparent that, in addition to patrilineal
descent, matrifilial and other non-agnatic links to land are important over
large areas of the continent, entailing rights and obligations of shared
custodianship if not of joint ownership. A man typically proclaims a deeply-felt
attachment to the land of his mother; and the same sentiment may be extended

(though less ardently) to the land of his mother's mother and that of his mother's father. It also appears that prolonged residence may in itself be a qualification for ownership, regardless of descent; and that in certain places and circumstances particular parts of the landscape may be owned by individuals, as distinct from corporations.

Second, while the ownership of sacred sites is normally unequivocal, that of the unnamed intervening tracts tends to be less firmly declared and at various points indeterminate. In general, the concept of territorial bounderies is not well developed. The proportion of designated to undesignated areas depends to a large extent on geographical and ecological factors. Named sites in desert regions, for instance, act as isolated reference points in an other-wise featureless expanse. In more densely-populated and topographically-diverse coastal regions, by contrast, they make up a much greater part of the total estate; and, in addition, the intervening tracts, being relatively small, them-selves often bear names.

Third, ownership of land is typically seen as dependent upon ownership of symbols representing or emanating from ancestral powers (icons, designs, songs, dances, ceremonies, and so on). Because the creative acts of the heroes were particular rather than generalized, and because the mythological record of their movements over the landscape is detailed and definite, ritualized affirmations of ties between man and land tend to be topographically specific rather than diffuse.

Let us now turn to resources. Probably everywhere in Aboriginal Australia the highest secular value is generosity. Readiness to share with others is the main measure of a man's goodness, and hospitality an essential source of his self-esteem. As Aboriginal children seem as demanding and self-centred as children anywhere, the altruism of adults is most plausibly explained, not as a natural propensity, but as the outcome of a programme of moral education in which greed is condemned and magnanimity extolled. It is likely that this pervasive and highly-developed ethic of generosity emerged as a cultural adaptation to the exigencies of hunting and gathering, and conceivably conferred improved fitness on those who adopted it.

The ethic of generosity applies primarily to resources, and only indirectly or (at a certain level) not at all to land. Ideally, estates are inalienable, indivisible, and non-transferable. Rights in relation to land (e.g. those governing the performance of a particular ritual celebrating the mystical association of a particular creator with a particular sacred site) are strictly defined on the basis of descent or filiation, and tend to be circumscribed and jealously guarded. Such possessiveness is not normally extended to the resources of an estate. Here, on the contrary, magnanimity is the operative principle, to the extent that access and benefit are normally accorded as a matter of course to a wide network of tribesmen over and above the actual owners. Despite assertions to the contrary in the older literature, notions of trespass are in my estimation poorly-developed or non-existent, being submerged or nullified by an over-riding ethic of hospitality and open-handedness.

This is not to say that generosity is either indiscriminate or unlimited. Degrees of open-handedness bear a rough correspondence to degrees of relatedness (i.e. the closer the kin, the more unconditional and ungrudging the willingness to share). Generosity is no doubt also conditioned by considerations of security and abundance, which in turn depend on seasonality, spatial distribution, accessibility, and so on.

The Blyth River example:

To illustrate the foregoing abstractions, I describe the situation among the Gidjingali of the northern Arnhem Land coast, whom I have known since 1958. At that time they numbered about 300, and they were divided into 19 land-owning groups. I shall begin by giving a detailed account of the estate of one such group, with whose members I became closely associated.

The estate is located on the coast about 4 kilometres west of the mouth of the Blyth River. The total area, of approximately 2 square kilimetres, contains

15 named locations, as shown in Table 1 and on Map 1.[1] The estate as a whole

is called Djunawunya, which is also the name of a specific part of it, viz. a

large central area consisting of an extensive recurved chenier and a fresh-

water swamp (1a, 1b). Seven sites are believed to have been created by super-

natural powers. Fishtrap (2, 13, 14) is a giant counterpart of the conical

cane-trap said to live under the sea north of the Djunawunya coastline (though

it is also believed that He is buried in a grave under a blow-out near the

eastern end of the estate, formed when He cut through the dune "like a plough",

and then expired). Fishtrap and Kingfisher (8,9) are exclusive to Djunawunya

(at least among the Gidjingali), while Water Goanna (3) is an important

creator elsewhere. Fishtrap is the estate's main symbol of identity, while

Water Goanna links it with certain others.

The people of eastern Arnhem Land believe that everything in the universe

belongs (at least in principle) to one or other of two divisions name dua

and yirritja. Sites, their owners, and their creators belong to the same

moiety, in the present case dua. It will be noted that one of the sites shown

on Map 1 viz. Munanamirra-adjirrapa (15) is separated from the rest by part

of an adjoining yirritja estate. Ownership of land in different places is not

uncommon in Arnhem Land and presumably represents some aspect of flux, such as

the acquisition of deceased estates. Frank Gurmanamana, my main collaborator

and a Djunawunya man himself, was unable to offer an historical interpretation

in the case of Munanamirra-adjirrapa, although he conceded that it might once

have belonged to a now-extinct clan. His explanation was mythological:

Flounder (munanamirra) emerged from the sea, created Munanamirra-adjirrapa

(Flounder-stood-here), then returned to live with Fishtrap.

The remaining eight named areas are not attributed to specific acts of

creation, though in one case (Mumordon-gitj, 10) Fishtrap is said to have

conferred the name. The tree indicated at 11b is the beach camping site

	NAME	DESCRIPTION	DIMENSIONS	CREATOR
1	Djunawunya	(a) recurved chenier	.5 sq km	
		(b) freshwater swamp	.15 sq km	
2	Malaba	freshwater creek and swamp	1 km	Fishtrap
3	Djindjinganda	small rain forest and spring	.01 sq km	Water Goanna
4	Djinamurra	small rain forest	.02 sq km	
5	Marraburda-ayurra	southern tip of recurved chenier		
6	Gugalburr	grassland, inundated during wet season		
7	Manadjilaburna	wet season channel	1 km	
8	Djon-djindjirrapa	drainage outlet from freshwater swamp (1b)		Kingfisher
9	Guwarrawurda	high-tide salt flat	.006 sq km	Kingfisher
10	Mumordon-gitj	portion of recurved chenier enclosed by trees to form 'pocket'	.0003 sq km	
11	Djanbi-madjirrapa	(a) high-tide salt flat	.04 sq km	
		(b) old tree (Scaevola taccada)		
12	Djunawinba	high-tide salt flat	.07 sq km	
13	Bulga-bulga	blow-out through dune		Fishtrap
14	Manangurramba	(a) recurved chenier	.03 sq km	Fishtrap
		(b) section of adjacent tidal creek	1.3 km	
15	Munanamirra-adjirrapa	recurved chenier	.07 sq km	Flounder

TABLE 1   Djunawunya named sites

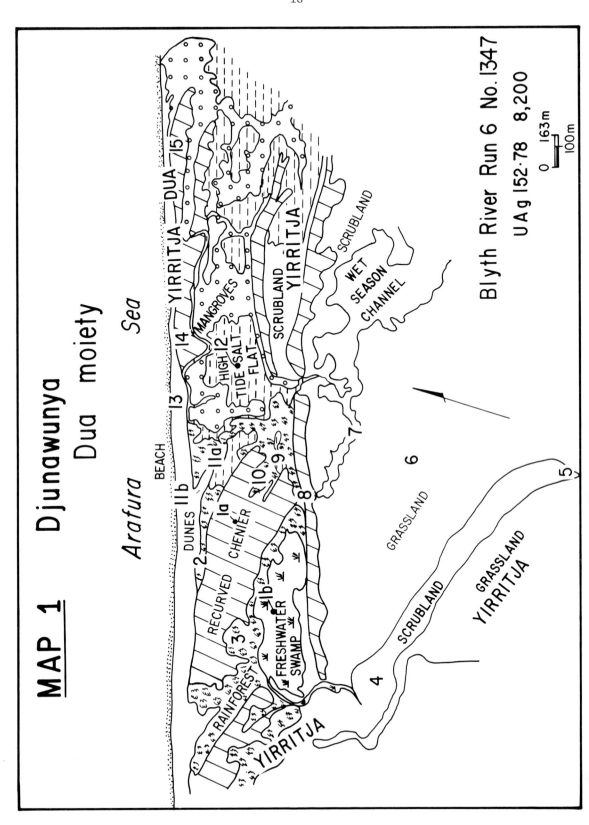

MAP 1   Djunawunya

Dua moiety

Arafura Sea

Blyth River Run 6 No. 1347

UAg 152·78   8,200

0   163m
     100m

of a colony of spirit men (Marawal), who also have a home out to sea and
who may be seen travelling by torchlight between the two places.

While patrilineal descent has been an important factor in determining the
present ownership of Djunawunya, it has not been the only one. The
acknowledged owners of the estate are the members of three patrilineal groups
named Kalamagondiya, Karrapam, and Milingawa, which for convenience I shall
refer to as PG1, PG2, and PG3. In 1960 they contained 25, 6, and 4 members
respectively, giving a total of 35 (19 males, 16 females). It would appear
that this tripartite situation arose not as a result of growth and division
but through amalgamation. It is important to appreciate how it came about.

PG1 may be considered as the original owner, in as much as its
association with the estate is longer than that of either PG2 or PG3. PG2 was
previously part of a small inland dialect group. Early this century, one
of its few remaining members married a woman from a _yirritja_ estate adjacent
to Djunawunya and chose to live with his wife's people. His children grew
up in the region and came to be associated with Djunawunya. Today their
descendants (i.e. the living members of PG2) are regarded as co-owners. The
circumstances in which PG3 came to share ownership were much the same, except
that in this case the husband who chose uxorilocal residence came from a
coastal estate about 15 kilometres east of the mouth of the Blyth River.

To complicate matters further, FG, the oldest living male member of
PG1, is a member not by birth but by adoption. His father, who belonged
to an inland dialect group, married a woman from a _yirritja_ estate on the
western bank of the mouth of the Blyth River. When he died, his wife returned
to her natal community taking with her FG, her only son. Her sister had
married a man of PG1, and the latter's son (i.e. FG's mother's sister's son)
became FG's guardian. For many years now, FG has regarded himself, and
been regarded by others, as a full member of PG1. His father's patrilineal

group, however, is _not_ regarded as a co-owner of Djunawunya. Why amalgamation
occurred in the cases of PG2 and PG3, compared with adoption into PG1 in the
case of FG, is not entirely clear, but it is probably related to the fact
that FG went to live with his mother's people while still a boy, whereas
the other two changes of residence were made by men after marriage.

We see, then, that the ownership of Djunawunya, while governed pre-
dominantly by patrilineal descent, has also been affected by residence. To
generalize from this example and comparable cases not only among the
Gidjingali but from other areas as well: long-term residence may confer
de facto ownership status on non-agnates. This is transmitted patrilineally,
and with the passage of time the original non-agnatic basis of membership
is forgotten.

In theory, and to a large extent in practice, the production of symbolic
representations associated with Djunawunya, such as paintings or sculptures
of Fishtrap, is carried out not by the owners but by their sisters' sons.
The latter treat this prerogative with great seriousness. Any failure
(imagined or otherwise) by the owners to acknowledge it inevitably produces
an outburst of public indignation; and men regularly express anxiety (for
which there would appear to be little basis in reality) about the theft or
abuse of their mothers' emblems. Such arrangements and their attendant
sentiments are by no means peculiar to Djunawunya but occur throughout the
Gidjingali tribal area and far beyond. I should add that men also have rights
in respect of their mother's mother's country, but the details need not
concern us here.

If we regard the representations of sites and their creators as being
analogous to title deeds, we have a situation where the latter are vested
in patrilineal corporations but held in trust and proclaimed on appropriate
occasions by uterine kinsmen. In as much as ownership and custodianship may
need to be viewed as complementary functions, links to land through females

are as vital as those through males. Traditional land ownership in Australia has been represented in anthropological textbooks as a paradigm case of patriliny, and in my own previous writings I have presented the Gidjingali as a conforming instance. I am disposed now to believe that it would be more accurate to describe their system as cognatic with a patrilineal bias. I also believe that such a description will be increasingly seen as preferable for Aboriginal land tenure in general.

If I have accepted the patrilineal paradigm too readily in the matter of land ownership, I have been one of its longer-standing critics on the question of land use. In particular, I have challenged the notion (more or less standard in Australian ethnography until twenty years ago) that patrilineal bands were dependent for their survival upon the resources of their own estates. Let us again examine the situation among the Gidjingali.

Traditionally, the owners of Djunawunya, together with those of four other contiguous estates on the western side of the Blyth River, formed the basis of a single community called the Anbarra. In 1960 the Anbarra numbered about 130. For a good deal of each year prior to European settlement they camped together on one or other of the constituent estates. Men fished along the coast and tidal creeks, or went inland to hunt for wallabies, while women gathered shell-fish, food plants, reptiles, rodents, and other small animals. Neither sex was restricted by territorial boundaries, and the camp constituted a base from which people ranged over the whole Anbarra region. Men tended to build fish-traps across creeks in their own estates; but they left the general camp to visit them and brought back part of the catch.

The main ceremonies took place during the Dry season. The Anbarra played host to members of neighbouring communities, and on other occasions were guests at rituals held elsewhere. Between ceremonies, small groups of close kin and affines often left the main community for a while and lived by themselves on their own estates.

In August or thereabouts the Anbarra crossed the Blyth River to enjoy the cycad nut, which flourishes on the east side. For a month or so they were guests of another Gidjingali community called the Marawurraba. Then both communities crossed to the west side and proceeded to a large inland swamp to harvest corms of the spike rush, and to hunt magpie geese which collect in great flocks toward the end of the Dry as the smaller waterholes disappear. Ownership of the swamp is divided among patrilineal groups of three different communities; and during October and November five or six communities gathered around the edges to exploit its rich resources. By December mosquitoes are barely tolerable in this area, and people began moving back to the coast. For the next few months the Anbarra camped on a sandy point at the river mouth. High winds help to keep the mosquitoes at bay, and over this period the Anbarra often acted as hosts to people from the interior.

Reciprocal altruism among the Gidjingali was based on considerations of mutual benefit. While it is possible that owners could have survived on their own estates, there is no doubt that, in the absence of techniques for food preservation and because resources and conditions differ from place to place, generosity and hospitality helped to raise the living standards of all. Such considerations are likely to have been important among hunters and gatherers everywhere.

Concluding remarks:

For those 'white' Australians who have assumed, or been assigned to, the task of 'uplifting the natives', one of the most depressing things about Aborigines has been their reluctance to adopt responsible attitudes toward private property. I am not talking here about correct attitudes to the private property of the invaders which, of course, they learnt at the point of a gun. Rather, I am referring to the almost total failure on the part of the advance guard of bourgeois culture to foster in Aborigines an attitude of retentiveness toward whatever wealth or property they were able to obtain from the new economy. Money and European commodities, given to individuals either in payment for labour or as charity, were distributed for the most part in accordance with traditional values and expectations; and, in the absence of tangible returns to the donor, would-be reformers tended to regard this apparent compulsion to share as a mindless dissipation of individual effort, or an inexplicable, if not delinquent, failure to satisfy self-interest.

There is no doubt that the ethic of generosity has been a serious obstacle to assimilation or, more precisely, the fulfilment of a hope that at least some Aborigines could be taught to accept and act upon the dominant values of mercantile culture, where success is measured largely in terms of an ability to acquire, accumulate, and retain wealth. The Aborigines, it is sometimes said, have been unable to make the transition from a system of primitive communism to the competitive individualism of the modern industrial state. But the notion of individuals trying to leap across an evolutionary gap is a misguided one. What has happened since 1788 is that innumerable Aborigines have spent their lives in a state of dilemma, not to say anguish, torn between pressures emanating from two conflicting value orientations, one indigenous to the continent, the other introduced.

This dilemma, though often acute and demanding our sympathy and understanding, is not entirely unforeshadowed. When I said that 'white' reformers were unable to foster in Aborigines an attitude of retentiveness, I chose the word 'foster' deliberately, rather than, for instance, 'inculcate'. I did so because in traditional Aboriginal society disinclination to share, either spontaneously or on request, was commonly felt and sometimes acted upon. The difference between Aborigines and Europeans is not a constitutional one.

Rather, whereas the morality of hunters and gatherers, by defining the
good man as the generous man, inhibits acquisitive and retentive impulses,
bourgeois morality, by rationalizing them, allows them to flourish.

As we might expect, individuals in traditional society differed in
industriousness as well as in skill. At the end of each day, food passed from
the 'haves' to the 'have-nots', usually carried from one campfire to another
by wives or children. But below the melody line, a continuo of grumbling was
evident -- complaints of stinginess, neglect, ingratitude, and so on. Normally,
the public pressure on individuals to share the visible product of their
labour with others was virtually irresistible; and it was well understood
that the ethic of generosity exposed the busy to exploitation by the lazy.
Accordingly, various counter-strategies were adopted, probably the most
effective of which was to eat during the food-collecting activity itself.
Betty Meehan[2] has recently brought to our attention the significance of the
so-called 'dinner camp' -- that is, small gatherings of close kin who met at
a pre-arranged place in the middle of the day to consume the fruits of the
morning's work. By the time they returned to the general camp, bearing the
outcome of what was apparently a pretty lean day, the greater part of the
product was already in an advanced state of digestion.

In a nomadic economy lacking techniques of food preservation, generosity
was most in evidence in relation to food resources that, at any particular
time, happened to be abundant. A tightening-up was apparent in contexts of
scarcity, and especially with reference to valued items of some durability.
I mention two examples. First, according to Isobel McBryde,[3] stone axe heads
over a considerable part of Victoria came from a greenstone quarry near
Lancefield. The outcrops were owned by a group of Wurundjeri, who controlled
both mining and distribution according to strict conventions. Only certain
members of the group were entitled to procure stone from the outcrops.

My second example concerns _pituri_ (_pitjuri_), a nicotine-containing drug
('tobacco') from the leaves of the plant, _Duboisia hopwoodii_. According to a
recent review of the data by Pamela Watson,[4] many Aborigines with access to
this plant may have been addicted rather than merely habituated. This grows
in the Mulligan River area of western Queensland, and quids prepared by
special drying techniques spread from this source over an area of some half
million square kilometres. Expeditions to the Mulligan River were made over
distances of 200 kilometres, often through hostile territory, to obtain
supplies. And there is a suggestion that, so great was demand in relation to
supply, trade in _pituri_ was characterized by tough bargaining rather than the
more usual formality and politeness associated with balanced reciprocity.
Watson comes to the following conclusions: "Because of the drug's value,
knowledge of _pituri_ became monopolized. The exact location of _D. hopwoodii_
plants was a secret closely guarded from both Blacks and Whites; knowledge
of the techniques of artificial drying was restricted, and so too were rights
in production and 'wholesale' distribution of the drug. Those benefiting
from this knowledge monopoly were totemic clans whose rights to _pituri_
were religiously based and old men who appear to have _used_ pituri to
sustain their authority[5]..."

No doubt this is an unusual case, and unfortunately the data are mostly
from 19th century ethnography and far from complete. Nevertheless, it might
be an interesting theoretical exercise to speculate why monopoly for the
purposes of self-aggrandisement was so rare among hunters and gatherers; and,
conversely, what were the necessary and sufficient conditions for such a
development to occur, especially in the face of a universal ethic of generosity.

NOTES

1. I thank Dr A. Short (Geography Department, University of Sydney) for
    giving me geographical advice on the landscape; and Mr J. Roberts
    (Geography Department, University of Sydney) for preparing the map.
    The map and table contain data obtained during a field trip in
    May 1981, financed by the Australian Institute of Aboriginal Studies.

2. In Shell bed to shell midden. Australian Institute of Aboriginal
    Studies. (Forthcoming.)

3. In Wil-im-ee Moor-ring: or, Where do axes come from?, Mankind, 1978.
    Vol. 11, 354-82.

4. This precious foliage, B.A. (Hons) thesis, University of Queensland
    1980.

5. Op.cit.: 73.

KUNYUHYUNGKI NGARRIKADJUNG MUNGOYH;   BALANDA BIRRIMWAM NGARRINANG KUNKERRNGE.

WE FOLLOWED FOR A LONG TIME THE OLDEN WAYS; 'WHITE PEOPLE' CAME, AND WE SAW
A NEW WAY.

PRISCILLA GIRRABUL

I am very happy to come and see you all in this country, and to talk to
you. This is my first trip to Canberra, to come and see you at this
conference. I've got a few things to say to you all, but I can't tell you
everything.

The first thing I want to talk about is the olden times, my people,
Aboriginal people, what they were living on, about our culture. Food, fish,
no [introduced] animals. Only wallaby, porcupine [echidna], all those things
like goannas, and men used to hunt for them. Women could too, with dogs.
Women used to hunt separately, hunt for food, our own food, bush food.
Mother and child, and grandmother, used to hunt, for the others that stayed
in camp. When they went out hunting they would bring back some food to the
camp, and share it out, to men, to children, and old ladies. That's the
story I heard from my father and my mother and my grandmother. Just like
yourselves, you hear a story from your own people. Men used to use spears,
no guns, nothing that you have. We used to have spears, only stone spears,
wooden spears, no wire spears. Today, people use wire spears and shovel
spears. That's from you. They are all your things. The olden-time people
used to use stone spears, wooden spears. Going for fish, they used wooden
spears. Stone spears for kangaroo or wallaby or emu. That's the type of
thing we used to use, way out in the bush.

Nowadays, since the balanda ['white man'] came to Australia, Northern
Territory, they came and taught us their ways. First the missionaries. I
was brought up by the missionaries. I was in the mission school, way out at
Oenpelli, not in Darwin, nor in Canberra. Not in Sydney, no. I was in

school at Oenpelli, that's all. That's where I learnt from <u>balanda</u>, who taught me. Out of your language. But I did learn my own language. Nowadays my children are learning a lot, from your language and in your language. So they are learning both ways. Some children are learning mostly your ways. They get taught, and they use more papers than I did. So you people must think right back, to the way we lived.

As I said before, women used to go out hunting. When a woman was pregnant, old ladies delivered the baby. No doctor, no nurses, as you have. We didn't have them at that time. In my time, one of the old women delivered me when I had a baby, when I had my son. That wasn't long ago. So nowadays ladies come to the hospital, Darwin hospital, they have their baby, the baby goes back to its country and we are still teaching them in our ways. I can't tell you more about women's business. That's because there are a lot of gentlemen here. It's not good for me to talk about women having babies, it's secret, for the ladies only. But the ladies can hear me about women's business.

Now, I've got a few more things to say. About mining companies. About the land. That land, it belongs to Aborigines. We have got our own land, just as my people a long time ago did. In our land there is something that you know about that we didn't know. Under the ground. My people didn't know about it, they just used to hunt and live, go to sleep; next morning they would go out hunting. They never knew what was there, under the ground. But you do. Europeans know more than us; they know more than what we know about our country. Maybe uranium is there under the ground, or other metals: gold, tin. Now, at this time we know what's in there, but not in my time, the old people's time. No. We didn't know there was uranium under the ground. We only knew our land. And that <u>is</u> our land. I've got land. My father died, and I'm his eldest daughter. I've got no brother. I had a brother, who had a different mother from me, but he's dead. In my country, in my land, I'm the boss.

Mining companies, I think, put a big pressure on Aboriginal people. We

know about these metals: gold and uranium, and that the government sends
mining companies, that want to go out to Arnhem Land, to mine, just like they
did to Nabarlek. And this man, the owner of that land, can hardly walk, he
only has one leg, and he didn't understand much, about the land, or about the
mining company, and he didn't know what to do. He didn't know that. So he
just gave up, and let it happen. We don't know what the uranium is for. So
people are very, very frightened, they are frightened of <u>balanda</u> coming into
their area, looking for these minerals. So I won't say anything more about
that. You might have understood me as I was talking: about two things,
about today and the mining companies, and about the olden times.

Remember this: my people used to live an olden, olden way. No clothes,
like these we're wearing today. People never wore these ones. They wore
something, pandanus skirt or maybe paperbark. But not in my time. I've
learnt to wear your things. But the olden times people, they wore nothing,
just went naked. They went without clothes. They used stone axes for cutting
out sugar bag -- wild honey. They didn't have sugar. That's why Aboriginal
people, in olden times, didn't have many sicknesses. No diarrhoea, no malaria,
no leprosy, no other sicknesses. Maybe these were carried from Europe or some
other places, maybe from China.

Those are some of the things I had to say, about the olden times. Woman
must take a place of a father. Or of a husband, for her children's area.
You cannot push the mother, you cannot push the child, nobody can. No other
Aboriginal man can come and tell me: "Priscilla, go away from your country",
or: "It's not your country". I would say to him: "It <u>is</u> my country. <u>You</u> go
away. Find you[r] own country. This is my father's land, my great grandfather's
land".

So, people used to live before in an old way without the things that
the <u>balanda</u> brought. Now at this stage, we're using your food, your animals.
But not before, in our time. We only had fish, wallaby, kangaroo, porcupine,

goanna, all those things, that's all. No buffalo, no bullock, no horses, no pigs. No.

That's all, maybe I'll tell you about some other things, next time.

COMMENTARY

                                        SUE KESTEVEN

Biographical note:

Priscilla Girrabul, ngalkangila, was born about 1920 [the 1956 mission record says 1925], near a hill called Nimbabbirr across the billabong from Oenpelli. Ngalkangila is her 'skin' (subsection) name. In these comments, I refer to her by this name.

Her father's clan was -Djok, and his country was Kudjumarndi, known to non-Aborigines as Myra Falls, which is to the south of Nabarlek. Ngalkangila tells a story of a snail-like Rainbow Serpent associated with Kudjumarndi which, as a consequence of that visit by that strange Rainbow Snake, is a dangerous place. Her mother's clan was -Mirarr, and her country was Nimbuwa, to the north of Nabarlek.

When Ngalkangila was little, Oenpelli had only stringybark houses then, with ant-bed floors. Women made the floors. Iron was used only in Mr Harris's time. [Note that epochs are marked by referring to the name of the resident superintendent; the mission concerned was the Church Missionary Society.] There was a garden at Oenpelli, with custard apples, pineapples, cassava, sweet potatoes, watermelons, pumpkins, peanuts. People who worked for the mission got cooked tucker. Others had to get bush tucker for themselves. But there was still no dining room, and no spoons, they used mussel shells instead.

Ngalkangila was placed in the mission dormitory at Oenpelli when she was a child. She and some others ran away from there once and went to Mikginj; the missionaries sent pursuers and, when they were brought back, Mr D. said:

"I'll go and get your supper now" and came back with a whip and gave them all a thrashing. "Balanda [non-Aborigines, especially those of European descent] used to come every day and make bininj [Aborigines] work, and if they didn't, they got hiding". There is affection shown by Ngalkangila for the old days, although she will also say that the missionaries 'cruelled' them; as an example, she will tell you not only of thrashings, but also of the missionaries' wives forbidding breast-feeding beyond a few months.

When she finished school she married a man of the -Manilakarr clan. Together they went off to the buffalo camps at South Alligator, Manmalarri, Madjinbardi (Mudginberri), Cannon Hill, Woolner, Lake Finniss. They went to Lake Finniss by canoe, down the East Alligator, round by sea and up the South Alligator River. At holiday time they would go to Pine Creek to see her mother and father. They also worked at Marrakai. There was a big mob there: Gagudju, Erre, Mengerrdji, Wardadjbak, a big mob, Kundjeyhmi and Kunwinjku too, they used to go together. At Madjinbardi, Ngalkangila was working that time as a cook. They got paid half money, half rations. Ngalkangila didn't drink liquor at that time.

When her husband died, Ngalkangila returned to live at Oenpelli. She worked in the hospital, as a nurse. The mission sent her to Darwin for training. While whe was there, she went to Channel Island to learn how to look after people with Hansen's disease (leprosy). People with leprosy were taken away from their communities and sent to Channel Island. In 1962 there was a typhoid epidemic at Oenpelli, when Ngalkangila had to work around the clock.

Ngalkangila married again. This husband drowned at the East Alligator Crossing.

In Ngalkangila's country, at Tin Camp, some years ago, an Aboriginal man was extracting tin in a small-scale mining operation. The equipment has fallen to pieces since, but Ngalkangila wants to set the enterprise up again. Since she is an 'old lady', she needs the help of young men. And since a few wet seasons have wrecked the road into the area, she needs to borrow equipment to make it again. She herself has no driving licence, and in any case her eyesight is not good. She does, however, have a liquor permit for Kudjumarndi, and by means of this 'carrot' intends to visit her country again very soon with some young men to establish her mining enterprise.

This sort of mining enterprise is acceptable to her, but her country is also rich in uranium and she has been pestered by mining interests to allow them to go there. They offer her 'bribes' (for example, the possibility of a helicopter trip into her country). The material benefits are tempting, but the cost -- another Nabarlek on her land -- is high. The outstation school teacher reported to her once that when flying over her country he had seen fresh tracks made. Her anger and distress at this information were great. She immediately asked the Northern Land Council to investigate the matter.

Notes on Priscilla Girrabul's contribution:

Ngalkangila invites people to reflect on changes in the Aboriginal life-style; the impact of Europeans in her area has been enormous. She has seen great changes in her lifetime. Until this conference occasion, she herself had never been farther south than Pine Creek.

Aborigines have golden memories of the past -- of a happy time before the balanda, 'white man' came and brought complications. And yet, Aboriginal people have wanted to use 'white man's' things, to eat his food -- and consequently, they feel a debt to the balanda. Balanda are said to know more. They may know more about some things, but they don't know how to live in the bush. But their knowledge of certain matters gives them power, and this scares Aborigines.

Mining negotiations put a great deal of pressure on Aboriginal people. Their time is taken up with meetings. A decision to do nothing is not regarded as a decision by non-Aborigines. Aborigines are forced to make decisions when they are not in command of knowledge which will let them know what the consequences of those decisions will be. So, today, Aborigines have to learn two ways: the old way and the new way. Some people are learning only the new way; but some -- especially those on outstations -- are learning both ways, as far as they are able. There are still constraints, however, and often balanda ways are adapted to Aboriginal ways, so there is 'mixing'.

Land has passed down from the ancestors, and the present status is a reflection of past events -- even if there appears to be a paradox, or a conflict, or an incompatible set of precepts. If that is how things were said to be by the old people, that is how they are, and they are not open to argument -- or the argument can be refuted by reiterating what the old people said.

Women own land equally with men. They inherit land from their fathers, but can also speak in some contexts for their husbands' land, because this is the land of their children.

Women were independent, and depended upon to ensure that no-one lacked food. Women had their own 'business'. This has been eroded by balanda hospital practices, and the presence of a shop and 'job' hours have eliminated or thwarted the necessity to hunt, although it is still the prime recreational pursuit.

AN ADDITIONAL NOTE

CATHERINE H. BERNDT

It would seem impolite to both Priscilla and Sue for me not to add a further note, if only because of our earlier and still-continuing interest in the people of western Arnhem Land and their neighbours. (Apart from our Man, Land and Myth in North Australia. The Gunwinggu people, 1970, a more recent comment is 'Oenpelli then and now: a brief overview', A.I.A.S. Newsletter, No. 14, Sept. 1980: 38-49; this includes, on p. 45, a photograph taken by John von Sturmer in 1980, of a midjan rite at

Oenpelli, arranged by Priscilla for her small grandson.)

We first visited Oenpelli late in 1947, returning for a longer period

of research in 1949-50, and at irregular intervals since then; we had

already met a few Oenpelli people and other western Arnhem Landers on

wartime Army Aboriginal settlements at Adelaide River and Katherine in 1945.

In 1947 and in 1949-50, Oenpelli was very different indeed from what it is

now. (The new system of orthography introduced a few years ago by

missionary linguists accentuates that impression: e.g., 'Kunwinjku' in

place of 'Gunwinggu', the use of 'h' to indicate a glottal stop, and so on.)

But the substantive changes have been overwhelming.

By 1949-50 the dormitory system had been abandoned, but not the nexus

between Sunday morning church attendance and Sunday 'rations' (of food from

the mission store). A fairly stable nucleus of people was caught up

directly in the routine life of the mission station. Others were involved

less centrally or less regularly; most adults spoke little or no English,

and spent at least a couple of days a week in hunting and food-collecting.

Aboriginal visitors came and went, usually from and to other settlements;

the official permit system kept non-Aboriginal visitors to a minimum, and

combined with the lack of all-weather roads and airstrips to ensure that

tourists were rare. The station itself and its balanda (European) staff

were small, and at that time they took little interest in the Aboriginal

languages and culture. None of the few motor vehicles around was Aboriginal-

owned. Liquor was available across the East Alligator River in the

'buffalo country', and at the main road settlements from Darwin southward,

but not in the Reserve. Mining, almost non-existent, was not envisaged

as a serious possibility. Aboriginal people in and around Oenpelli felt

that they had the whole countryside to move about in, to use all of its resources (animals, plants, birds, fish, etc.) and to engage in religious ritual affairs at appropriate places -- with no outside interference to take into account: only the demands of the mission on one hand, and Aboriginal customary rules about ownership, usage, and social relationships on the other. Of course, there were plenty of signs of change, imminent as well as in process, and by the late 1950s they were becoming more conspicuous. They escalated quite rapidly during the 1960s, even more so in the 1970s. Today, much of what we saw and heard during our first visits has passed into the category of 'memory culture', and second- and third-hand memory culture at that.

We knew Priscilla's own father, and her first husband, in our early time at Oenpelli. But I saw very little of Priscilla herself. We did not talk much together until early in 1966.

By then, her son was helping to teach in the school. He had some 'cowboy' records, Priscilla told me, and liked to try them himself on his guitar. He had introduced her (and consequently, as it happened, introduced me too) to that kind of singing. As she and I sat talking, we heard from across the camp the beat of clapping sticks and a songman's voice, singing; and we began to reminisce about the days, and evenings, when people had to provide their own entertainment (no travelling films, for instance), and several songmen were active during evening ceremonies and in daytime practising. We sighed about one young man in particular, long dead by 1966, who was a superb and tireless composer and singer. Priscilla observed, in English, "They [were] very good, like comic songs, [they] used to make us laugh... They [were] like cowboy songs, like Slim Dusty...' And she added, 'Cowboy songs are right for this country, they very good for us people, they right for us...'

But for most of the time, on that occasion, we were discussing other things: her family, for instance, her parents and grandparents and other relatives, with several women sitting nearby in their own camps joining in when a topic concerned them. On another point: she helped to clarify for me the distinction between two kinds of named social divisions -- the gunmugugur, often translated these days as 'clan', and the yigurumu, which is linked with it but not identical -- and, Priscilla insisted, 'deeper than gunmugugur, and we not using it all the time'. (Priscilla's gunmugugur, or 'clan', is -Djorg, from her father: in current mission-based spelling, -Djok. The hyphen at the beginning leaves room for a feminine or masculine prefix, Ngal-, or Na-.) Her yigurumu, also from her father, is 'Nagamurg!' [No prefix; the initial Na-, in this case, is different.] Each gunmugugur has its associated yigurumu.) She was very careful in explaining these: the general relevance of the concepts, and the specific examples she used in illustrating them.

Especially, however, we talked about 'country': places, and their spiritual and social associations, the spirit-characters who live on eternally at various sites. She reminded me of the places belonging to her own immediate relatives, including her son (from his father). Above all, she spoke of her own 'country'.

One part of what she said focused on the country itself, in its traditional and continuing significance. She talked enthusiastically and nostalgically about the dangerous and tabu (-djamun) waterhole where the Rainbow Snake lives, its small 'sort of neck' just visible above the surface of the pool; and the other spirit-Dreaming djang at that site, the sweet-scented flower of a special tree and the wild honey that goes with it. Aboriginal healers (margidjbu) associated with that country, Priscilla said, could dream about that place. A margidjbu could take the spirit of a sick person there: if the spirit sank down in the water, the patient would die; if not, the patient would respond to treatment, and survive. The dream would be a _vision_ of that place, more beautiful than the actual scene might be, with flowering branches bending low over the quiet pool.

In her other comments, she expressed anxiety about the future of her country; how vulnerable it was, and difficult to protect. She had spent a fair amount of time away from the Oenpelli area, as well as in other _balanda_-controlled circumstances (such as the dormitory) in the mission station itself, and she was wary about what might happen next. By the mid-1960s, the advance guard of tourists and mining and road-building activities was already presaging a new kind of invasion, and a new life-style. So, she worried about her country: how she could make sure it was safe. She was making plans to go back to it, to watch over it 'in case some _balanda_ came and took it', because there was a 'lot of tin there, lot of metal or something ... and nobody there looking after it...' It is a responsibility, as well as a positive asset: part of her own heritage, _and_ of the wider Aboriginal heritage in western Arnhem Land. In the current situation, balancing the prospects for protection against the prospects for alienation or destruction or deterioration (and not only through mining developments), she has due reason for her continuing concern.

ABORIGINAL WOMEN, RESOURCES AND FAMILY LIFE

CATHERINE H. BERNDT

Aboriginal women traditionally played a vital part in the affairs of their communities; in family maintenance, in the use and deployment of natural and social resources, and in the religious sphere. In general, however, their contributions and responsibilities have not been sufficiently acknowledged or appreciated by outsiders. The position has been improving to some extent, but not everywhere. The change has not kept pace with the overall trend toward recognition of the positive qualities of Aboriginal people. One reason is the way Aboriginal women's traditional roles and status have been reported in the past. Such reporting has suffered from preconceived opinions, biased observation and biased selection of data. All this has had the circular effect of a self-fulfilling prophecy. It has certainly influenced the attitudes and behaviour of other Australians toward Aboriginal women. As well, it has influenced other Aboriginal people themselves, particularly those who have grown up in non-traditional settings, so that they are more likely to accept such opinions as a true version of women's traditional position. One consequence is that reliable, and valid, information on the subject of this chapter is much scarcer than it ought to be.

Attitudes, and reporting:

Aboriginal women have shared some of the same disadvantages that have affected women in general; but, for them the main difficulties in this respect did not rest in their traditional situation. Disadvantages and difficulties were imposed on them from outside, adding to those they already had. Negative attitudes toward them and about them, since the early colonial era, have been expressed in two main ways.

One is through direct personal contacts, through actions and relationships.

From the beginnings of European settlement and for a very long time afterwards, most of the newcomers seem to have regarded the Aborigines as an inferior population: as curiosities, nuisances, objects of charity, useful only for the services they could be induced or compelled to offer. Aboriginal women in particular were not taken seriously except in terms of employment or sexual relations or both. This view was in keeping with the more widely prevalent European image of women, one that emphasized domestic affairs, childbearing and childrearing, and women's potential as sexual partners. The assumption seems to have been that this is how Aboriginal men regarded their womenfolk.

The second means of expressing attitudes is through verbal, especially written, materials. What concerns us here is, specifically, the reporting of women's roles and status in traditional or near-traditional circumstances and in community affairs generally. In many cases, such statements mix a minimum of facts with a maximum of interpretation. Or they take, as evidence of 'how things were' in a traditional Aboriginal environment, life-history material from very different settings (e.g. from recollections of a 'strict' mission-dormitory upbringing). Such accounts are of course valuable in themselves, just as 'memory-culture' reminiscences always are; but that is another matter.

An example of how not to draw conclusions about the past from very tenuous evidence is provided by Huffer's (1980) study of Aboriginal women at Mornington Island. After commenting (pp. 16, 23) on the "powerful influence" of a strict mission upbringing on Lardil people of thirty and older, who "had received their education and training in the controlled atmosphere of the dormitory system", and "had learned much about the traditional beliefs mainly by talking with the old folk", she goes on to assert (p. 150): "The women were inferior in the magico-religious practices. Their role was to gather bush food, while the elderly people stayed in the family camp and cared for the children."

In other regions where dormitory systems were operating, under various regimes and in a variety of styles, there were reservoirs of people outside them

who could maintain more active kinds of linkage with the traditional past.
The small dormitory at Oenpelli, despite its equally powerful breakdown-
potential, was set in the context of a larger population with, up to a point,
re-vitalizing consequences for those children who were exposed to both kinds
of influence. That was the case too at Balgo, in the north of Western
Australia. Although the dormitory arrangements there were tightened up for
a time, especially during the 1960s, before the system was abandoned, early
in 1958 there was only a girls' dormitory, flexible enough to accommodate
contact with relatives in the camp situation. In the late afternoons, little
groups of girls would be busy collecting an assortment of grass-seeds, some
helping their mothers and other women, others on their own; winnowing them in
wooden dishes, grinding or crushing them, shaping them into little dampers,
and cooking them on open fires that they tended themselves in the traditional
way. And in the evenings they would probably be sitting in the camp with
adults, watching and listening to one of the ordinary ceremonies that were
the customary form of entertainment at that period, returning to the mission
dormitory when the dancing and singing were over, and the camp fires burned
low indicating that it was time for sleeping.

In traditional, all-Aboriginal circumstances, such experiences were an
intrinsic part of an on-going process: contact between adults and children
of both sexes and all ages, more or less continuously, in teaching-and-
learning situations, covering the total range of information necessary for
ordinary living, but graded according to life-stages and particular contexts.
Relations between people and between people and land, use of resources, and
the aesthetic dimension that was equally necessary to living, were taught
and learned in the course of such contacts; and the different 'bits' reinforced one another in an overall, widening pattern.

The coming of Europeans played havoc with the process and the pattern,
and with information about both: what the newcomers wrote and said about

them, and what survived of them to be passed on to on-coming generations
of Aborigines. But it is clear, from what was still going on until a few
decades ago in regions that were the last to be drastically disrupted
(Arnhem Land, the Western Desert, parts of the Kimberleys), that much,
perhaps most, of what people did and said took place in mixed-sex groups, or
across sex lines. Even when they acted in sex-specific roles, they did so
most often in interpersonal transactions, and most typically within a kinship-
oriented framework: as mothers and sons, fathers and daughters, sisters and
brothers, and so on. Sex contrasts on a corporate basis were evident to
some extent in socio-economic tasks, but more conspicuously in the religious
sphere. These contrasts appear to have caught the attention of outsiders,
to a much greater extent than the more low-key aspect of cooperation and
interdependent closeness between men and women.

Nevertheless, a great deal that has been written about Aborigines
generally refers to women even when women are not specified -- subsumed under
the frequently ambiguous term, 'man'. It can be just as misleading to talk
and write about women as if they could be isolated, or segregated, from
discussions of men. I have focused on women in several other places (e.g.
C. Berndt 1974, 1981), but here I think it more useful to take a slightly
broader approach.

Knowing the land:

Many people of European descent in Australia think of land as a saleable
commodity, a piece of the earth's surface that need not be any more than a
stretch of ground: if bulldozers and other earthmoving equipment have cleared
it completely, so much the better; they can manage without even a blade of
grass or a spider or any living thing to link them with what was there
before; they can start anew, from 'scratch', imposing their own private view
of how it should be, what it should look like. There are exceptions; but
even people who think in terms of land contours and vegetation are still

very far from the more inclusive concept of land, of 'country', which
Aboriginal people traditionally took for granted.

From all the evidence available, for traditionally oriented Aborigines,
today as well as in the past, to speak of 'my land', 'my country' is to make
a shorthand, tip-of-the-iceberg statement. It is a pointer to a complex
interlinking of life-forms and things that all belong together in a diversity
of ways. And all of these, in conjunction, make up a constellation of resources
which Aboriginal people used, and with which they were intimately connected.
That was true for women, as much as for men -- and for children of both sexes.
To say that land was a resource, then, is to say much more than some
Europeans take it to mean.

It has become fashionable these days to repeat that Aborigines were
perfectly adapted to their natural environment: that they lived in harmony
with that environment, knew all the details of it, and all its specific
resources in so far as these were relevant to them. Such statements have
become almost a set of clichés, used by people of widely differing backgrounds.
But -- how much use has really been made of Aboriginal knowledge and
information in this respect? How much collaboration has there been with
Aborigines in studying the natural environment and all it contains?
Anthropologists have done this to some extent; but mostly they are not trained
as zoologists, botanists and so on, and have not been in a position to
specialize in such matters. On the other hand, zoologists and botanists (etc.)
have not shown much readiness to collaborate consistently with Aborigines
in pursuing their studies. It is true that they have differing aims and
interests from those of Aborigines, who had made a thorough study of their
own environments. But up to a point they could probably have asked some of
the same questions, and been concerned with some of the same answers.
Expeditions to 'remote' areas from southern cities, reporting 'discoveries'
of 'new' fauna and flora and still-unknown living habits of various species,

seem in the 1980s strangely out of key with the verbal acknowledgement of Aboriginal information on such matters. The only excuse, in some regions, is that Aboriginal people are no longer available there, or no longer know-ledgeable, because of the past and continuing impact of the outside world.

Traditionally, for women and for men, it was not simply a matter of being able to identify the signs and tracks of various creatures, knowing where and when to find them. It was also a matter of knowing their behaviour patterns; their waking and sleeping and mating habits, how they produced offspring, whether and how they reared them, what foods they ate, how they obtained these -- the complete picture, in practical details, but also in its aesthetic aspects (vividly depicted in song, and in art and dramatic representations). This kind of picture, an orally and graphically transmitted record, was conveyed through a long process of careful teaching and learning, by (to repeat) women as well as by men. The empirical detail and clarity of this information-picture is not necessarily obvious to outsiders, because it was not incorporated in a single package, or set of packages. But knowing the land, knowing a particular area, involved more than identifying a place, or locating a place name on a map. It meant all of these facets, and their interrelationships, how they belonged together -- including their relation-ships with people.

Talking about land:

When I first went to Yirrkalla in north-eastern Arnhem Land, in 1946, I was faced with a situation in which only one woman spoke a little English -- and understood less. At that time there was no preliminary material available for learning any of the dialects in that region. (No mechanical aids such as tape-recorders were available, either.) I began to learn her dialect, not only by building up a set of vocabularies, but also by writing down as much as possible of everything that she and other people said in my hearing. The fact that I did not understand much of it, except for the simplest items, did not matter, because later I was able to come back to it and discuss it with her, and with others, correcting and amplifying, and using it as an assortment of jumping-off points for exploring a number of different topics.

Quite early in my acquaintance with her, when she had already told me some details about herself, including the main names and the location of her own country, she decided that it was important for my education to know more about that country and about other sites that she knew well. So she listed for me several series of places, leading in different directions, with a couple of the main English-name areas as orienting labels: 'Caledon Bay', 'Blue Mud Bay', going 'south', going 'west', and so on. She added details for many of the names, which made sense to me later when I came back to them. The point here is that the couple of hundred names included in this initial part of her teaching-programme for me represented a topic she considered to be unquestionably important -- important for anyone who wanted to understand the local socio-cultural environment, and important for her as a person living in it.

Some years later, at Balgo, in the north of Western Australia, I wanted to add to my understanding of 'country' that women I knew had already talked about in various kinds of context. None of them could read or write, but I annotated the symbols they drew on sheets of brown paper I had brought for the purpose. Apart from their 'own' country, their own clusters of sites, each of them insisted on going further, and following the 'tracks' of the mythical person-ages associated with these. They added details of terrain (waterhole, soak, sandhills, rocks); events relating to human beings (birth-place, death site, etc.); and, in particular, the links with minor as well as major mythical characters. One problem was to get them to call a halt when there were other commitments in which all of us were involved.

These are two, very slight, examples of the interest, enthusiasm, and careful concern for detail that Aboriginal women in all the areas I know have shown, not only for their 'own' country, but also for a wider territorial span that they see as having links with it in one way or another. Of course, in urban areas in the south the picture is necessarily different: the almost-uncompromising break in transmission of information, and absorption or partial absorption in a European-type life-style made that sort of detailed connection impossible for them, even when they were interested. 'Own country' had to be phrased in broader terms; or, when actual sites were named, the mythical-spiritual linkages were vaguer or barely known. In the north, however, virtually all of the many hundreds of myths, stories and songs and personal life-history accounts that have been told to me by women include large and small place-names, knowledgeably annotated -- as an intrinsic and crucial part of the narrative or song. In accounts of creation, throughout the continent, women as well as men were active participants, moving across the country, shaping the landscape, naming various sites, putting plants and creatures and human populations at places they decreed were right and proper for them; and leaving their own spirit-essence, or part of it, at sites that now commemorate them. Women knew such accounts, in varying depth according to their age and competence; and some were highly skilled and impressively dramatic narrators and singers. Supplementing and complementing these are the almost-casual references in conversation to this place or that, and to 'who' or 'what' was there -- in the case of spirit beings, still _is_ there. In regions under threat from outside, such as mining and other intrusions, a note of anxiety has become increasingly evident in such accounts. But this represents a neo-traditional type of commentary on material that has already been documented, known, and established in the verbal resource-record of the region -- not a sudden access of renewed interest in sites that outsiders are now 'discovering' for their own purposes.

Living in the land:

A woman's 'own country' was (is) her main spiritual-personal-social resource centre. It was always of pre-eminent significance to her. The primary criterion rested on a charter of patrilineal descent, through her father and his fathers and their fathers. Other factors could be involved to reinforce that bond or add new ones: place of birth, for instance, or place of 'conception'. Actually, in some regions, this last would be the site where, so a woman reported, she first experienced the 'quickening', indicating that a spirit-animator had joined with a potential foetus to render her pregnant. Beliefs about such animating spirits, and the dreams or other events that conveyed the pregnancy-message, were and are quite varied; but their common theme was the transmission of spiritual life, the eternal link with the Dreaming, which gave continuity to human existence despite the transient quality of human physical manifestations.

Through other kinds of bond, a woman had secondary rights in her mother's country, for instance, and in her mother's mother's and even her father's mother's country. Because marriage ideally took place between persons who were already related in terms of kinship, and whose 'own' territories were not too far apart, she might have some measure of kin-based rights in her husband's 'own' country; but this sort of acknowledgement was usually quite slight, if it was mentioned at all, even in cases where it might have been relevant.

The significant aspects of a woman's association with her husband's 'own country' were: (i) That she helped to sustain and renew its resources by contributing to the religious rituals which had such spiritual continuity as their major intent; women's cooperation was crucial to the success of such religious tasks, and women worked with and for their husbands (and children) in this respect; (ii) That all of its resources, except for those secret-sacred items that were looked after by adult men of that country, were open to her, to use as she saw fit. Rights were, customarily, inseparable from obligations. Obligations included following the rules about avoiding places that were physically or ritually dangerous, sites to which entry was forbidden except to specified persons or categories of persons. Other kinds of obligation had to do with supplying food and other goods, and specified services, within a given range of people -- and rights to receive food, and so on, in direct or indirect return.

What is well established in the literature is women's role in the family-support system. They provided the mainstay of the family diet in the shape of vegetable foods, small creatures and so on. Like men (and the literature notes this too) they might eat fruits and other snacks (animal and vegetable) in the course of a day's foraging; but, unlike men, they nearly always had something moderately substantial to bring home to their families, and perhaps for others.

As Kaberry (1939:14) stated succinctly, the "division of labour between the sexes ... is in a very real sense a matter of co-operation". Aborigines used what I have called (1974) a 'two-sex model', recognizing and even dramatizing contrasts between males and females, but setting these firmly within a framework of interdependence. They did not see differences as negative features in human interrelationships, provided that they were kept within a matrix of commonality and broadly shared basic assumptions. Men and women contributed different benefits, in different ways, to the overall wellbeing of their communities.

So, women drew on the food and other resources in their husbands' 'own' countries, and in the range of territory about which they moved with their husbands and families. They came to know those resources intimately. They had a declared interest in the 'country' -- country in the most comprehensive sense, of land plus: all the multifarious 'existents', all the life-forms that inhabited it along with its human population, including plant life that had spiritual as well as physical roots in the soil.

For women as for men, 'resource development', 'development of resources', has meant or threatens to mean the exact opposite: the destruction of resources in this wider sense; and undevelopment, if one can put it in that way, the blotting out of an intermeshing complex of spiritual and material forms that can never be reconstituted in anything remotely resembling the traditional patterns.

Women, being involved

For women as well as for men, the three-fold frame of social-natural-spiritual was fundamental to ordinary living. We could summarize it, as an interrelated whole, as 'the social environment in the natural environment and in the spiritual environment -- and vice versa'. For women, too, religion was instrumental as well as expressive, underpinning and justifying the socio-economic dimension as part of the total fabric of physical and spiritual living. Myth and song and sacred ritual, like ceremonies for relaxation and entertainment, were facets of women's world, in which they had active roles to play. A woman's 'own country' and special sites continued to have special significance for her even though she might move a little distance from these on marriage and help to care for her husband's country -- to care for it ritually, as well as using its various resources.

Women were concerned just as much as men were with natural and social (human) resources, including land, in their particular areas. Within the overall perspective of interdependence, both men and women had relative independence in a wide range of tasks and obligations, rights and privileges. It was not a matter of members of each sex following their own interests or looking to their own welfare. Both women and men contributed in traditionally stipulated ways to the welfare of their particular community -- which included their own welfare, but not at the expense of others. In Aboriginal belief, it was not necessary, nor was it desirable, for everyone to behave in the same way or do the same things, or to have authority or power in the same spheres all the time. In some respects, men appeared to be dominant. In other respects women were, though usually less conspicuously so.

'Developments' (variously interpreted) and changes in all these fields have had a formidable impact on Aboriginal women. They include changes in women's access to resources, and in their rights to make effective decisions. Women have 'lost ground' in more ways than one. They have been affected as persons: for example, in regard to their own country, their spiritual home, from which they draw spiritual sustenance; and in regard to their husbands' and children's territory, as a residence-area, a home-area, a place of living. Not least, they have been affected in their key role as dependable nurturers of their families, especially of small children, by wide-ranging upsets in the process of making a living and ensuring an adequate food supply. The whole network of social obligations and rights has been subjected to a 'demolition job'. Local people have scattered, or been persuaded or enticed out of their former territory, and/or outsiders have come in; and the care of young children has been at least partly taken out of women's hands. On all these counts, women have been disadvantaged. Consultation and discussion have not been entirely lacking, but they are much less visible and consistent than in the case of men. That applies to urban and rural women as well as to those who are still traditionally oriented.

It is fair and reasonable to regard women as being traditionally 'partners' with men. On the basis of the evidence available, however, it is not reasonable to regard them as junior partners (I.M. White 1974). That issue is not resolved by going to the other extreme and categorizing men as junior partners, as some writers now seem to be suggesting.

Two things are urgently needed now, in the face of current 'developments'. One is for Aboriginal women to be heard much more prominently than they have been in the last few years, and on a wider and more representative basis. That means 'speaking out' on their own behalf. In the past, as far as the outside world was concerned, they have been very much a silent majority. However articulate they might be in their own languages, they were not able to communicate in fluent English; and they were hesitant because, however sophisticated they might be in their own culture and in their own communities, they did not have enough experience in the wider Australian society to make themselves heard effectively. (Among the bright points in this regard is a forthcoming volume edited by Fay Gale, the outcome of a symposium on Aboriginal women held during the 1980 A.N.Z.A.A.S. Congress in Adelaide. The title was suggested by Aboriginal women from Borroloola: 'We are bosses ourselves: the status and role of Aboriginal women today.')

The second thing is that this increased effort, this extra encouragement for Aboriginal women to assert themselves positively, needs to be achieved, not at the expense of Aboriginal men, but in conjunction with them. The traditional partnership of men and women, their cooperation in every aspect of social living, is even more imperative now than it was before.

REFERENCES

Berndt, C.H.   1974 Digging sticks and spears, or, the two-sex model. In F. Gale ed.: 64-84.

Berndt, C.H.   1981 Interpretations and "facts" in Aboriginal Australia. In Women the Gatherer (F. Dahlberg ed.). Yale University Press, New Haven and London.

Gale, F. ed. 1974 Woman's Role in Aboriginal Society. Australian
            Institute of Aboriginal Studies, Canberra (Second ed.)

Gale, F. ed. We are Bosses Ourselves: the status and role of Aboriginal
            women today. Australian Institute of Aboriginal Studies,
            Canberra. (Forthcoming.)

Huffer, V. with Elsie Roughsey et al. 1980 The Sweetness of the Fig.
            Aboriginal women in transition. New South Wales University
            Press, Sydney.

Kaberry, P. 1939 Aboriginal Woman, Sacred and Profane. Routledge,
            London.

White, I.M. 1974 Aboriginal women's status: a paradox resolved.
            In F. Gale ed.: 36-49.

ABORIGINAL PERSPECTIVES OF THE LAND AND ITS RESOURCES

WESLEY LANHUPUY

The theme of 'contemporary and traditional Aboriginal perspectives of the land and its resources' contains assumptions alien to Aboriginal people. For Aboriginal people there is no separation between land and resources: there is no separation between us and what was our country and there never will be, because of our spiritual belief and understanding. The 'contemporary' and 'traditional' division could also lead to misunderstanding by non-Aborigines. These confusions in non-Aboriginal minds are partly due to talking about Aboriginal people in English. The English word 'land' has narrow connotations of economics and geography. The implications are dramatically broader for Aboriginal people when talking about their country, called Yirralga (traditional land) by traditional owners. It encompasses all things. English-speaking Aboriginal people talk about ownership in the context of responsibility, but the way spiritual and ceremonial practices are linked with that land is hard for me to put down on paper for this symposium.

This combination of Aboriginal responsibility and ownership of the inter-related clans of, for instance, north-eastern Arnhem Land, is derived from Aboriginal law, ceremony and customs. Non-Aborigines, therefore, require a total anthropological and sociological comprehension of Aboriginal life in order to understand what responsibility to the land means.

To reiterate some of the words that Aboriginal people have said in the past, in trying to explain to the rest of the Australian nation, our relationship with this country would be going over old ground. However, I believe this is necessary, because I do not think it has been heard as often as it has been said. When European Australians have listened, they have generally listened with their own conception of what land means, and not with the understanding of responsibility in the sense Aboriginal people would. The late Larry Lanley, when Chairman of the Mornington Island Council, referred to the land as a 'Mother' -- a Mother who provides Aboriginal people with everything they need. He said an Aboriginal cannot survive without his land -- he will die without it. In a speech given to the Canberra Press Club by the former Chairman of the Northern Land Council, Galarrwuy Yunupingu, he called the land his 'backbone'. He said he only stands straight, happy and proud because he has his land. He referred to the land as an art, allowing him to paint, dance, create and sing, as his ancestors did before him. He saw the land as the history of his nation, saying that it tells Aboriginal people how they came into being and by what systems they must live. He called the land "my found- ation", and said also that "without land I am nothing".

In my work as an Executive Officer of the Bureau of the Northern Land Council, I oversee the interaction between my people's responsibilities and aspirations for our country and the demands of modern development knocking on our door. The following (an extract from a Gapuwiyak Council letter) is an illustration of the scope of feeling and responsibility Aboriginal people have for their country.

> 'We need freedom from these pressures as we make our adjustment
> to new life styles. Development is taking place. Our young
> people are learning both the traditional and new skills. We
> have trained health workers, powerhouse operators, trainee
> mechanics, stores staff, builders and office staff. Give us
> time to grow. We are all just learning about these new things.
> We want to fit together many of the new traditional parts
> of our life with this new work but we need time. We need
> to be free from the pressures that European culture and mining
> have placed upon people in other areas.'

Even though Aboriginal people have acquired some of the superficial trappings of 'modern' economics this should not be seen as a diminution of our responsibilities for our country. While these changes have negative aspects, they have also increased our capacity to fulfil ceremonial obligations to our country. Consequently, customs and laws are also strengthened. We will continue to use modern technology selectively

to pursue the vast responsibilities we have for this country of ours.
Aboriginal people are capable of accommodating change, but we do need time.

The Northern Land Council has often expressed its opinion that it won't
stand in the way of development, unless we are totally ignored in respect of
social factors that must be taken into account. We see and have foretold
that this political shortsightedness will threaten our livelihood and that of
the culture that has been and is so unique. Like technology, we are able to
utilize effectively non-Aboriginal expertise. The Bureau of the Northern
Land Council is a clear example of this. However, such expertise must be
subordinate to Aboriginal people's aspirations.

Our past contact with non-Aboriginal academics has been a mixed blessing,
as has been our contact with all other elements of non-Aboriginal society.
This is not to deny the value of some academics' contributions as information
disseminators of Aboriginal ideals to the rest of the Australian nation. The
political consequences of this increased awareness of non-Aborigines have
produced a broader understanding of the aspirations of Aborigines in the
Northern Territory and to a limited extent in other states of Australia. For
our brothers and sisters in other parts of Australia, their time is yet to come.
This time will come only when unity among groups in support of our cause and
future unite to fight the injustices that we have all been subjected to.

The recent decision of the Northern Territory government to proceed with
50 or more exploration licence applications has brought about fears in the
minds of those of my people living in Arnhem Land. These fears have come
about because of our experiences in other mining towns -- for example, Gove
and Groote. Aboriginal people can be as much traumatized by rapid change as
anyone else in this world. The other factor for such movement is that we wish
to protect sites of significance, sacred areas that we have in this country.
We shall protect these places from intruders and developers who may have
interests in our land, whether it be for exploration purposes in search of
minerals, or for any other intrusion.

Most people at this symposium will be aware of the fact that Aboriginal people want to live a life-style of their own, and this is evident in movements that are being witnessed in Arnhem Land today. My people are continuing to move out from missions to their own outstations or homeland centres. I believe that the reason for this movement is not only to divorce themselves from the pressures of laws governing them in local communities. It also enables them to make decisions that affect their lives on a day-to-day basis, on their own lands, without question by other clans and groups. When such decisions are made, they are implemented accordingly.

Adjustment to the European way of life is so alien to Aboriginal people yet so much is expected of us by way of adjustment, within a very little time span. I would like to take this opportunity to call upon the government of Australia and say be patient and understanding of our aspirations in securing our style of living. Development is being implemented in a way that is unsatisfactory to us at present. It must be slowed down to a rate so that my people have a chance to keep pace with it. Otherwise our social and cultural practices will be nothing but a memory for which our great grandchildren will have to search in national libraries and galleries.

I believe this is a suitable forum for the Aboriginal people represented by the Northern Land Council to call on other Australians to recognize and acclaim the genius, compassion and humanity of the late Professor W.E.H. Stanner. I would like to leave you with the following words of his that demonstrate the positive role academics and other Australians can play if their hearts are true and they listen with understanding. The quotation is from the Boyer Lectures, 1968, <u>After the Dreaming</u>. The Australian Broadcasting Commission, Sydney: 50-1.

> "I listened to one elderly man speaking on the matter. He was something of an orator, with a power of words, a sense of pause and gesture, and very evident ability to phrase the conventional wisdom of his audience. I had the sense that he expressed well what many of his fellows were feeling and thinking. He turned

his back to the open waters of Carpentaria, and looked north, west and south to the great stretches of Arnhem Land which no one -- no one, that is, except the Aborigines -- wanted only a few years ago when we knew nothing of the mineral riches that have been discovered. In a dramatic way he pointed to and declaimed the names of territories and places within the tribal domain. "All of them", he said, "are our country". He then named the places already or soon to be lost under the special leases created over them. I could not follow all he said because I depended on an interpreter but there was no mistaking the substance of his remarks or the fact that he was unhappy and unreconciled. Were they to be compensated? Would yet more land go? Would the sacred places really be protected? These were among the questions he asked, but no one present could answer him with the scruple and certainty that alone could set his doubts at rest."

ABORIGINES IN SOCIAL HISTORY: AN OVERVIEW

G.C. BOLTON

This paper is divided into two parts. The first is a necessarily superficial overview of the approaches taken by European-Australian historians toward the Australian Aborigines; it is directed to readers who are neither anthropologists nor Australian historians. The second portion deals with historians who have touched on issues specifically relevant to the question of Aboriginal land rights.

The history of European-Aboriginal contact in Australia is usually seen as passing through four major phases: 1) conflict. This is characteristically the pioneer phase, when farmers and pastoralists are establishing themselves on former Aboriginal lands. Home government exhortations to treat the Aborigines as British subjects are quickly disregarded. Conflict situations could be found in different parts of Australia from the first alien settlement in 1788 to the close of the frontier period, about 1900, though isolated incidents occurred as late as the 1930s. 2) segregation. This is the phase when the Aborigines are seen as a dying race: 'smoothing the dying pillow' is the habitual cliché. The remnants of the Aborigines are directed into reserves and deprived of many of the rights of citizenship. In northern Australia, where Aboriginal labour is essential for the pastoral industry, a quasi-feudal relationship develops between patriarchal employers and low-paid Aborigines: the arrangement described by A.P. Elkin in a controversial phrase as 'intelligent parasitism'. 3) assimilation, or the opening of access to Aborigines to participate in the rights of Australian society and to conform to majority Australian patterns of social life and economic opportunity. This is advocated in some quarters in the 1930s, but does not fully become Commonwealth policy until 1951. Vestiges of the restrictive 'reserve' system survive longer in some states, and are not yet extinct in Queensland. 4) acknowledgement of Aboriginal rights. This follows Aboriginal demands

for the maintenance of a separate identity without necessarily rejecting
assimilation, and for the restitution of Aboriginal land rights and cultural
distinctiveness. The orgins of this demand can be found in the Second World
War period, but it achieves prominence only in about 1969, and has not yet
supplanted assimilation as official policy throughout Australia.

Before 1950:

   During the periods of conflict and segregation Aborigines figured only
marginally in histories written by European-Australians, and then usually as
a 'problem' encountered by pioneer European settlers and soon surmounted.
Tribute was occasionally paid to some faithful Aboriginal offsider of a hero
of European exploration, but otherwise they stood entirely outside the
mainstream of Australian historiography. In recent years historians of the
'New Left', such as Humphrey McQueen, have attacked the survival of these
stereotypes in secondary school texts. It may be preferable to quote the
Australian historical tradition at its best in the form of W.K. Hancock's
Australia (1930):

> The Australian Aborigines, shut off for centuries
> from the co-operative intelligence by which nations
> who are neighbours have created their common civilisation,
> never imagined that first decisive step from the economy
> of the chase which would have made them masters of the
> soil. Instead they fitted themselves to the soil,
> modelling a complex civilisation of intelligent
> artificiality which yet was pathetically helpless
> when assailed by the acquisitive society of Europe.

Yet even so sensitive an observer could see no remedy other than segregation:
"It might still be possible to save a remnant of the race upon well-policed
local reserves in Central and Northern Australia".

   The first histories specifically devoted to Aboriginal-European relations
were written in the late 1930s by two young reformers who wanted to break
down the segregation system and to restore the old concept of the Aboriginal
as entitled to share fully in the rights of Australian citizenship.

E.J.B. Foxcroft, later a senior Commonwealth public servant, wrote Australian Native Policy (1941). This largely deals with 19th century Victoria, and shows how the humanitarian policies of the Colonial Office under Glenelg lost out to the exigencies of a frontier society which followed the Cape Colony's precedent in using 'native policy' as a control mechanism. The finale was a reserve system and the near-extinction of the Victorian Aborigines. Paul Hasluck reviewed Aboriginal policy in Western Australia in Black Australians (1942), taking his story to 1897 when the Home government relinquished control of Aboriginal welfare to the self-governing colonial government of Western Australia. As a Liberal minister for territories, 1951-63, he was responsible for introducing assimilation as official policy and for initiating substantial reforms. Because both Foxcroft and Hasluck published during the Second World War, the immediate impact of their books was slow, but they helped to create a climate of opinion in favour of change.

Crawford, Mulvaney and the pre-historians:

In 1952 R.M. Crawford published his short but important Australia, in which one of the ten chapters was devoted to an account of Aboriginal society; one more than most comparable works. Two years later Crawford appointed to a lectureship in his Department of History at the University of Melbourne John Mulvaney, subsequently holder of Australia's first chair of pre-history at the Australian National University. Mulvaney was a pioneer among a group of pre-historians, such as Jack Golson, Isobel McBryde, Sylvia Hallam, and Rhys Jones, whose work during the past 25 years has utterly transformed our knowledge of what is known of the Australian past before European settlement -- a transformation which owes much to the development of carbon-dating. Among the major reinterpretations offered by the pre-historians, the following are important:

1) Human occupancy in Australia can be dated with some certainty at least to 35000 BP and probably very considerably further.

Controversy still persists about the pattern of spread
across the continent.

2) It is not true that the Aborigines were insulated from
external stimuli of a kind which might provoke change and
adaptation. Trade and conflict with the inhabitants
of Papua New Guinea is now well attested for north-eastern
Queensland. Macassan bêche-de-mer fishers and others are
known to have established a pattern of commerce with northern
Australia at least for five centuries. It is possible,
however, that some isolated sub-groups suffered for want of
external contacts. And Rhys Jones holds that the Tasmanian
Aborigines lost many of the skills of the mainlanders, possessing
far fewer artefacts and a more simple technology.

3) It is not true that the Aborigines made no major impact on the
Australian environment. Their use of fire for hunting and
cropping was systematic, and revealed considerable capacity
for organization in an ecology lacking the plant species which
lent themselves to conventional agriculture. Their 'fire-stick
farming' created the northern grasslands and park-like expanses
of southern Australia which proved attractive to European
pastoralists. Aboriginal development of the soil has been
shown to be purposeful, and ecologically provident to a
degree not always present among European-Australians and their
governments.

These reinterpretations have made for a much greater appreciation of
the qualities of traditional Aboriginal society, and have exercised a
noticeable, if indirect, influence on contemporary assessments of Aboriginal
potential. Because research in this field is advancing so rapidly, much of
the most recent material is available only in specialist journal articles.

Mulvaney, in The Prehistory of Australia (1969), summed up the state of knowledge ten years ago. A more recent work, haute vulgarisation of the best type, is Blainey's Triumph of the Nomads (1975). The journal Aboriginal History (beginning in 1978) contains valuable bibliographical material. It is noteworthy that the first of five volumes in Section A of the Bicentennial History will be devoted almost entirely to the making of the Aboriginal society of 1788.

Modern historians and anthropologists, 1950-70:

Because until the 1940s Aboriginal numbers were believed to be dwindling, the few anthropologists who were concerned with Aborigines saw their task as one of recording and analyzing all that could be recovered of traditional Aboriginal society while that was still possible. Little attention was paid to the adaptive techniques by which detribalized and part-Aboriginal communities survived as 'marginal men' in a non-Aboriginal-dominated society.

A marked reversal in demographic trends from the 1940s saw a sharp and continuing increase in detribalized and part-Aboriginal numbers. This coincided with a gradual broadening of scholarly interests. A.P. Elkin, doyen of Australian anthropologists, in the course of contributing to the development of federal assimilation policies, wrote two articles (which appeared in the American Anthropologist, 1952; Quadrant, 1957) establishing a typology of Aboriginal-European relations. His leading students, R.M. and C.H. Berndt, published the first anthropological study on culture contact (From Black to White in South Australia, 1951). They later became involved in problems arising from the acculturation of Aborigines in Western Australia and elsewhere. Their work, with that of their colleagues and students, came increasingly to focus on the social anthropology of contemporary issues which are of concern to Aborigines. [Note the shifting emphasis in the revised edition of the Berndts' The World of the First Australians (1981) in contrast to the first edition of 1964; also the anthologies edited by them, for instance, Aboriginal Man in Australia (1965), Australian Aboriginal Anthropology (1970) and Aborigines and Change: Australia in the '70s (1977).] R.M. Berndt took a leading role in encouraging the Social Sciences Research Council of Australia (now the Academy) to plan a series of studies on Aborigines in Australian society "elucidating the problems arising from contacts between Aborigines and non-Aborigines and formulating policy implications from these; drawing together existing knowledge in various parts of Australia and undertaking such further research as can be carried out over a period of three years". Because of external funding, it was possible to enlarge considerably the scope of this project. The major event of the early 1960s was the national conference on Aboriginal studies proposed by W.C. Wentworth, then a federal Liberal M.P., and convened by Professor (then Dr) W.E.H. Stanner, and held in Canberra in 1961. The papers presented at that conference were published under the title of Australian Aboriginal Studies (1963); and the Australian Institute of Aboriginal Studies was established. This body was to have far-reaching implications for research in the fields of traditional and changing Aboriginal society.

The later 1960s were a time of quickening interest in questions of race and minority rights. In 1967 a national Referendum, by voting that Aborigines should be included in census enumeration, implicitly endorsed the principle of federal intervention in Aboriginal policy-making. In 1968 the Australian Broadcasting Commission's Boyer lectures were given by W.E.H. Stanner. After the Dreaming was an influential statement of the shortcomings of public policy, coming as it did from an experienced and restrained scholar.

1970-79:

Then, in 1970, came the deluge -- in so far as publications were concerned. The Academy of the Social Sciences published the first five of its

series of volumes under the general label of <u>Aborigines in Australian</u>
<u>Society</u>. Edited and directed by C.D. Rowley, the series now numbers
fourteen, and covers a wide range of material on contemporary Aboriginal
problems, including Rowley's trilogy (1970-71). The cumulative effect of
this series has been to provide a multi-disciplinary survey of Aboriginal
policy which offered an authoritative basis for future work. No attempt has
been made to impose an interpretive orthodoxy on the series.

An explicitly radical critique of Australian Aboriginal policy may be
found in the three-volume anthology edited by F.S. Stevens, <u>Racism: the</u>
<u>Australian Experience</u> (1971-72). Initiated by a Sydney committee in support
of the United Nations Year against Racism (1970), the articles linked
Australian prejudices against Asians and other non-European immigrants with
attitudes toward Aborigines -- a linkage seldom, if ever, properly explored;
the third volume, concentrated on Aboriginal policy. Most were strongly
critical of the policy of assimilation. "Although the term 'assimilation'
might have some emotional appeal it can only be achieved through the total
cultural genocide of the Aboriginal people", claimed Stevens. Despite its
exaggeration, Stevens' work is significant for two reasons. He and his
contributors linked the improvement of Aboriginal conditions with the
vocabulary and methodology of the American campaign against racism -- not
surprisingly, because Stevens, now associate professor of industrial relations
at the University of New South Wales, spent four years between 1956 and 1960
as a manual worker in California, sharing the experiences of the under-
privileged. Moreover, they introduced into academic publication the mood
of growing resentment present among an increasing proportion of the
Australian Aborigines.

At the academic level, work has proceeded during the last ten years at
two levels: one seeking to provide such information out of the social

sciences as will help to shape public policy constructively; the other operating more at a consciousness-raising level and seeking to arouse indignation and repudiate assimilation. The latter approach tends to be a little less careful in its scholarship and to concentrate on the more disgraceful aspects of European exploitation of the Aborigines. So far, the two groups have worked concurrently without raising much debate on the fundamental question of the appropriate role of scholarship in the social sciences. Problems may arise with the increasing provision of courses about Aboriginal society to be taught in schools and tertiary institutions. Several books of documents have been produced, among which F. Gale and A. Brookman, Race Relations in Australia: the Aborigines (1975), is to be preferred to S.N. Stone, Aborigines in White Australia: a documentary history (1974) and J. Woolmington, Aborigines in Colonial Society, 1788-1850: from 'Noble Savage' to 'Rural Pest' (1973). So far, the history of European-Aboriginal relations has been thoroughly surveyed only for one state, Western Australia. But monographs abounded. In a survey made in 1977 A. Markus cited over sixty publications appearing since 1970. This was published, together with a select bibliography by Barwick, Urry, and Bennett in the first issue of the journal Aboriginal History -- whose appearance marked an important step in securing scholarly recognition for this branch of history.

In recent years historical writing about Aborigines has reached out beyond regarding them either as hapless victims of undifferentiated European aggression, or as the more or less passive recipients of good and bad policy-making. The work of the Townsville school of historians such as H. Reynolds and N.A. Loos suggests that, within the limits of available resources, Aboriginal adaptation to European aggression was often speedy and versatile; but it also draws attention to the death-roll resulting

from frontier contact. Barwick's research on Aboriginal use of 19th
century rural technology has shown a different example of initiative and
adaptability.

So far most Aboriginal contributions to historiography have come in
the form of autobiography, usually with editorial assistance: Lamilami,
Roughsey, Clancy McKenna and -- an advance into family history --
Philip Pepper of Lake Tyers are examples of this genre. In an historiographical essay of 1979, R.H.W. Reece pointed to the likelihood of historians
emerging from among the urban Aboriginal community, and speculated that some
might be preoccupied with a view of the past as '200 years of murder, rape,
and dispossession'. The Aborigines who attended the Bicentennial History
conference of February 1981 questioned whether it was proper or feasible
for non-Aborigines to write Aboriginal history, and claimed that academic
standards of historiography were inappropriate to Aboriginal history. We
have not heard the last of this debate. As against this, Mulvaney has argued:

> Aboriginal stockmen adapted to the horse as readily as American
> Indians; Tasmanians adopted the dog so rapidly that it
> transformed their social life even as it was under brutal
> European assault. Aboriginal sportsmen have achieved
> celebrity in many fields of European endeavour, not least as
> cricketers in England over a century ago. Many explorers praised
> the initiative and endurance of Aborigines in the patronising
> prose of the period; but such guides cannot be dismissed
> as mere variants of Uncle Tom. Neither can the Gippsland
> informants of A.W. Howitt or his proud friend Barak, elder
> at Coranderrk. Those great folk heroes, Burke and Wills,
> perished in a land of Aboriginal plentitude. Forty years
> later two Aboriginal men from Charlotte Waters accompanied
> Spencer and Gillen across the continent and returned alone,
> safely and without fuss. Such subjects are as much a part of
> culture contact as are the very real and depressing effects.

One thing is certain. Scholars can no longer write history about the
Aborigines in terms of generalizations applicable to the whole of Australia
for the last two centuries, nor can they expect to work within a received
interpretative orthodoxy. There is a stimulating ferment of healthy
pluralism about the present state of study of Aboriginal social history.

It is less easy to identify any consistent historiographical pattern which might illuminate the issues arising out of the question of Aboriginal land rights. A study of constitutional history might have to begin with the debate between C.H. McIlwain (1923) and R.L. Schuyler (1929) about the validity of claims for British parliamentary sovereignty in overseas dominions. Although this debate arose from differing interpretations of the American revolution, its implications went wider: if as McIlwain contended the colonies fell to the British crown by right of conquest, an indigenous people would have no claims to the protection of British citizenship, but nor were the laws of England about property and inheritance necessarily applicable to them; if on the other hand countries such as Australia were colonies of settlement to which immigrant Britons brought their own laws and institutions under the supervision of Westminster and Whitehall, this implied a complete denial of any political standing for any prior occupants of the soil.

The legal status of Australian Aborigines was touched on by Hasluck (1942) and Sawer (1966), but it was not until this year that A. Frost in Historical Studies offered an explanation for the failure of 18th century colonisers to acknowledge Aboriginal rights in Australia. He showed that the eighteenth-century British defined the practice of agriculture and the construction of habitations as necessary prerequisites to social and political organization. Without them, no community could be accepted as constituting a policy capable of exercising land rights or any other rights. This misconception was understandable enough in eighteenth-century Englishmen, but it remains to be discussed whether the work of anthropologists during the last three decades had produced evidence which might call for a re-assessment of the legal situation. It is also possible that light is shed on the question in the controversy between Hiatt and Stanner and others (Oceania, 1962, 1965) on the definition of 'horde', 'estate', 'range', 'domain' and 'regime' as principles of Aboriginal territorial organization.

ABORIGINES IN THE URANIUM INDUSTRY: TOWARD SELF-MANAGEMENT

IN THE ALLIGATOR RIVER REGION?

JOHN VON STURMER

I Introduction:

For Aboriginal-watchers — indeed, Northern Territory- and
Australia-watchers — the Alligator Rivers region provides essential
viewing, with its uneasy blend of uranium, conservation, tourism,
Aboriginal rights: a convergence of vital issues along what many people
consider has been the European-Aboriginal frontier for over one hundred
years, the 'Leichhardt Line'.[1] Subject to a fact-finding study
(Christian and Aldrick 1977), the deliberations of an important government
commission, the 'Fox Inquiry'[2] — which assessed the ingredients and
created the recipe for the 'mix' — a succession of environmental impact
statements,[3] a plan of management,[4] two mining agreements,[5] two land
claims,[6] the activities and reports of special monitoring agencies,[7]
it has almost certainly been the object of more words, thoughts, plans
and strategies in the last decade than any other part of northern
Australia.[8]

Thus far the stress of the inquiries, impact studies, monitoring
assessments has been on fact-finding, the production of base-line data.
Against this, there has been little analysis of the overall picture.
On the one hand, the 'insiders', the 'actors' in the 'uranium equation',
have been too caught up in the day-to-day demands of the situation to
adopt any reflexive pose. On the other hand, 'outsiders', including
the Press, while possessing the advantages of distance — geographical,
emotional, perhaps ideological — generally lack the knowledge of the
'actors and factors' necessary to make more than superficial remarks.

Tatz[9] makes a bold foray into these largely uncharted waters: an attempt to plot the factors from a set of partial views, the mostly unsystematic and narrowly focused perceptions of some of the 'actors'. The result is a sort of political science bricolage, 'a science of the concrete', which produces analytic concepts at once shadowy and suggestive. It is new, and old, territory: while the 'exotics' (the mining companies, the Australian National Parks and Wildlife Service, the Northern Land Council, the Northern Territory government) are busy carving out new niches, the 'endemics' (the Aborigines and the few Europeans who have long been associated with them in the region) are developing — sometimes actively, sometimes by default — new survival strategies: predation, parasitism, scavenging... All the lifeforms, new and old, have antennae raised at the ready to deflect too close scrutiny or criticism.

Lack of analysis, a defensiveness which inhibits real debate, the development of a new political-economic-administrative system (indeed, in its interaction with the environment, a new eco-system), the survival strategies of the 'endemics': these are some of the issues touched on in this paper. They are undercurrents to the central theme: the meaning, relevance, effectiveness and future of the policy of Aboriginal self-management. What are its objectives? How and when will they be achieved? How do they 'fit' with what might be called 'the new pragmatics': resource development in the context of organic change? Where are Aborigines going?

II The great 'white' disillusion:

McKenzie, Chapman, Gray, Webb, Shepherdson, Sanz[10]...: names inseparable from the history of Northern Australia, the long-termers, years in the front line of European-Aboriginal relations, people of true vocation and commitment, knowledge founded in experience and hard practice, often authoritarian, paternal but caring ... The rough-hewn communities they helped create, with few resources and mostly minimal support (and interference) from 'down south', were new things. They cohered, often against the odds, drawing together widely disparate Aboriginal groups, even traditional enemies. They provided schooling, employment, housing, food, health care, law and order. Facts should not be ignored: the school was often no more than an extension of the dormitory system, reinforced by Aboriginal monitors and police; employment compulsory and mostly unpaid; housing often rudimentary and subject to periodic inspections; food rationed, spooned out to the elderly, and supplemented (at least in the case of Aurukun) by compulsory hunting excursions on Sundays after a compulsory church service. Even in the best of missions and settlements, irreparable damage was done as a result of the transfer of power, control, decision-making from Aboriginal to European. But there are other facts which also should not be ignored: for example, it is idle to argue that there was not a strong measure of Aboriginal collusion in the transfer, more cooperation than resistance. Indeed, under no easily observed compulsion, people voted with their feet. They quit the bush and flooded into the settlements.[11] In retrospect, the best of the communities worked: a high degree of self-sufficiency, an economy carefully geared to local productivity, low on violence, a relationship of mutual respect between the few Europeans and the many Aborigines.[12]

And now? Almost everywhere the 'Holy Grail' of self-sufficiency recedes further into the distance, the machinery of community or settlement propped up by elaborate budgetary allocations and procedures, the interventions of a multiplicity of government departments and agencies, and the maintenance of huge teams of non-Aboriginal functionaries keeping essential services, schools, health and outstation resource centres, office and store, in operation. No longer a handful of missionaries sitting around a small table, remote from the world, sharing their collective experiences, wisdom, aspirations, over their afternoon tea. Now a complex of cliques and cabals, groups of Europeans who factionalize across wide ideological gulfs — the 'two-year termers', some after the quick quid, dealing in cars, booze, playing cards to ease the pain of isolation, others 'after the experience' or 'finding themselves', others just playing one more round in the game of departmental musical chairs; and the few remnant 'lifers', bitter, unproductive, dissatisfied in their martyrdom. 'Nine-to-fivism', a scrupulous adherence to office hours, and then a retreat to house, family, the luxuriance of greenery and sprinklers, barricaded behind fences, sometimes a dog or two... Little attempt to ease in newcomers; little collective wisdom to pool; a relationship between 'black' and 'white' dominated by mutual disregard or exploitation.

But surely, some will retort, there are still some people with a sense of vocation? Of course, but they are soon appalled at the realities: houses blasted from within, victims of families in a state of guerilla warfare; schools which everyone acknowledges have failed: massive absenteeism, parents aiding and abetting their children's truancy; child neglect, bashed wives, bashed husbands; attempted rapes of pre-school children; a diet of bread and damper, meat, sugar; steady boozing with intermittent binges; sham jobs, clock-watching; filth, squalor, vandalism, the relentless lack of purpose. Facts, undeniable.

And one day or another they suddenly acknowledge the facts; and they quit. 'And', comes the chorus, 'isn't that all to the good?

Doesn't that mean that Aborigines will be left to run their own affairs? A pity perhaps, even a waste; but a necessary step toward self-management'. The chorus requires a massive act of faith: that it is inevitable 'things will get worse before they get better'; that it is only a matter of time before all Europeans leave, even the uncommitted and the lifers; that the 'community leaders' will soon 'emerge' but will need time to 'spread their wings'. In the meantime, write off the present as the fruits of oppression, 'white' brutality, 'black' powerlessness, helplessness.

Some observers — Aborigines and Europeans — deny the act of faith: they say that it is doubtful whether things can get worse or, indeed, that they can ever get better; that the European 'advisers' will be there forever; they say that if the Europeans leave, the communities will collapse, will, in the words of an Oenpelli man, 'stink like dead buffalo'; they know better than to put everything down to oppression; they know that leaders, people of capacity, decision-makers, people adept at dealing with Europeans and European institutions exist, but question whether they can take any effective action in a climate of complete indifference, or resist the easy temptation to pursue a path of dedicated self-interest. They see that the problems don't rest just with the poor, the helpless, the powerless; they point also to the affluent, the capable, the masterful, to those Gerritsen calls 'the dominant men'.[13] A former Council Chairman, admired and feared by 'black' and 'white' alike, a man of property, a man of the world, whose house — in the words of a sympathetic colleague — 'would make a Calcutta tip look like the Sheraton', delighted when his son and heir falls from grace, gleeful that one source of competition is out of the road, at least for the moment. Traditional owners who demand payment for land on which their own houses are to be constructed. Trips to Darwin for conferences, land claim hearings, 'consultations' cynically greeted as an opportunity for 'sitting fees', reimbursement for 'travel expenses', a 'party': wrecked motel rooms, a television set in the swimming pool, suspensions for driving under the influence, gaol sentences waived in favour of fines so that the 'work of the community' can continue. Some of the 'rising stars' — 'moddled and coddled by the missionaries', as a battler on the front line puts it, a man renowned and villified for his pro-Aboriginal stance — moving softly from one highly paid official position to another, performance carefully screened from public scrutiny or comment, positions for which the normal appointment conditions of job applications, interviews, Public Service Board appeals, are waived.

This is not the folklore of the 'Rights for Whites' Movement in Katherine; it is not the fodder fed by the daily papers to the lady taxi-driver who casually refers to the 'rock apes' as she passes a group of Aboriginal women on the drive to Darwin airport. They are simply the everyday facts with which the informed, the concerned, the sympathetic must cope, and which they feel they must suppress in their efforts to promote the Aboriginal cause. And if they can't or won't suppress them, they must find excuses. They do not relish the stories. Their initial reaction is 'Don't tell me!' They bear continuing witness to a life-style in which, it seems to them, there is no bottom line, in which no one can be called to account, in which abuses, hypocrisies, profligacies, excesses of every kind pass without comment.

It is a situation which cannot be painted dispassionately though it invites calm and accurate documentation. The picture could be made more cheerful with a few dabs of bright colour. There are, of course, men and women of integrity, Aboriginal and European, who have not succumbed.

But the reality of the crisis should not be disguised. Are Aborigines simply 'chucking it all away?' Is there nothing to slow the sinister trajectory already in motion: self-management without the necessary resources (among others, finance, knowledge, clearly articulated aspirations), increasing difficulty in getting and retaining good staff and advisers, a downward spiral of decreasing talent, knowledge, expertise, professionalism, capacity to cope? Is self-management handing over to Aborigines problems which the 'white man' not only largely created but was unable to resolve, government of the weak by the weak, dereliction of responsibility by the society at large dressed up in fancy words?

III Self-management: problems and issues:

What is self-management? Mr Viner, then Minister for Aboriginal Affairs, stated (1978: 3442) in a speech in the House of Representatives that:

> In essence, the policy of self-management requires that
> Aboriginals, as individuals and communities, be in a position
> to make the same kinds of decisions about their future as
> other Australians customarily make, and to accept responsibility
> for the results flowing from those decisions.

The key elements are decision-making, responsibility, and self-sufficiency, 'the economic face of self-management' (ibid.). The major objective: an end to dependency.

I am unaware of any exhaustive assessment of this policy — and it is not my intention to undertake that task here. There is general concurrence that Aborigines (rather than government officials, academics, or anybody else) should be defining their own objectives; but the obvious difficulties in the policy should not be glossed over. I present some of them in the following series of questions:

1. How is self-management possible without a measure of economic
    independence?

2. <u>All</u> Aboriginal societies have historically been engaged in relations
    with each other; <u>all</u> have entered into a set of relations — often
    dating back many years — with particular Europeans, European
    organizations and enterprises and, through them, with Australian
    and global society. In these circumstances, at what level is
    self-management possible or desirable, if at all? To what extent
    are people able to make effective decisions without being aware of
    all the issues and pressures impinging on their lives? To what
    extent can culturally determined and very different notions of
    'futurity' be reconciled?

3. A related question: given that the internal articulation of
    Aboriginal societies is complex and (before contact, one assumes)
    self-regulatory, how does self-management — which, paradoxically,
    becomes a question only when a society enters into a set of
    relations with another society, either in a relationship of
    equality or as a sub-component — maintain the internal articulation?
    And if the demands of the set of relations thereby established
    require or bring about adjustments to the internal articulation,
    what impact does this have on the society, particularly on its
    self-regulatory character and what might be loosely termed
    'social policy'?

4. To what extent are supra-societal (Aboriginal) organizations
    necessary for self-management? How do they receive their delegation
    to act as 'self-managers'? What self-regulatory mechanisms are
    available in their operations? Or, putting it another way, how

can they be made accountable to their 'clients'? Are democratic

processes applicable to their formation and operation?

5. What, in the Aboriginal context, is the relationship between

decision-making and management, between policy and implementation?

To examine these questions, let us look at the Alligator Rivers region.

IV Self-management in the Alligator Rivers region:

1. The economics: In his ministerial statement, Mr Viner (1978) readily

acknowledged that many Aborigines live in circumstances where the

'prospects for self-sufficiency are minimal'. 'In fact', he continued,

'nearly all remote Aboriginal communities do not wish, for a variety of

reasons, mainly cultural, to move to areas of greater economic potential'.

For this reason, he argued, there are 'limitations on what it is possible

to do by administrative means other than through grants from the

Government...' The precise measures proposed — 'land ownership;

expansion of employment opportunities; training programmes; support

for limited economic initiatives; home ownership; support for outstation

movements; increased Aboriginal contribution to financial and other aid

projects' — suggest that the policy makers did not distinguish between

self-management for individuals and self-management for societies, or

proceeded on the assumption that the one entailed the other.

The deficiencies in this view will be touched on at various points

later. The more immediate point to note is that self-management — at

least at the group or societal level — requires a high level of economic

independence. The Minister was correct in asserting that there are

cultural (and other) reasons why communities in remote Australia do not

relocate; he is simply noting the fact that communities wish to remain

communities. However, it seems odd to link the notions of remoteness

and limited economic potential. Western Cape York Peninsula (Weipa,

Aurukun), north-east Arnhem Land (Groote Eylandt, Yirrkala), parts of the Kimberleys and Central Australia, the Alligator Rivers region, these are all areas of which much of the potential is known, not just suspected, areas in which the 'dramatic breakthrough' to self-sufficiency might come, 'from mining and the organised distribution of royalties' (Viner 1978).

Policy would seem to dictate that Aborigines should share in the proceeds of any development occurring on their land. In the Northern Territory under the <u>Aboriginal Land Rights (Northern Territory) Act</u> 1976, and specifically in the Alligator Rivers region under the provision of the two mining agreements, the reality matches the spirit of the policy. Thus, any assessment of the social impact of uranium mining on this region must make it clear that the 'up-front moneys'[14] (there have been <u>no</u> royalties distributed hitherto) have allowed a higher degree of (economic) self-management at both the individual and societal levels than was the case immediately before the advent of the mining — for individuals, 'money-in-the-hand', enhanced purchasing power, an increased capacity to create indebtedness among others; at a societal level, the creation of structures, which not only act (or are to act) as brokers in the distribution of individual payments, but make decisions about the size of the payments against perceptions of need, notions of forward planning ('What will be good for our children and our children's children'), and individual demands. The Gagudju Association, the members of which are largely traditional owners of the Kakadu National Park, was established to handle moneys from the Ranger project. It has purchased vehicles (for outstations), assisted in the provision of housing and outstation servicing, purchased the Cooinda Motor Inn (and imposed restrictions on alcohol sales to its members)[15], established a school, entered into negotiations with the Jabiru Town Development Authority concerning

contracts and other business opportunities, and leasing of the special
areas set aside as Aboriginal 'transient camps' within the new town.
It is involved in consultation with the Australian National Parks and
Wildlife Service over the running of the Kakadu National Park. It
employs its own staff, including a European executive officer; and has
its own lawyer and accountant. In short, it provides a formal political
and administrative structure in which Aboriginal members can make
decisions about matters of importance using their own financial resources,
and with which other agencies can establish contact.

The Kunwinjku [Gunwinggu] Association, which it is intended will
handle moneys from the Nabarlek project, is still in the process of
incorporation. Despite a much wider membership than the Gagudju
Association its financial future is much less assured[16]. Attempts to
broaden its economic base may bring it into conflict or competition with
other Aboriginal structures which already exist in its sphere of influence.
Alternatively, it may be asked or required to take over the functions of
other structures which have proven 'unprofitable'. The general
expectation is that it will assume a broad mantle of responsibility in
the manner of the Gagudju Association; but the latter operates in what
was 'virgin territory': there were no councils, housing associations,
outstation resource centres, mission bodies before its creation.

It is significant, to the implementation of self-management, to
distinguish between two broad conceptualizations: one, that self-
management is not possible without immediate economic independence; the
other, that reality dictates gradualism. I know of no detailed costing
of what would be involved in guaranteeing the financial independence
of any group of Aborigines in Australia or how one would set about the
task; certainly there are no figures available for the Alligator Rivers

region. Without them it is difficult to establish the rational basis on which the mining agreements were formulated, if it was the intention of the negotiators acting on behalf of the Aborigines of the region to use the agreements as a way of implementing self-management. There can be no certainty that this was their intention; but it is an interesting issue because it brings into sharp relief the question of why 'up-front moneys' and royalties were set at the levels they were, and why such elaborate (and awkward) categories were set down for their distribution. The answers to those questions have not yet been adequately investigated. It might have been argued — with force — that 'up-front moneys' should have been much higher, guaranteeing a high level of initial capital to the associations, and 'tied' — that is, the purposes for which income was to be expended should have been carefully specified in advance. The latter would have been an interesting requirement for it would have demonstrated to everyone that agreement to the mining was not just a bowing to inexorable pressure but simply one component of a social strategy, a 'development package', carefully designed and agreed to by the Aboriginal society as a whole. In short, it would have meant that incorporation, the creation of a structure with clear goals, would have been a pre-condition of the agreements. The mining would then have been an enabling mechanism, the 'financier'. In reality, the incorporations were late starters. By the time they got off the ground, much (in the case of Nabarlek, most) of the money had gone.[17] Individualism had won the day (a very short-term victory). Now, there is an awareness that the society has been the loser. It would be wrong to put a too sanguine construction on what people say, for their motives are complex and fine words do not always mean fine actions. However, there is now an awareness among some people in the area that if mining is to bring real benefit to the life of their society, the financial return must be large and immediate to allow comprehensive policy formulation. In other words, it can be used to finance a new social order which may offset what are seen as the potentially harmful effects of intrusion. It is likely that this will be a significant issue in the negotiation of future mining agreements.

Against this, gradualism raises — indeed creates — difficulties: there is never enough to go round; each distribution of funds produces the conflicts, irritations, inequities documented by the Australian Institute of Aboriginal Studies monitoring project.[18] Inevitably it creates a demand for more of the same. It produces a society ordered — or disordered — on the basis of raised expectations and institutionalized individualism (see later in this paper), not on a realistic assessment of the 'art of the possible' which looks long and hard at the links between goals and means, behaviours and outcomes. It produces a society which requires continuing, and expanding, subsidy. As an outside observer one wonders how long the cornucopia can continue to flow. When the mining project comes to an end, what then?

Another issue which relates to this discussion is the relationship, now and in the future, between mining revenue (and other revenues) and government funding. There has been much conjecture about the likelihood that the Aborigines of the region will be asked to contribute from their own revenues to the provision of 'essential services' and other facilities; and there have been a few minor moves in this direction. However, whatever attitude governments choose to take, it is possible that Aborigines will take initiatives of their own, for example, to set up their own educational and health facilities. This is not altogether in the realm of potential actions: the Patonga school established by

the Gagudju Association may provide a precursor for other initiatives
to meet 'felt needs' not met by government, or to shake off its
controlling hand.

A further issue is the increasing role that the mining companies
themselves may play in what might be broadly called the 'welfare arena'.
For example, Queensland Mines Ltd. has shown a preparedness to pick up
the tab for providing services and facilities normally provided either
directly or indirectly by government: electricity, water, housing,
school, teacher accommodation, health visits, shopping, vehicle servicing,
banking, and so on. These are not part of the formal mining agreement;
and I am unaware that they are subject to any formal arrangement between
government and the mining company. One need not speculate too much on
the reasons why mining companies would be willing to undertake such
functions: from varying perspectives, a sense of responsibility, a
desire to keep traditional owners onside in the event of future projects,
a public relations exercise to demonstrate that mining is a good thing...
Whatever the reasons, the practice requires careful scrutiny. While no
doubt attractive to the beneficiaries, to those people who argue that
'the developer should pay', and to governments happy to be relieved of
the costs of providing equivalent services, it runs counter to the self-
management policy: decisions are removed from Aborigines as effectively
as they were under any mission, Aboriginal responsibility is vague, and
dependency is reinforced rather than ruptured.

2.   Education for decision-making: The social history of the Alligator
Rivers region is yet to be written.[19] The contact history goes back
to the settlements at Raffles Bay (1827-29) and Port Essington (1838-49)
on the Cobourg Peninsula. Less than twenty years after the founding of
Palmerston (later Darwin) in 1869, a Jesuit priest reported that the

'Alligator tribes', from over 200 km. away, were regular visitors.
How dubious are notions that Aboriginal societies were closed, immobile,
uninterested in change in the face of such evidence! The building of
the Pine Creek railway (1889), gold mining, luggers, the buffalo
industry, the formation of the reserves, World War II ...: important
events in the continuing saga. Major issues which require answers are
the causes of the rapid population movement, the massive depopulation,
the accommodation to missionaries and buffalo hunters...

Of course, properly speaking, the contact history of the region does
not start with the arrival of Europeans (or Chinese or Japanese).
Macassans had been visiting the northern coastline since 1700.[20]
Moreover, Aboriginal societies themselves had never maintained a state
of hermetic isolation from each other. There was always formal and
informal contact, and much interpenetration. In this sense, Aborigines
have always been in the world: individual societies always part of a
wider political and economic universe. It is a pity that this issue
has received such little attention for the study of traditional
'diplomacies' and 'foreign policies' might have shed much light on
Aboriginal attitudes and responses to all 'outsiders'. The Alligator
Rivers region continues to be the source of mass movements and relocation
of identifiable populations.[21] Processes of adjustment, incorporation,
re-identification and separation are essential components of the social
dynamics of the region.

I have made the point elsewhere[22] that uranium mining has brought
a massive injection of non-Aboriginal people into the region. Not that
it is large in numbers, but a deluge given the small size of the resident
Aboriginal population. Aborigines are now, and for the first time, a
minority in their own land; only a few years ago they were a majority,

in population terms if not political terms the dominant public. The

implications for self-management of this sudden and dramatic shift

have yet to be thought out in full. Much will depend on the extent

to which non-Aboriginal 'population pressure' is increased or compounded

by additional mining projects and tourism in the Park. Much will also

depend on the residential options taken up or brought into operation by

the local Aboriginal people: the maintenance or abandonment of the

existing major communities and the outstations; a drift to or avoidance

of the mines, centres of Park activities, the new Jabiru town; a

movement out of, or, in the case of former émigrés, a return to the

region... However, regardless of the choices and responses which people

might make, and while the capacity for self-management has almost

certainly been enhanced by mining revenues, it is obvious that another

condition for self-management, the continued existence of a distinctive

Aboriginal social field, is now at some risk. The Aboriginal response

is likely to be a maintenance of what is at least current practice, if

not deliberate policy: a marked biological and cultural separation.

Analysis must not stop at the shifting pattern of relations within

the region itself. The reality is that the Aborigines are enmeshed,

some people would say helplessly, in the wider Australian polity and

economy. While not more than one or two Aboriginal people may know the

name of the present United States President, and perhaps no one that

of the Japanese Prime Minister, decisions made in these and other

countries help set the scene for the 'self-managing' which they are to

enjoy as of right. This makes mockery of the demands made by many

people that the Aborigines of this region act as the nation's conscience

in the 'Great Uranium Debate': winners neither if they adhere to the

stereotype of people living in harmony with the environment nor if they

break with the stereotype and seem to join with the developers. Notions
of 'National Interest', nuclear non-proliferation, energy crisis are
meaningless to people whose field of vision is almost exclusively local.
A cruel illustration of the point is the grandiose rhetoric which
surrounds the creation of the Kakadu National Park, the leasing of
their land by traditional owners to the Director of the National Parks
and Wildlife Service 'for the benefit and enjoyment of all Australians'.
What does the expression 'all Australians' mean? Let me illustrate.
Thanks to modern technology, this year's Carlton-Collingwood clash in
the VFL Grand Final was screened on video at the Gunbalanya Sports and
Social Club only a week or two after the event. The game was watched
avidly; yet not just one person, about six or seven, asked me where it
was being played. They knew it wasn't Darwin, so they turned to the
next point of reference. 'Katherine?' they suggested — a town of 3,000
people, soon, some planners predict, to be outstripped by Jabiru. There
were 113,000 spectators at the game, only 14,0000 less than the population
of the entire Northern Territory.

And the expression 'for the benefit and enjoyment...'? Again at the
Social Club, a man in his late thirties, excellent bark painter, my 'cousin'
[in a traditionally part-avoidance relationship] — after passing me a beer
in the two-handed fashion proper to this relationship — asked: 'Nakurrng,
these tourists, who pays them?' To him it was incomprehensible that people
would cram themselves in buses with lots of other people to drive out along
the vast dreariness of the Arnhem Highway to take photos of the murky waters
of Cahill's Crossing on the East Alligator River. What was the purpose of this
activity? Why would anyone do it? Surely someone must be paying them. Fishing,
yes, that could be understood: barramundi can be eaten. But, then, why
shouldn't the fishermen pay? Aren't they stealing another man's tucker?

What -- in the terms of the Land Rights Act -- constitutes their 'right to forage'?[23] If the Oenpelli abattoir must pay royalties to the traditional owners on the buffalo slaughtered on Aboriginal land by and for what is an Aboriginal enterprise, why should the wielders of rod and lure be immune? Such was the thrust of his argument.

Being in the world is one thing, making decisions which in reality amount to little more than permitting 'intrusion by agreement' is another. There are some difficult analytical problems in comparing, say, the intervention of a mission organization into the life of an Aboriginal society with the intervention of mining companies or a Park authority. There is a clear difference in scale, but this may become less conspicuous as the focus of the analysis turns from the scene of interaction to the ranks marshalled and ready to enforce the intervention were it to be threatened by the locals. There is a clear difference when one looks at what the interventions are intended to achieve, missionaries trying to change people's minds and behaviours, a 'bringing of the light', the imposition of the 'good life', miners wishing no more than to take the money and run, Park people less easy to characterize, perhaps the assumption of borrowed clothing, a landscape untainted by civilization, more interesting for its flora and its non-human fauna than the humans who helped shape and model it. Again the clarity of the distinction may fade if one considers the impacts of their interventions, potential or real, on the locals: it is certainly more complex than pointing to the alienation of the mind, on the one hand, and of the land, on the other. It may fade, too, if one examines the wider intentions of the interventions, a desire in all cases to impose a world order: Christianity, development, conservation. Complex and highly integrated local orders, systems which work, ideologies finely attuned to local conditions, may receive sympathy but little real understanding from the proponents of the 'greater verities', the 'grand inevitabilities' always in a state of becoming, continually anticipated but never fulfilled. Nor are the 'true believers' likely to look too closely at the basis of local decisions when they appear to coincide with their own plans, hopes and aspirations. They will attempt, at least initially, to focus on matters of apparent mutual accord, common interest. Missionaries, mining companies, Park authorities, are apt not to explain their real motives; they concentrate on telling people what they will do for them, of the rewards for allowing the intervention; the real reasons can perhaps come later when, they believe, the locals can understand. It is a strategy which works in the short term. In the long term it may prove less successful. The locals may say, 'We've seen that missionary... that mining company... that Park mob. We don't like it...'.

I do not here wish to argue the pros and cons of the interventions. The thrust of my argument would be that any intervention with an end external to the society in question is unjustifiable. However, until there is a true global society it is unlikely that any component society will be free from unsolicited interference. The question which I wish to address here is how to rupture the endless cycle of trial and error (the karma of development!); how, without providing an apologia for development or other interventions, to recognize their inevitability and to devise means to lessen their destructive capacity.

One is the provision of a broad political education geared to the recognition that the regional society shows every intention of wishing to continue and to run its own affairs. It would have to address itself to the specificities of the regional 'mix': the various organizations and structures; their philosophical underpinnings, functions, responsibilities, interrelationships; the broad issues — environmental

and cultural maintenance, industrialism, world energy requirements —
and their political implications. A small but significant number of
Aboriginal people in the region are aware of the need for such an
educational programme. They toy with the notion of going to university
(a sadly unrealistic aspiration at this stage). More concretely, they
pressure members of the Australian Institute of Aboriginal Studies
monitoring project to mount courses. They are not concerned with numeracy
and literacy, the great sacrosanctities of the present education system.
Rather, they are concerned about how the world works, how their own world
relates to it, and the prospect of cultural survival. It is education
for local control, not for mobility.

A second means is the localization of decision-making. On the basis
of Aboriginal experience in the Alligator Rivers region, it is vital to
distinguish between decision-making and consultation. In the context of
Aboriginal self-management they are almost always treated as the same.
The organizational analogues of this confusion are discussed later. For
the moment, we need to recognize that consultation is essentially a process
in which decisions are made outside the region, and brought to its people
for ratification. The consultants rarely expect changes to their proposals
(experience teaches them otherwise). 'No' answers are ignored (they
simply occasion a further consultation) and silence is regarded as assent.
When I first entered the Alligator Rivers region, there was nothing which
horrified me more than the obtuseness of the meetings called in the name
of consultation. It provoked me to write a paper (1981: 13-30) about the
basics of such interactions. Matters which are perhaps more important
are yet to be treated: real consultation, the sheer grind and leg work
necessary to establish the informed climate in which proper decisions can
be made, the steady and systematic building up of knowledge of the

protagonists, their interrelationships, their stances, their goals, in order to understand not so much what is being said as what remains unsaid; the determination of the conditions in which real decision-making can occur locally. The reality is that, despite the plethora of meetings, the locus of decision-making lies effectively outside the region; and none of the monitoring agencies or committees of review concerned with the region has arrived at really satisfactory ways of engaging Aborigines in its deliberations. Until this matter is resolved their assessment of what is happening or what should happen will largely ignore Aboriginal perspectives. Often this is against the will and the wishes of the agency or committee involved; in other cases it appears to be a matter of policy. In this respect, the agencies and committees involved in so-called social issues have a good record, and those involved in so-called environmental issues, a less satisfactory record.

This brings us to the third requirement, the need for the Aborigines to retain (or regain) control over information about their land, and to assert (or re-assert) their responsibilities to it. A major component of Aboriginal world view is the mutual responsibility of people to land, land to people. One of the consequences of the mining has been the creation of special agencies — notably the Office of the Supervising Scientist and its associated Alligator Rivers Region Research Institute — to monitor the effects of mining on the environment, the land. These bodies were set up under the Environment Protection (Alligator Rivers Region) Act 1978 which defines 'environment' as including "all aspects of the surroundings of man, whether affecting him as an individual or in his social groupings", an identical definition to that used in the Environment Protection (Impact of Proposals) Act 1974 under which the Ranger Uranium Environmental Inquiry was conducted. The commissioners of the Inquiry did not hesitate to

consider 'the position of the Aboriginal people' and recognized that
there were "a number of serious problems which will arise respecting the
culture and future welfare of the aboriginal people if mining in the
area goes ahead, and these have to be considered". They also recognized
that there was "an important question of the impact of mining operations
on the National Park".[24] They dealt with these and many other matters
in their Second Report. In short, they did not distinguish, in their
deliberations, between physical and social impacts on the environment.
Yet the distinction is made fairly forcibly — and perhaps legitimately[25]
— in the present environmental monitoring programme, backed up by a
massive machinery: a system of authorizations, government departments,
research teams, university contracts, specialist workshops, a powerful
coordinating committee on which there is no local Aboriginal representation.
It is the world of high science and technology, not the world of the layman,
even if he happens to be the landowner, or if he and his descendants are
at most risk. Some observers see it as rather naive scientism, lacking
coherence, absenting human beings from the models in the vague hope that
they can somehow be tacked on later.

These may be hard words to direct at people and organizations of
obvious goodwill and integrity. Yet, it is impossible not to single them
out for special scrutiny and comment for they alone seem to be immune to
the strictures of self-management: their engagement in the region is
entirely contingent on the mining; they were never required to negotiate
with the local Aboriginal people; any suggestion that they should
accommodate their style of operation to local requirements tends to be
greeted with suspicion as simply creating annoying and unnecessary
constraints; they justify their presence on the basis of an expertise
which transcends all other considerations and of assurances that they are

working 'for the good of the people'. How much simpler and better had they been employed by and answerable to the land owners! Now it is rather like the pastoralists having to hand their land over to CSIRO in the interests of scientifically-based management! The Alligator Rivers region demands an applied science with a human face.

A fourth means is the education of the 'interventionists'. If we argue that Aborigines must develop a national or global consciousness, we must also agree that the representatives of the wider forces — the miners, the conservationists, the scientists, the public servants, and the politicians — must come to grips with the local realities, the local issues. Without the dual trajectories — the locals looking outwards, the non-locals looking inwards — the knowledge necessary to establish a basis for mutual accommodation will not arise. Even then, knowledge may simply reveal basic irreconcilables. For example, how do the notions of futurity held by miners match with notions of futurity held by Aborigines? In broad terms we can distinguish between a notion (and system) of progress and a notion (and system) of maintenance, between expendability and renewability. Let us take another example: the locus of decision-making. Aborigines insist that they cannot make decisions about another man's land; to do so is, in the words of the late Albert Barunga of Mowanjum, 'like taking another man's leg'. Non-Aborigines appear not to share this difficulty, though it may be a relative matter: a conservationist may be less happy preserving a venomous, but endangered, reptile species in his backyard than somewhere in the vast remoteness; and so to miners; and so to others.

Let it be said that there are few observable grounds for optimism in the current Alligator Rivers region scene that these requirements will be fulfilled. There is no machinery for the sort of broad political education

envisaged here. Indeed, the meagre adult education facilities at Oenpelli
have been dismantled. The 'consultations' continue unabated, developing
a life and reality of their own as yet another field of action for what
I shall call the power-brokers (see the discussion below). Information
about the region seems more and more to be held by external agencies.
There are not even the haphazard checks provided normally by the media:
no regular newspapers, no television, poor radio reception. Local
Aboriginal organizations find planning difficult without the necessary
information: for example, when the next mining payments are due, and
how much. And the prospects of informed, understanding outsiders look
bleak against the realities of half-baked induction programmes and the
still total lack of any language courses.[26]

3. <u>Brokers and associations: toward social equity</u>: The internal
articulation of Aboriginal societies is complex and to some extent, yet,
to be fully worked out. The loosely clustered kindreds important in
day-to-day life cut across the demands of lineage affiliation crucial in
establishing personal identity, and for the ownership and transmission of
property: land, sites, ritual, stories, songs, dances... There are now
other elements: loyalty to community vies with loyalty to one's own
estate... In Oenpelli there is strong and general agreement that the
owners of the land on which the community is sited should run it. This
might lead, as it has in other places, to pressure on those people with
no traditional ties to the land and no close kin ties with the owners,
the 'outsiders', to leave, to return to their own land. This is an option
which is open, as attested by the formation of the outstations. Yet, as
people argue, almost all residents have close sentimental ties to <u>that</u>
land: it is their birthplace, their home of many years, the place where
their parents or their grandparents died...

Over twenty years ago Sharp could write (1958: 1-8) of the Yir-Yoront
of western Cape York Peninsula as a 'People without Politics'. But it
is now becoming an anthropological commonplace (despite Gerritsen's
remarks: see Note 13), to accept that Aboriginal societies are and always
have been, if not political in any institutional sense, then given to
intense and unremitting politicking.[27] It seems to some observers that
the elaborate categories, the appeal to precedents and unchanging custom,
facilitate rather than inhibit individual action. It is as though the
whole universe is negotiable; that the most tenuous link can be used to
justify or legitimate interest: 'I have right to talk for we all come
from two grannies' or, an extreme case, 'My wife been camp here once...'
Land Claim hearings are more likely than not to reinforce this view of
Aboriginal society.

If European intervention undermined the importance of traditional
Aboriginal power bases, it as often as not created new bases. The Church
was one. It is no accident that many of the present Aboriginal
spokespeople in northern Australia have a strong church background, and
speak an English often heavily larded with biblicisms. Now the rhetoric
is sometimes turned against the former mentors: the old fire-and-
brimstone missionary becomes 'Old Pharaoh' and the new outstation leader
is Moses leading his people back to 'the promised land'.

The Church is still seen as an important route to power, even if
its importance is fading. Now, there is a proliferation of political or
quasi-political structures which can serve the same function —
community councils, housing associations, the school, the health centre...
Of these the community council is generally the most significant. Its
operation deserves close examination for it represents most clearly that
version of self-management which consists of a transfer of power from

the missionary (or the community superintendent or manager) to his
Aboriginal substitute, the Chairman, from European 'outside overseer'
or 'business manager' to Aboriginal 'town clerk', and so on.

Some researchers (e.g. Sansom 1980: 182-3) have found it useful to
talk of Europeans as brokers. But the analysis could easily be extended
to the Aborigines who are replacing them. Indeed, it is interesting to
compare the 'white' and the 'black' brokers. If the Aboriginal brokers
insist that they should have houses, vehicles, trips, they are only
emulating what they see as the non-Aboriginal model. Where they may
differ is that they may show fewer scruples or more aptitude in extracting
a 'fee' from their 'black' clients — not a new development for, in most
cases, they were already what might be called 'second-level' brokers,
mediating between the missionary and the Aboriginal community. Self-
management has simply meant that they have jumped a rung.

Aboriginal communities now often seem like a battlefield in which
every man of talent seeks an independent power base. Not all bases are
European-created; some are distinctively Aboriginal (outstation,
ceremonies). The latter have at least one major advantage: the 'bosses'
— a word retained for leaders whose field of operation lies exclusively
in the Aboriginal domain — have the power to attract large mobs. This
is especially true of the ceremonial 'bosses', though their power, if
not spasmodic, is only 'official' at the times of ceremonial activity.
Moreover, in addition to providing an economic base (for they have to be
paid for), ceremonies demand that all participate. It is unlikely that
one will ever achieve power without having passed through the various
ceremonial stages. Moreover, there is some evidence that there are
attempts by those who have negotiated successfully with European or

European-style organizations or enterprises to convert at least part
of their 'winnings' into ritual 'capital'.

The European-created structures are less successful bases for creating
'mobs'. For one thing, except in the case of the councils, and
correspondingly one of the reasons why the councils continue to enjoy
prestige, the structures provide little control over staff recruitment.
For example, schools and health services are still subject to the dictates
of government departments located <u>outside</u> the community. Were they to
become independent community-based facilities they could be expected to
follow the same pattern as the councils. This may be one of the reasons
for continuing demands for Aboriginal school principals, especially from
the main contenders (and in a climate of almost total indifference from
those with nothing to gain).

Another factor is that they relate to <u>balanda</u> information and skills
— that is, to the European domain. This is a difficult position from which
to gain respect. It is an isolating mechanism; and perhaps it explains
why Aboriginal brokers holding positions in these structures may be
courted, feared, but are never acknowledged as 'bosses'. The perception
is founded on a fairly reliable truth: that they are indeed <u>not</u> 'bosses'
of the knowledge, the information which legitimates their power base.
They simply know enough about Europeans or are sufficiently fearless in
their dealings with them to give the illusion that it is they who maintain
the 'cargo' — when, in reality, the 'cargo' would probably come anyway.
A classic example is the provision of social security payments. It could
be argued that block payments to communities would enhance the brokerage
operation, allowing the brokers to claim credit for its allocation to the
community, then determining how it should be distributed. Individual
payments would seem to work against it. However, in reality they do not.

All the cheques arrive on the same day; if they fail to appear — a common occurrence — it is blamed on the council; the brokers are prepared to accept culpability to the extent that they may make arrangements for other council funds to tide over their clients — the pensioners, mothers, invalids — until the cheques arrive; and even if the fact that the cheques arrive at and are distributed from the council building were not enough, and that the cheques are cashed at the bank agency staffed by council employees, the Chairman may make the linkage quite explicitly: 'That money came through me. Give me loan ten dollars'.

Another issue is that the directionality of 'mob recruitment' is reversed. Putting it a little crudely, a base in the European domain requires a flow of money, goods and services outwards from the broker to his Aboriginal clients; a base in the Aboriginal domain brings a flow of money, goods and services from the clients to the 'boss'. In short, the first form of brokerage is entirely dependent on the European domain.

The demands of the brokerage system are not met until there are sufficient niches for all potential brokers. I have likened Aboriginal communities to a race in which each European-style agency or structure is a horse and every broker a jockey betting on his own performance. It is a fail-safe system in that the losers can always invoke Aboriginal law; their kindred will, somewhere or other, give them access to one or other of the place-getters. The stakes then have more to do with status and power than money.

Complaints are made that the system is unproductive, just another form of 'nigger farming'. Again, the Aborigines could claim that they are simply emulating the 'white' model (it certainly wasn't the missionary in the big house who planted the garden or who caught the 'killer'). Nevertheless, the basis for complaint is real enough. Moreover, there are two other problems equally serious: one, that the system logically entails what I shall call 'institutionalized individualism'; the second, that it inevitably entails growing inequities in the society.

It is perhaps easier to treat the problems in reverse order. Money flows into the society through the brokers who will channel it first to themselves, then to close relatives, and then outwards in dwindling amounts through increasingly distant kin linkages. Job opportunities will tend to go to close kin or members of the 'mob' who have already entered into client relationships with the broker-as-patron. Distant kin who enter into a patron-client relationship for economic reasons, and in the lack of any other basis to the relationship will be aware that they have demeaned themselves, become ' 'nother man's slave'. All other economic avenues will be pursued before such a step is taken. In this connection it is interesting to observe that the only bark paintings made by any of the brokers (based in the European domain) are to keep their hand in, an exercise in what is seen as traditionalism, not to make money. Indeed, it is almost axiomatic that it is only the powerless who are productive. The big money is with the European-based brokers. They have the best food, the best clothes, the best houses. And as the mining revenues flow in, they will continue to demand their 'cut' — either directly, or by getting powerful positions on the bodies which allocate or distribute the money, or by setting up business enterprises which they will operate 'for the good of the people', or by acting as middle men in cash transactions (mostly involving vehicles), or in promoting the claims, legitimate or otherwise, of hopeful beneficiaries. Some observers claim this is all to the good: the emergence of wealthy entrepreneurs who will serve as a model for 'their people'. Others see them as ruthless exploiters, sucking the life-blood of their fellows. The problem with the first view is that

if they serve as a model of anything it would be of the principle of
'renewable waste': they seem to have no greater drive or capacity to
retain their income than their fellows; they simply spend faster and
more lavishly. The money enters the community ... then leaves. The
second perspective is harsh; but closer to views which are volunteered
from within the society itself. Why then doesn't the society itself
exert some controls?

This is a difficult question to answer. A simple and rather glib
answer is that the resources are derived from outside the society, and
that controls can only exist in a situation where the mode of consumption
is tied to the mode of production. In a situation where the 'mode of
production' — being able to 'mau-mau' Europeans or to play the European
rituals convincingly — rests in the hands of talented (and sometimes
unscrupulous) individuals, it is not surprising that they can 'consume'
without license. They do provide a model: everyone seeks his own
'channel', his 'captive European', his tame organization. And the
reality is that as many 'channels' are created as there are potential
'operators'. It is this process which I call 'institutionalized
individualism'.

I would not wish to argue that this is a new development in
Aboriginal social organization. The relationship between production and
consumption is so close in a hunter/gatherer economy that 'rugged
individualism' must always have been a way of life. But there is another
point that needs to be made in this connection: any surplus was used
for social ends. Its distribution among a wide network of kin created
a momentary dependency which enhanced the prestige of the distributor.
The dependency could be made less momentary if an individual controlled
a campsite with close access to environments which always, or at certain

fixed times, were highly productive. In spectacular circumstances the potential surplus could be converted into ritual capital by allowing the land owner to sponsor a ceremony. In short, the notion and the reality of dependency are not newcomers to Aboriginal social life. It is incorrect to blame the 'dependency relationship' on welfarism; it would be more correct to argue that welfarism accorded well with certain essential features of Aboriginal social organization.

What does this mean: that Aboriginal societies continue headlong along a pre-existent trajectory, that the 'original affluent society'[28] has gone berserk, requiring less and less effort and skill by its members to survive? This is a gloomy prognosis, and may or may not make sense of certain observable phenomena: the waning knowledge of the landscape, the increasing number of ceremonies coupled with a dwindling emotional commitment, the abandonment of so-called 'increase ritual'.

The formation of the associations alluded to above (see under IV, 1), offers some prospects of societal as opposed to individual self-management. Success will hinge on their capacity to incorporate and to reflect <u>all</u> the features of Aboriginal social structure and organization; to deflect fissive pressures; and to incorporate <u>all</u> other organizations operating within their sphere of influence within a single hierarchically-ordered structure; to develop long-term goals and strategies; to develop management as well as decision-making skills; to resist the 'delegation' of decision-making, negotiation and information to non-local bodies; and to maintain a viable economic base. There are some Aboriginal people in the Alligator Rivers region who have demonstrated a capacity to perceive societal objectives and a willingness to keep family priorities in abeyance until these objectives are achieved. Moreover, the Kunwinjku

Association has made significant moves to reflect traditional structures, affiliations and decision-making procedures in its own structure. This provides some grounds for hope, however slender. But there is a long way to go: the notion of a single chairman with over-riding powers seems inappropriate to an Aboriginal organization. The mining agreements promote rather than inhibit fissive tendencies;[29] there have been no efforts to consider the long-term implications of the associations for the continued existence of the community council/chairman/community adviser/town clerk complexes;[30] there are decision-making but no management skills (see IV, 5 below); outside agencies have either failed to consider their future relations with the associations or maintain unnecessary controls (see IV, 4 below); their financial future has already been discussed, at least as it relates to mining (see IV, 1 above). If they are to work, the associations must constitute literally a system of local government and be able to ensure social equity. They must be able to make rules, and to enforce them. The question then arises as to how much they will require external supervision.

4. <u>Land Councils, Associations and regionalism</u>: In implementing the policy of self-management the federal government has placed much emphasis on supra-societal or pan-Aboriginal organizations: the Aboriginal Development Commission, the National Aborigines Conference, Aboriginal Legal Aid, the Land Councils.

There has been much criticism of the Land Councils in particular for their structure seems to be totally at odds with the principles and reality of land ownership: centralized, bureaucratic,[31] council members appointed by delegation from particular regions, charged with the final decisions on <u>all</u> land falling within the Land Council's sphere of influence.

Against this, land ownership links particular people to particular places; the owners resist — except in special circumstances where they are culturally defined and sanctioned — any efforts by others to 'speak for the land'. The Land Rights Act recognizes land ownership yet never confronts the difficult question of translating it into appropriate administrative machinery.

Without treating this matter in detail, several general comments can be made: self-management and delegation of responsibility work in opposite directions; in any case, delegation based on democratic principles is inappropriate where there are already structures in existence which can reasonably be said to represent 'the will of the people' — it simply becomes a means for individuals with no basis of legitimate authority to promote themselves into positions of power (or as someone has suggested, a way of promoting a 'social undesirable' out of the system). Unless the 'delegates' can be made accountable to the land owners — difficult where few of the land owners would know all the council members and where none is involved in appointing any other than the local delegates — there is a very real danger of creating an emergent group of entrepreneurs similar to those already described (under IV, 3 above), but with greater resources and even less answerable to their society of origin.

The alternative direction would be to make the fact of ownership paramount; to allow decisions to be made locally; to provide structures — the associations being formed in the Alligator Rivers region would be appropriate — which could record and ratify these decisions; to create a Land Council which consisted of delegates from component associations (the real locus of field activities) whose only powers would be to report decisions made locally, and to discuss matters of general moment. In short, the Land Councils should be regionalized — not, as current developments within the Northern Land Council suggest, by delegation to

regions (essentially by the appointment of field staff attached to

regional offices, the prime responsibility of which is to report to the

central Bureau), but from regions. The Land Councils would continue to

serve important functions: advice on request to the land owners and

associations on the political, economic and other implications of matters

about which they are required to make decisions; a court of appeal and

redress for particular land owners or others dissatisfied with their

treatment at the hands of the regional association; a forum for the

discussion of long-term goals and objectives... In short, it could serve

as an information base, a component in a multi-tiered system of

accountability, a 'think tank', a powerful political lobby.

5. Decision-makers or managers? In the implementation of the self-

management policy there has been little distinction made between decision-

makers and managers. Indeed, there has been an implicit assumption that

it is the decision-makers who should be trained or involved in management.

Thus, communities have full-time chairmen sitting all day in an office

struggling to write letters conveying their decisions to this or that

government department. Correspondingly (a phenomenon described in different

terms under IV, 3) many people take up management (or functional) positions

in the expectation that these will provide them with a power base (that

is, more involved with decisions than management).

The reality of self-management in communities is that, by and large,

decisions are made by Aborigines and implemented by Europeans. Thus it

is the latter, the managers, who bear final responsibility. They stand

between the 'powers-that-be' (the funding bodies and the decision-makers/

brokers) and the functionaries, the Aboriginal workers. Some at least of the Aboriginal workers attach themselves to European 'bosses' in the expectation that they will provide stepping stones to positions of power. Somewhat disjunctively, the European 'bosses' are required to train their 'workers' eventually to take over their jobs. This situation is characteristic of the Alligator Rivers region as it is elsewhere.

Much of the thrust of thinking in policy circles is to devise ways of training Aboriginal 'decision-makers' to 'run' European employees. However, the harsh reality is that any employee who is prepared to concur in the plans and style of his or her 'black boss' is likely to be a long-term survivor. This will have nothing to do with the person's capacity to fill the position. The other strategy is to create an efficient and professional European bureaucracy, and then to talk about Aboriginalization.[32] Neither strategy is likely to be particularly successful. I am reminded that there is commonly a distinction in Aboriginal ceremonial life between 'owners' and 'managers'. In one ceremonial context one may be an owner, in another a manager. The distinction, and especially the alternating bipolarity of its operation, may be applied more generally once its mechanisms are properly understood. Only the managers, the workers, have real say. The owners are dependent upon their endeavours and are unable to complain. In short, the systems of accountability and production are tied to a system of (mutual) dependence.

At a higher level, the 'policy managers' — the people midway between the policy-makers (at ministerial or senior departmental level) and the 'field operatives' — have in my experience insufficient knowledge of the dynamics of the societies with which they are meant to deal to be able to provide suggestions which might lead to the refinement of policy, in one direction, or which might assist the 'front-liners', on the other. Given the large number of departments now involved in Aboriginal matters,

following the dismantling of the old monolithic Welfare Branch structure
and more recently the handing over of functions from the Department of
Aboriginal Affairs, there are now large numbers of these people; they
have to hold meetings 'to co-ordinate their activities'. There is no
information-sharing, for there is no real information to share; they lack
research and assessment skills; they are overburdened and frustrated by
what they see as the failure of policy; and they retreat, by necessity,
to the application of departmental guidelines.

Without wishing to hurt the feelings of particular individuals — for
my intentions here are far removed from conducting a witch hunt — it must
be stated that this is one of the most unsatisfactory components of the
Alligator Rivers region formula. There are strong grounds for suggesting
that the number of departments involved in face-to-face dealings with
Aboriginal communities in the endless and relentless 'consultations'
should be reduced, and that there should be special courses and programmes
mounted so that people at this level can acquire appropriate professional
skills. Moreover, there should be special inducements offered for people
who wish to seek these skills and to maintain long-term commitments to
particular societies.

V   Final remarks:

The preceding discussion should give little cause for rejoicing.
Aboriginal societies are in a state of crisis, and there are no ready
answers to what appear to be deep-seated problems. It is doubtful whether
anything will be achieved by more of the same: more education, more
health services, more conferences for community leaders, more money...
The situation needs a radical re-think.

The first requirement is a set of objective benchmarks for assessing
societies and the quality of their interactions. What is tolerable

behaviour? What makes a good society? What makes a bad society? All is
not lovely in the ethno-relativist garden: it is important not only to
be able to describe and to analyze, but to judge. Certainly Aboriginal
studies have to be more than apologetics.

It is probably unclear from my paper, taken as a whole, whether I am
for or against self-management. In fact, I am not certain what it is;
and even if I were I would probably remain undecided, finding it necessary
to balance the notion of freedom against the possibility of its
implementation. Quite apart from my own views, the policy requires close
and critical analysis: not only what it is, but what it is intended to
achieve. This is the second requirement.

The third requirement is that if things are not working, they must be
made to work. There is a grave danger that self-management will be
declared a failure; that even sympathetic Europeans will turn their backs
on the 'black struggle'; that governments will tire of endlessly funding
the waste, vandalism, exploitation which are increasingly hard to disguise
from voters; that the Aborigines will be left to their own devices or,
for the lucky ones, forced to depend upon the revenues of mining and other
agreements entered into on their behalf by a remote Land Council.

It is this latter situation which has been discussed at some length
in this paper. Mining revenues, depending on how much, and how, when and
to what or whom they are paid, can provide a more or less independent basis
for social maintenance and planning, in short, a form of self-funding
government. Its structure and machinery remain to be determined. If it
is to be achieved, it will depend on translating political processes,
structural principles and systems of accountability (law and order) which
regulate and give momentum to the society into a mechanism which can mesh
with, and which is sufficiently knowledgeable and informed to deal with,

the wider society and its representatives. Moreover, the point must be made forcefully that there is little justification in creating a system of local government in order to keep local responsibilities in local hands yet vesting effective power in an external agency.

It might be that mining money will be seen differently from government money: as something produced from the land and hence something which can be incorporated in a world view where people and land stand in a relationship of mutual welfare. It cannot be assumed that this is the way it will be seen for, at the moment, money comes by way of compensation for disturbance, not as a share of proceeds. Few Aboriginal people in the Alligator Rivers region understand the relationship between mining and income from mining. It is unlikely that this understanding will improve until Aboriginal people become full participants in mining and other enterprises.

And the greater question: to be full participants in Australian society? In partial answer it must be asserted that, for this objective to be achieved, there is nothing to be served by disguising the truth. The reality of Aborigines in Australian society must be laid bare, it must be told as it is. Researchers will need to formulate a theory and history of contact which goes beyond the frothings of oppression, exploitation, colonialism, which accounts for current realities, and which is explicable to all Australians. Aboriginal organizations, government departments and mission organizations involved in Aboriginal affairs must be prepared to be subject to the same public scrutiny as other parts of the society; the veils of secrecy draped discreetly over the facts 'in the Aboriginal interest' must be torn aside — a role here for the informed investigative reporter, the politician, as well as the researcher. Governments must be prepared to set forth specific policies, programmes

and objectives in the context of a coherent social theory; at present
there is nothing more offensive to people engaged actively in the
Aboriginal scene and coping with the day-to-day realities than to receive
yet another glossy publication filled with pictures of happy smiling
children, brimming billabongs, flocks of magpie geese against the setting
sun, cave art, rock paintings, and the success stories: film, tennis,
football stars; welder, typist, mining company employee...[33]   Policy
must be more than a public relations exercise.

But, one might say, confronted with the harsh realities, what
policies are possible? Isn't it better to put a rosy complexion on things
in the hope that they will improve? There is at least one positive aspect
of current policy: it recognizes that the situation is highly variable,
that solutions and programmes applicable in one area might not work in
another. The logic of this perception is yet to be fully worked out;
indeed, policy implementation often works in the opposite direction —
the creation of pan-Aboriginal organizations which are supposed to
develop general strategies in areas where the policy already recognizes
that this is impossible, perhaps even undesirable; the movement of
personnel, the 'implementers', willy-nilly from one situation to another,
the internal demands of department, institution, council, taking precedence
over the demands of the 'field'... Logic demands longitudinal examination
of particular situations, the steady and systematic accumulation of
relevant facts, of the 'actors and factors' in concrete terms, not just
boxes, labels and arrows. It requires, too, the careful determination
of local goals and objectives, assessment of feasibility, and the
development of strategies for their implementation; and the assimilation
of researchers, government personnel and relevant others to particular
local social fields.[34]

The Australian Institute of Aboriginal Studies' social monitoring project in the Alligator Rivers region might provide the basis of a model of what is required. The model is imperfect in many respects. Indeed, we have argued that the project itself is not as directly answerable to the local people as it might be,[35] that it deals with 'actors and factors' which seem to be in a continued state of flux, that the 'action' personnel representing government and other agencies dealing directly with Aborigines often lack expertise and, in many cases, are not even located in the region. Nevertheless, local people participate in the project as Steering Committee members, or as staff, or as important sources of information or advisers. Moreover, many of the other 'actors' show active goodwill by sharing information, and seek and offer advice. And machinery exists — principally through the inter-governmental Standing Committee on the Social Impact of Uranium Mining on the Aborigines of the Northern Territory — to act on advice or information.

And it must not be forgotten that the project would probably not exist were it not for the uranium mining. There have been several other approaches made to the Institute for projects similar to the one mounted in the Alligator Rivers region. They have in all cases been linked with large mining proposals. This seems to me to miss the point. It may be that it is the areas for which there are limited economic prospects which even more require close attention: in short, in the lack of other resources, a research and planning resource.

NOTES

1.   The explorer Leichhardt travelled north through the middle of the region on his way to Port Essington in 1845. See Leichhardt 1847.

2.   Ranger Uranium Environmental Inquiry. First and Second Reports 1977. Australian Government Publishing Service, Canberra. This Inquiry is commonly referred to as the 'Fox Inquiry' after the senior of the three commissioners, Mr. Justice R.W. Fox, Mr. G.G. Kelleher, and Professor C.B. Kerr.

3.   Queensland Mines Ltd. Draft Environmental Impact Statement, Nabarlek Uranium Project, Arnhem Land - Northern Territory, December 1977; Queensland Mines Ltd. Final Environmental Impact Statement, Nabarlek Uranium Project, Arnhem Land - Northern Territory, January 1979; Noranda Koongarra Project, Supplement to Draft Environmental Impact Statement, October 1979; Ranger Uranium Environmental Inquiry, First and Second Reports; The Jabiluka Project Draft Environmental Impact Statement, prepared by Pancontinental Mining Ltd. as proponent on behalf of Pancontinental Mining Ltd. and Getty Oil Development Co. Ltd., December 1977; and The Jabiluka Project Environmental Statement, prepared by Pancontinental Mining Ltd., July 1979.

4.   Kakadu National Park: plan of management, 1980. Australian National Parks and Wildlife Service, Canberra.

5.   Ranger Uranium Project: management agreement between Peko-Wallsend Operations Ltd., Electrolytic Zinc Co. of Australasia Ltd., Australian Atomic Energy Commission and Ranger Uranium Mines Prop. Ltd. 1979, Australian Government Publishing Service, Canberra; Ranger Uranium Project, agreement under S.44 of The Aboriginal Land Rights (Northern Territory) Act 1976, between the Commonwealth and the Northern Land

Council, signed 3 November 1978; Mining agreement between Queensland

Mines Ltd. and Northern Land Council, signed 22 March 1979.

6.   One was heard as part of the Ranger Uranium Environmental Inquiry

(see Second Report 1977); the other is the subject of an interim report

(2 July 1981) entitled Alligator Rivers Stage II Land Claim: report by

the Aboriginal Land Commissioner Mr. Justice Toohey to the Minister for

Aboriginal Affairs and to the Administrator of the Northern Territory.

See, also, Alligator Rivers Stage II Land Claim, 1980, prepared by

I. Keen for the Northern Land Council.

7.   The Office of the Supervising Scientist was set up on the basis of

recommendations made by the 'Fox Inquiry' (see especially Ch. 17 of that

Inquiry's Second Report). The functions and powers of that officer are

spelt out in his First Annual Report (being the Supervising Scientist's

Report for the year ended 30 June 1979, Australian Government Publishing

Service, Canberra: 3-6). The Supervising Scientist is concerned

primarily with impacts on the physical environment.

The Australian Institute of Aboriginal Studies holds a brief from

the federal government to monitor the social impact of uranium mining on

the Aborigines of the Northern Territory. See Social Impact of Uranium

Mining on the Aborigines of the Northern Territory, Report to the Minister

for Aboriginal Affairs by the Australian Institute of Aboriginal Studies,

for the period 1 April to 31 September 1979 (Parliamentary Paper No.

346/1979); for the period 1 October 1979 to 31 March 1980 (Parliamentary

Paper No. 168/1980), Commonwealth Government Printer, Canberra (1981);

for the period 7 April to 30 September 1980, Australian Government

Publicity Service, Canberra (1981); and for the period 1 October 1980

to 31 March 1981, Australian Government Publishing Service, Canberra

(1981).

8.   In addition to the writings already cited, see, for example,
Jones (1980), and Harris (1980).

9.   'Aborigines and uranium: policy and practice': a paper given
at the Second International Conference on Hunting and Gathering Societies,
held at Laval University, Quebec City, by C. Tatz in September 1980:
19-24. See Tatz 1982: 118-64.

10.   W.F. McKenzie (Aurukun); J.W. Chapman (Kowanyama, Mitchell
River, and Edward River); F. Gray (a trepanging camp at Caledon Bay,
and Umbakumba); T.T. Webb (Milingimbi); H. Shepherdson (Milingimbi and
Elcho Island, Galiwin'ku); S. Sanz (Kalumburu).

11.   Of course, there may have been 'hidden' compulsions: disease
(e.g. leprosy), the departure of young mobile men to work on luggers,
pastoral properties, mines and elsewhere thus creating imbalances in the
labour force available to local groups engaged in hunting and gathering.

12.   This situation was, of course, not unique to Australia, as is
clear from the excellent ABC radio programme, Taim Bilong Masta (1981)
about Australians in New Guinea.

13.   'Thoughts on Camelot: from Herodians and Zealots to the
contemporary politics of remote Aboriginal settlement in the Northern
Territory': a paper given by R. Gerritsen to the Australasian Political
Studies Association, 23rd annual conference, August 1981. Australian
National University, Canberra.

14.   So-called 'up-front moneys' are paid at the completion of
particular phases of the projects, e.g., the commissioning of the mill.

15.   The restriction may extend to all Aborigines, but this raises
questions of philosophy and legality.

16.   The Nabarlek project is much smaller, and of much shorter duration,
than the Ranger project. Moreover, the provisions of the Nabarlek

Agreement are likely to mean that relatively large sums will be channelled to small sub-groups of the Association, leaving relatively small sums to be put to 'societal development'.

17.   For a detailed discussion of the financial aspects of the mining agreements and the history of disbursements up to April 1981, see S.L. Kesteven 'The effects on Aboriginal communities of monies paid out under the Ranger and Nabarlek agreements' (forthcoming).

18.   See Kesteven ibid.

19.   A useful preliminary sketch was prepared for the Australian Institute of Aboriginal Studies by G. Barker 1978 'Alligator Rivers region: historical sketch to World War II' (manuscript). Early in 1981 the Australian National Parks and Wildlife Service commissioned the Australian Institute of Aboriginal Studies' Uranium Impact Project to undertake a research project on the social history of the Kakadu National Parks region. Mr. R. Levitus was engaged to carry out this study: his preliminary report was completed early in 1982.

20.   See, for example, R.M. and C.H. Berndt (1954) and C.C. Macknight (1976).

21.   For example, the migration of Dangbon- and Kunwinjku (Gunwinggu)-speaking people from the Mann River to various points including the tin mines at Maranboy, and later to Mudginberry and Oenpelli and, even more recently, to Jabiru; and the rapid 're-colonization' of the Mann River during the last 10 years. Some of the earlier movement is mentioned in McCarthy and McArthur (1960: 149-50) and R. and C. Berndt (1970: 5-7 et seq.).

22.   'The social impact of mining on Aborigines in remote areas - with special reference to uranium mining and the Aborigines of the Alligator Rivers region, Northern Territory', a paper given by J.R. von Sturmer to the Australian Institute of Petroleum Ltd., September 1980 Congress, Sydney, on The Future for Petroleum in the Pacific Region.

23.   See the definition of 'traditional Aboriginal owners' in the Aboriginal Land Rights (Northern Territory) Act 1976:s.3.

24.   Ranger Uranium Environmental Inquiry, First Report, p. 5.

25.   Note the thrust of the discussion (Ch. 17) and the recommendations (pp. 331-3) about environmental research, standards, monitoring and supervision in the Ranger Uranium Environmental Inquiry, Second Report.

26.   See the recommendation of the Project Director on p. 79 of the Report to the Minister for Aboriginal Affairs on the Social Impact of Uranium Mining on the Aborigines of the Northern Territory (for the period 1 October 1980 to 31 March 1981). Australian Institute of Aboriginal Studies, Canberra.

27.   See, for example, J.E. Bern (1974 and 1979: 47-60), J.R. von Sturmer (1978, especially Ch. 11), and F. Myers (1980a 197-214; 1980b: 311-26).

28.   To use Marshall Sahlins' phrase. See his article first published (1968) as 'La première societé d'abondance', in Les Temps modernes, No. 268: 641-80, and in expanded Ch. 1, 'The original affluent society,' in Sahlins (1974).

29.   Especially under the Nabarlek Agreement, which sets up complex and different categories of Aboriginal beneficiaries. See Kesteven in Note 17.

30.   These complexes were not set up under any single piece of legislation or at any particular moment in time. To the best of my knowledge, a factual account of the development of these complexes in the Northern Territory is yet to be written.

31.   Acknowledged baldly in the recent choice of name to distinguish the administrative arm of the Northern Land Council from the Council as a body of councillors. It is now to be referred to as the Bureau of the Northern Land Council.

32.   This is the adopted policy of the Northern Land Council.

33.   The particular example before me is one which is issued by the
Department of Aboriginal Affairs: <u>Aboriginals in Australia today</u>
(Canberra, 1981).   This is only one of a large number of similar
publications.

34.   It seems to be insufficiently understood that Aboriginal societies
are <u>foreign</u>; and that, consequently, people entering them should be
prepared to make the same sort of effort they would presumably make were
they to take up residence in other foreign societies, e.g. China or
Indonesia. Generally speaking, government personnel (and researchers)
are not even given intensive language training before being thrust into
'the field'; and departments seem to have no hesitation in transferring
their officers on the spur of the moment and for administrative convenience
from one community to another — places more remote from each other in real
terms, it might be argued, than Ottawa and Moscow.

35.   See the discussion on pp. 20-1 of the Project Director's report
in the document mentioned in Note 26.

ACKNOWLEDGEMENTS

I would like to thank Ms S. Kesteven, Mr R. Levitus, Mr S. Williams and
Dr S. Wild for helpful comments.

REFERENCES

Bern, J.E. 1974 Blackfella business, Whitefella law: political struggle
        and competition in a south-east Arnhem Land Aboriginal community.
        Ph.D. thesis in Anthropology, Macquarie University.

Bern, J.E. 1979 Politics in the conduct of a secret male ceremony,
        <u>Journal of Anthropological Research</u>, Vol. 35, No. 1.

Berndt, R.M. and C.H. 1954 Arnhem Land: its history and its people.
     Cheshire, Melbourne.

Berndt, R.M. and C.H. 1970 Man, land and myth in North Australia: the
     Gunwinggu people. Ure Smith, Sydney.

Christian, C.S. and J.M. Aldrick 1977 Alligator Rivers study: a review
     report of the Alligator Rivers environmental fact-finding study.
     Australian Government Publishing Service, Canberra.

Harris, S. ed. 1980 Social and environmental choice: the impact of
     uranium mining in the Northern Territory. Centre for Resource
     and Environmental Studies, Australian National University, Canberra.

Jones, R. ed. 1980 Northern Australia: options and implications.
     Australian National University, Canberra.

Leichhardt, L. 1847 Journal of an overland expedition in Australia,
     from Moreton Bay to Port Essington... Boone, London.

Macknight, C.C. 1976 The voyage to Marege'. Melbourne University Press,
     Melbourne.

McCarthy, F.D. and M. McArthur 1960 The food quest and the time factor
     in Aboriginal economic life. In Records of the American-Australian
     Scientific Expedition to Arnhem Land, 2. Anthropology and Nutrition.
     (C.P. Mountford ed.). Melbourne University Press, Melbourne.

Myers, F. 1980a The cultural basis of politics in Pintupi life,
     Mankind , Vol. 12.

Myers, F. 1980b A broken code: Pintupi political theory and contemporary
     social life, Mankind, Vol. 12.

Sahlins, M. 1974 Stone Age economics. Tavistock, London.

Sansom, B.L. 1980 The Camp at Wallaby Cross: Aboriginal fringe dwellers
     in Darwin. Australian Institute of Aboriginal Studies, Canberra.

Sharp, R.L. 1958 People without politics: the Australian Yir Yoront.
In Systems of political control and bureaucracy in human societies
(V.F. Ray ed.). American Ethnological Society, University of
Washington, Seattle.

Tatz, C. 1982 Aborigines and uranium, and other essays. Heinemann
Educational Australia, Melbourne.

Viner, R.I. 1978 Department of Aboriginal Affairs Report, Ministerial
statement, November 24, House of Representatives, Canberra.

von Sturmer, J.R. 1978 The Wik Region: economy, territoriality and
totemism in western Cape York Peninsula. Ph.D. thesis in
Anthropology, University of Queensland.

von Sturmer, J.R. 1981 Talking with Aborigines, Australian Institute of
Aboriginal Studies, Newsletter, No. 15.

THE ABORIGINAL COMMONALITY

BASIL SANSOM

This paper is written to try to explain how and why Aborigines
of town and country, of mission settlement and pastoral station, of
fringe camps, Bagot and Palm Island share widely and generally in sets
of understandings that make them feel at home with one another. Nor do
these understandings merely come out of a common experience of relegation --
of being administered Aborigines in remote Australia or the welfare outcasts
of a 'white' society in the south (cf. Rowley, 1972a, 1972b). This would
only be a commonality based on settler imposition -- a sharing born of the
common necessity to react to conquest. There is, however, far more than
reactive adaptation to the Aboriginal commonality. It comprehends things
about life and the business of living with fellow-Aborigines that a Fourth
World people have in common right across an island continent.   In a
recent article about Aboriginal writers of autobiography, Barwick (1981:75)
has put the matter very well. She remarks that the Aboriginal authors
concerned "are aware of regional differences in Aboriginal society; they
acknowledge great difference in individuals' viewpoints. But because
they find themselves at home in Aboriginal communities scattered across
a continent, at ease with unrelated aunties and uncles who share a
loyalty to family and familiar territory, they recognize an Aboriginal
'world-view' based on common experience". The problem, then, is to show
Australians who do not share in the commonality of the Aboriginal experience
what that sharing entails, where an Aboriginal commonality has its roots,
and what in defiance of distance and separation such a commonality can be.
Here I work to show that the Aboriginal commonality is rooted in Aboriginal
ways of 'doing business'. These are familiar to people in Perth, Darwin,
outback Queensland and Alice Springs. These ways belong generally to the

Aborigines of Australia.

Widely appreciated ways for getting things in train, for dealing
with the problems that whitefellas pose, for bringing the dispersed people
of a region together for celebrations, for coping with financial difficulties
in family life, make Aborigines of town and country continentally 'all same'.
And this kind of similarity and the fellow-feeling that comes of it, while
known to Aborigines, is largely unappreciated by members of the settler
population. Settlers are prone to issue pronouncements about the difference
between Outback and inside, drawing absolute divides between 'bush' people
and people of the urban centres for whom they invent special labels like
"neo-Aborigines" (Wentworth cited by Jones and Hill-Burnett 1982). Because
this is so one has to crave recognition for the Aboriginal commonality, and
argue against established settler views of the essential difference between
Aborigines of 'tribe' and town. Further, one has to note that anthropologists
in the past have played no small part in playing down the reality of sharing
which Barwick has celebrated in Canberra Anthropology. In my writing of the
Aboriginal commonality, there is something of recompense - a balancing of
anthropological books that is long overdue. Let me illustrate the deficit
by citing a starred example.

Back in 1952, Sharp wrote (1968) a now noted anthropological essay
on the effects of innovation on native Australian social forms. In his
'Steel axes for stone-age Australians' he showed how the replacement of stone
blades by steel did a number of things. The substitution affected long-
established patterns of regional trade in which stone axes from a central
quarry were bartered for goods along lines that extended both to the
north and south of the Yir Yoront of Cape York Peninsula. In addition, the
ready availability of cheap steel axe heads undid traditional authority. Comman
in pre-contact Yir Yoront society was reinforced in part by the fact that
good stone axes were scarce. These scarce items (like fertile tracts of

manorial land in Europe) were held for their use to be licenced and approved
by acts on the part of Australian figures of authority. 'Boss-men' who
held axes let these tools out. For such favours, they got the reward of
compliance. Then and suddenly, the steel axe arrived both to subvert the
tribal eldership of bosses and to devalue a very modality and badge of authority
by giving it to everybody in much the same way that in American universities
the title and function of 'professor' is indiscriminatingly handed out to
everyone on the teaching staff. So the measure of innovation was both profit
and loss -- a gain of technological efficiency plentifully distributed among
both women and men; a loss of a scarce instrument of rule and utility that
had been jealously held by male figures of authority who expected subservient
returns from each borrower for every favour of lending that they rendered.

The story told by Sharp is eye-opening and a product of admirable
anthropological appreciation of a ripple effect caused by casting many pieces
of manufactured steel into that pond that was the total trade and authority
system of traditional Aboriginal society in a vast north-eastern sector of
Australia. Deservedly, Sharp's essay has been reprinted. Yet the well-
known paper has its tragic flaw. Its author is so possessed by the cultural
effulgence and the social integrity of traditional Aboriginal society that
he can only look to Aborigines of the cattle stations and town camps with
a pity mingled with contempt - the kind of mixed sentiment that Edward
Lear gave to Violet, Slingsby and Lionel when (together with the Quangle
Wangle) they soberly contemplated the death throes of caught sea creatures
(Lear 1947). Sharp confirms (ibid.:353) a terrible vision of cultural
dissolution when, with the 'collapse' of totemic ideas, "there follows an
appalling sudden and complete cultural disintegration, and a demoralization
of the individual as has seldom been recorded elsewhere". The process gives
rise to pathetic communities of "broken natives huddled on cattle stations
or on the fringes of country towns". The point is that Sharp never truly

got together with either the people of the cattle stations or those of town camps. He viewed each with an outsider's eye as people who had 'lost' their ceremonies together with their pride in self. The derelicts had given away what Stanner (1959-61) unfortunately has designated the 'High Culture' of Aboriginal religious expression and so are pictured as people of no culture at all. Sharp was wrong. The fringe dwellers and the Aborigines of cattle stations preserved an essential Aboriginality whether or not they continued to talk, as they say, 'in language' or perpetuated the ceremonies of man-making and the ritual celebration of Dreaming powers. Certainly there is a difference between 'tradition-oriented' (Berndt and Berndt 1981:514-16, 517-22) people who have and cherish the full panoply of traditional expression in art and dance and ritual enactment and the people who cease to speak 'in language' and no longer subscribe to the particular and tight integration of myth, rite, painting, song and ritual performance that is traditional Aboriginal religion. But these altered people have inventively created a new language - the developed Aboriginal English that, for linguists, has the status of a creole (Decamp 1971). This tongue, in turn, is the modality for the comprehension and expression of a recreated culture. The relevant question is: how do the adoptively created language and the emergent culture both relate to the old modalities out of which, after all, they came?

Some answers to my question are provided by Pat Baines whose current research on Aborigines of the settled South West of Western Australia shows that Nyungar people of the region have a new cosmology. Its details are enunciated in Aboriginal English to produce a sense of being that paradoxically is true to traditional forms and yet can radically depart from them. In preliminary analyses of recently collected stories, she has shown that these people have developed legends in which named familial heroes walk across the landscape and do deeds in places that are also named. These

histories are held in family possession and the ancestral figures who move
across country progress on the site-and-track pattern of the mythical ancestors
of traditional Dreaming stories (cf. Keen 1977). Nyungar stories are stories
of arrivals and departures, of human travels that cover country to take
it into walkabout embrace. The group that holds the story of those located
happenings that mark the remembered moments of each heroic ancestor then take
the ancestrally covered and so made-over territory into familial ownership.
The emergence of these new stories is associated with yet another innovation.
There is organized pilgrimage to the graves of those named ancestors whose
movements and acts are made legendary through the tales - and this on the
part of the descendants of people who finally put their dead to rest and
barred mention of dead people's names. The new Nyungar stories are,
nonetheless, reassertions despite apparent departures and breaches of tabu.
The characteristic progress of classic Dreaming stories of sites made
significant by happenings has been adhered to. But the old form is reasserted
as ancestral adventure. In all this, the story-form for taking country into
ownership is wholly traditional: on the other hand, the contents of the
stories are distinctly 'modern' for legend has replaced myth and human
identities walk the Dreaming tracks of collectively evoked adventure where
men (and only men, not women) have usurped the mythical figures of the
Dreaming.

Aboriginal families of south-western Australia are now united by their
sharing in stories of place just as Aborigines of the South-West always were.
The difference is that the 'modern' story vests in Aboriginal English and
appropriately asserts a continuing Nyungar presence and historical association
with places that have now to be held against a world of 'white' settler
domination. In the face of settler incursions, Nyungar need history not myth
to assert their claims of territorial provenance which say in effect "My
grandad was there before yours cleared that paddock and, of course, you

people got grandad to do the fencing and stretch the wire that keeps us out". I can hardly borrow more from Baines's unpublished work to reinforce my contention that emergent, vital and traditionally untraditional cultural expression is germane to developments in Aboriginal Australia. I would, however, refer doubters to Kolig's (1981) recent book on religious forms that have been recreated at Fitzroy Crossing by the Aborigines who now subscribe to the collectively engineered and novel modalities for religious expression that they have themselves brought into being. My main concern in this essay on the Aboriginal commonality is not with cultural production but with the social bases for the reproduction of persistently reasserted Aboriginal ways of doing business. This in one sense is fortunate. We now know quite a lot about social arrangements in town and country whereas studies of the emergent Aboriginal culture of expressive forms are scarce. I argue next that one index of the regeneration of the Aboriginal commonality is a well-documented and generally distributed manifestation. This is the recomposing household or fluctuating local group.

Concertina households:

The notion of the 'concertina household' is not anthropological though, perhaps, it should be. It comes of the collective wisdom of welfare officers in Perth who deal with Aboriginal people, ministering to their financial and housing needs. These welfare officers are aware that their Aboriginal charges cope with the vicissitudes of life (which include spells of employment succeeded by unemployment, falling into arrears with rental payments, imprisonment, the temporary separation of spouses or the breakdown of marriage, illegitimate births where a child has no supporting father, the removal of problem children into care, illness and problems attendant on the social incidence of drunkenness) by recomposing households. On the day of an officer's counselling visit the rented State Housing home at 23 Fairweather Street may harbour five people. On the next counselling visit,

the welfare worker can walk into a house in which (depending on the time
of day) up to thirty people can be found treating Fairweather Street as their
current address. Who is in a house at a particular time, on what grounds
and on the basis of what tie of relationship to the 'official' household
head would require an extended explanation. One would have inevitably to
deal with householding, with the nature of 'family', with a geo-ecology of
Aboriginal tenancy in Western Australia and with a sociology of signal
events. I shall deal with some of these things later. The immediate and
important point is to note that welfare workers in Perth know a phenomenon
and have a label for it - the 'concertina household'. This is a variable
entity that inhales into an expanded manifestation or noisily exhales into
compact and tight formation. And note that I was encouraged to this
metaphorical flight by the fact that Aborigines themselves describe the
fractious events often attendant on household reformation as 'noise'. So,
"That's a real noisy place now. Too many people. I reckon that place is
goin to spill right out. That Auntie Josie caan keep't". Here an Aboriginal
informant whom I have left unnamed predicts exhaling contraction of the
concertina. Writing of commonality, let me now invoke Yuendumu in the
Northern Territory, after having thus said something of Perth.

In 1979 Elspeth Young went to Yuendumu and her brief was to report on
the Aboriginal economy. Her detailed report was published in 1980. In it
she explains why she did not perform some of the standard routines of
economic investigation. As she came to understand the nature of the local
community, she concluded that she could not treat the household as a
budgetary unit, devise household schedules of need and go on to account for
the generation of need by referring it to household composition -- considering
the relationships between a 'normal' established household and the economic
world outside. Standard economic procedures failed her for reasons that
she explains (1981:68). At Yuendumu "a large permanent house can shelter

over twenty people during one week, and be occupied by a single nuclear
family the next.   This makes it impossible to assess accurately how many
of Yuendumu's Aborigines have permanent houses, or the density of occupation
in permanent or temporary accommodation......".   Young, furthermore, comments
in general terms on the three remote settlements of Yuendumu, Willowra and
Numbulwar remarking pervasive and persistent patterns of movement.   "In
general, Aborigines are highly mobile on a short term basis, following
patterns of movement strongly related to the location of members of their
extended family;   long term movement outside such a network, away from
tribal territory, is uncommon" (ibid.:242).   She thus characterizes the
northern Aborigines she knows as people of recomposing households and of
a stamping ground that is made up of the frequented haunts that are used on
and off by people who cleave to a region but have no lasting attachment to
particular residences within it.

The trends that Young describes have been documented before and notably
by Beckett who wrote of 'kinship, mobility and community' among part-
Aboriginal people of the far west of New South Wales -- an area familiarly
known as 'The Corner'.   He wrote (1965:20) that in the region about
Wilcannia:

> Each Aboriginal has a beat, an area which is defined by the
> situation of kinsfolk who will give him hospitality, within which
> he can travel as much or as little as he pleases, and where he is
> most likely to find his wife. Proximity is only a minor factor.
> When first working in Murrin Bridge, I was impressed by the fact
> that most of the people knew far more about Wilcannia - 200 miles
> away - and visited it more frequently, than they did Euabalong -
> only ten miles away - or Condobolin - only thirty. One explanation
> is that the Murrin Bridge people have lived near these last two
> places only since 1948, whereas their contacts with the Darling
> River people go back to 1934 and before; however, one might expect
> links to have developed after a decade. In fact, over the last
> seven years only one marriage has been contracted with Condobolin
> and only one with Euabalong, as against six with Wilcannia.

In the course of his analysis he noted other trends that I wish to stress:

(1)   The tendency for stabilized people attached to place to be older

rather than younger, leaders rather than followers.

(2) There was a high frequency of divorce.

(3) There were enduring ties between mothers and their children
     which contrasted with what might be called 'contingent fatherhood'.
     While a mother is generally a mother for as long as she lives,
     a father's recognition depends more markedly on his performances.
     A father gets credit and wins recognition from children to the
     extent that he shows active regard, affection and loyalty by making
     contributions to the 'raising up' of the boy or girl that he begot.
     (In this vein, Aborigines in and around Darwin call a father who
     has been only casually interested in the rearing of his children
     'that father for nothing'.)

Beckett's achievement in his Wilcannia study was to relate the characteristic
Aboriginal family of 'The Corner' to a pattern of mobility. This
relationship is, for me, an aspect of the Aboriginal commonality.

Of households, the 'beat', 'the line' and 'runs':

'Beat' is the word Beckett uses for the set of frequented places
joined by a track that each Aboriginal consolidates and then comes to regard
as an individual stamping ground. And I gather from my own enquiries that
Beckett's 'beat' is an adopted word, extracted from the Aboriginal English
of 'The Corner'. It is also, I find, a word now used (in the sense that
concerns us) by Aborigines of Brisbane and its hinterland. In the
environs of Perth, older Aborigines speak of 'runs' that join the townships
of the South-West -- Quairading to Merredin to Mukinbudin to Perth.

In Western Australia there are Aborigines whose pattern of movement
is up and down the bitumen strip that connects Perth to Broome. These
people speak of 'the line'. 'Beat', 'run' and 'line', while encysted words
of familial or regional argots, are exact synonyms - each stands for the
set of places that constitute a social ambit for a person of no necessarily

fixed residence but of a delimited countryside. In and about Darwin,
Aboriginal English yields "all that place bla Countrymen" as the phrase
to translate 'beat' or 'run' or 'line'. And the general point I wish to
make is that the varieties of Aboriginal English in Australia have similar
lexicons of words and phrases for recognized things. The relationship
between the Aboriginal English of the south-east of Queensland and that
of Perth is one of direct translation -- the task is to find the local
synonym in noun or verb or phrase. However, when turning the formulations
of Aboriginal English into Standard English, direct translation often fails.
One is constrained instead to write brief glosses to make things like the
'beat' or 'run' or 'line' realities. I am commenting on an aspect of the
Aboriginal commonality. When Alice Springs is compared with Perth,
people of The Alice are said to have "got it same but different really".
In other words, they know realities that are recognizably the same as
those constructed in Perth even though often they choose to label these
familiar things by using a contrasting and therefore interestingly variant
nomenclature for the things that a speaker drawn from Perth knows well but
talks of proudly in Perth style. Aboriginal argots co-exist in Australia
and the relationship between them is direct -- evinced in an immediacy of
unglossed substitution of one word for another. Same realities, sometimes
different labels. When one considers the reality that is signalled by the
beat of Wilcannia and Queensland, by the Darwin phrase 'all that place
bla Countrymen', by the 'runs' of older Nyungar of Western Australia and by
the 'line', one is led to doubt whether the Greeks ever had a word for it.
To remark this is also to note an aspect of the Aboriginal commonality.
It is grounded in social similarity that, linguistically, is differentially
expressed. And when ordinarily distanced people come unusually together,
they can join in an exercise of discovery. Essaying communication, they
find that they are same but different: people of similar (even identical)

perceptions but also persons distinguished by command of the special
style and tongue that comes of their origins and distinguishes their
respective verbal performances to bring spice and wonder to the discovery
of a commonality in understanding that is carried in different codes. So
Aborigines from far-flung parts are able fluently to join as they negotiate
the labels for shared world-views into being. The stage, so to speak,
is pre-set for enjoyable acts of easy and direct translation. The sameness
is an essentialism born of an intriguing likeness of the raw stuff in the
made over things of experience: the difference is nominal. This said,
the problem is to account for the pan-continental generation of essential
similitude. To do this it is necessary to characterize Aboriginal groupings
and then to define the values and modalities in terms of which members of
such groupings conduct their business in everyday living.

The Hinterland Aboriginal Community:

Beckett for Wilcannia and Young for Yuendumu, Willowra and Numbulwar
point up common characteristics of Aboriginal social organization in
distanced places. The forms that they describe conform to type. And I have
a label for the type. I originally provided it (1976) when asked to assist
in the preparation of a land claim in the Northern Territory. I
distinguished 'The Hinterland Aboriginal Community' as a widely distributed
and reasserted form for Aboriginal association. The type is characterized
by a listing of seven attributes which define it as a grouping made up of
Aboriginal people who:

(1) Regard a particular locational centre, often an Aboriginal
camp on a cattle-station, as their home-place.

(2) Despite the fact that this home-place is not necessarily a
part of their home-territory as defined in traditional
terms.

(3) These groupings of people are, furthermore, usually of mixed
tribal origin and, in consequence, their various members
speak a number of different languages or dialects. In such
mixed groups, the general use of a form of non-standard

English (usually called 'pidgin') facilitates communication between those members of the group who do not have an Aboriginal language in common.

(4) Vital social links between members of such tribally mixed groups are based on years of joint experience of work not merely on one, but on a number of cattle-stations as well as in other forms of European-controlled employment. As the people themselves are apt to put the matter: "We bin work together for years n years".

(5) Links forged by years of association in cattle-station employment or in other work, are reinforced by ties of marriage, of 'in-lawship' or affinity. Men who have worked together often take each other's kinswomen as wives. The result is that second and subsequent generations are produced whose members, while still 'mixed' in terms of patrilineally reckoned tribal origins, are closely linked both to their contemporaries and to their predecessors in the local group by ties of kinship and affinity.

(6) It should be noted that adult members of this type of grouping have not necessarily all worked together at one place or for the same employer for their entire careers. Rather than sharing a single station of employment, the people of the group have shared what may be called a 'work beat'. Such 'work beats' are made up, for example, of several cattle-stations, a couple of buffalo-shooting camps and, perhaps, a farm the owner of which offers seasonal employment. It is characteristic of such work beats that they expand or contract over the years, often because of either the success or the failure of Top End enterprises.

(7) Certain places that are part of a work beat gain particular significance. These are places that those persons who claim to be members of 'one mob' come to regard as their base or home-place. Given the seasonality of employment in Northern Australia, the home-place or base may often be defined as the place at which a person establishes his residence during the Wet season.

(8) A Hinterland Aboriginal Community in the north-west of the Territory is a group of people of mixed tribal origins who are now based on a particular home-place, who are united by ties of shared work-experience, by ties of kinship and affinity and who are generally to be found living together in the Wet season while, at other times of the year, some of the members of the group will be absent from their home camp for extended periods because occupied elsewhere.

I come now to a difficult part of my argument. Having been assertively firm in characterizing a type of community, I have by very use of the word 'community' prejudiced most of my readers who, I assume, generally associate the coming into being of any community of association

with settlement and the long-term attachment of persons to home and
neighbourhood. The point is that the important camps or other stopping
places of each set of people who belong to 'runs' or 'beats' or 'lines'
are places in which an Aboriginal presence is generally asserted and
reasserted over time. But this work is done by a set of people who, so
to speak, take turns at being the people of that Warehouse campin, or that
Big Tree station, or of Auntie Josie's place (23 Fairweather Street in
metropolitan Perth). The Aboriginal domination of sites and scenes relies
on a continuous and representative presence of people drawn from the
category that northern Aborigines call Countrymen. And all Countrymen are
fickle in their individual attachment to place, basing themselves on this
camp as home-place and then sortieing from it for a time on 'visits' to
other places. But a visit can be turned into a shift of primary camping
or residential allegiance. Thus Big Johnny of Wallaby Cross can become
that Crookeye of the camp next to the garbage dump in Adelaide River. The
home-base camps of Countrymen are home camps of convenience as are the
homes rented by Aborigines along the Perth-Broome line. In the long
term, one can say that the people of a region all taken together 'have'
certain places. These places are reassertively theirs because sundry and
assorted Countrymen continue to use them, on-and-off, and the beauty of
stories of place like those instanced earlier, is that the stories shift
to embrace heretofore unused but now frequented places. They also keep
a currently unused camp site in notional possession because a people's
right and claim to the shell camp lives on in told and retold tales.

    In general, the Countryside of Darwin Countrymen or the lines and runs
of the patronymic Nyungar groups of the South-West are territories for the
continuing reformation of recognized Hinterland Aboriginal Communities
based on prime regional locations. Prime base locations, which are
cyclically populated and repopulated, are contexts in which one witnesses

the composition and recomposition either of residential households or of
the kitchen-centred hearthholds of open-air encampments. Aspects of the
Aboriginal commonality are then patterned movement in created regions, the
wax and wane of groupings in residential association and the further
manifestation of intermittent association that is expressed either as
"on and off marriage" (cf. Sansom 1980) or as a high frequency of final
marital dissolution. There is a further consequence to note. Given
unsettled or broken marriages, there is an ongoing business of placing
'kids' and, sometimes, of placing recently placed children all over again.
The children are consigned to the care of suitable guardians in response
to shifts and starts in the management of adult marital association. In the
business of caring for the children of extended families, older women became
prominent. The system of social organization promotes older women as
'grannies' who watch constantly to oversee the proper treatment of clutches
of young descendants whose destinies are the business not only of their
parents but of all their interested kin. In the words of Anthropology,
the prominence of grannies is reflected in a tendency toward 'matrifocality'
in the current composition of local domestic groups -- a trend remarked
in various studies of urban Aborigines (e.g. Gale 1972) but emphasized
in particular by Barwick (1974) with reference to Aborigines of Melbourne.
To put the matter simply, there is at any time a proportionately large
number of households without dominant men in them and in which a granny
is the hearthholder or householder and so the family 'boss'.

Of cause and consequence:

To remark and detail the clustered and interrelated aspects of a
continental commonality is one thing: to account for its creation and
perpetuation quite another. Two further steps are required. The first
is to turn from produced common trends and forms to the culturally
established modalities for action that bring them into being. The second

step is to consider not internal Aboriginal affairs but the nature of the relationship between Aboriginal minority communities and mainstream Australian society.

To deal with Aboriginal 'business', I start by remarking a difference between Western and Aboriginal conceptions. Aboriginal business starts off from a notion of ownership that is worked out in ways that contrast starkly with a Western emphasis on property as the prime object of possession. An emphasis on property comes of the participation of Western economic man in the markets of a cash economy. The Aboriginal economy (past and present) is a service economy and, in it, the parties to transactions are not vendor and buyer. Instead, there is magister and minister (Mauss 1954) -- the owner of a business or a trouble or a problem or a ceremony and the person who helps in the business, aids in times of trouble and comes from far to offer service for the duration of a ritual enactment at a sacred site. Aborigines own slices of action and also own the signs and symbols that attest to a person's rightful capacity to initiate the staging of events of distinguished sorts and kinds. This is to recognize four orders of Aboriginal things owned. These are:

(a) Ownership of a warranty that licences an order of performance and/or the things that symbolize this socially acknowledged capacity;

(b) Ownership of a trouble or problem (in this the person who 'has' the trouble is victim);

(c) Ownership of an obligation to perform a deed or stage a programme of action; and

(d) Complex ownership of a business that one continually negotiates by winning and keeping the agreement of others to one's initiatives and their assent in one's authority. When it is accorded this is the authority that asserts and proves a person's leadership.

Social life is exchange. It takes a deal of flexibility of mind for a person of one set of practices for doing business to adjust his thinking and accept the values and procedures of a foreign system for exchange when the axioms of that system contradict all the imperatives and prescriptions of the system that contains him and which he knows. To understand how Aborigines do business nothing less than a conversion of market thinking into service thinking is required. Such conscious and appreciated transformations are not easy. But then, living on the other side of cultural difference, Aborigines of town and country are required to translate their service values into market values day after day as they move between Aboriginal community and the markets of settler society.

To extrapolate from the principles I have set out, it follows that:

(1) The regnant capital good of Aboriginal society is the actual warrant or symbol of capacity to stage events. The prototype of such ownership of capacity is in the responsibility of persons for the maintenance of sacred sites and the perpetuation of the memory of their significance through ritual re-enactment of the story that hallows a site by linking it to events that came of the Dreaming adventurings of personified powers. Nothing is more valued or important than the ownership of a sacred site.

(2) The troubles and recognized problems of known others are occasions for the generation of signal indebtedness, as when instances of sickness bring concerned others to the sick bed to be distinguished as serving helpers who "saw that sickfella through".

(3) When the onus is on someone to honour obligation -- for
     instance the preservation of the tabu on calling dead men's
     names -- then the action that follows is action in face of
     challenge. Successful performance redounds to a person's
     merit -- Ada and Masie would not <u>allow</u> that their dead
     brother's name be called. And, furthermore, Ada and
     Masie caused them to be punished for they in active
     defiance of cultural prescription, and to rubbish Ada and
     Masie, called the name that this pair were obliged by
     traditional prescription to submerge in unremembrance.
     Prescriptions of obligation back the assertive deeds that
     ensure that right things will be done in face of the threat
     of the perpetuation of wrong.

(4) Success in organizing activity brings both debt and
     recompense. In Darwin and its hinterland the completion
     of any successful group venture is celebrated in an act
     of finishing. People come up to the organizer of the event
     to declare themselves 'satisfied' (or unsatisfied) with the
     performance. The successful organizer of events then
     accepts plaudits. He also acknowledges debt. Each
     contributory act toward the organizing of a ceremony or
     the organizing of a hunting party is, in the outcome,
     balanced against previous contributions in an accounting.
     The organizer of ceremony ends up as a person who owes much
     to Peter Merrick for doing the Emu dancing but owes nothing
     to the painter who dressed the performers with ochres, for
     the painter entered the performance as a thrice-rescued
     drunk saved from police trouble by the mentor of ceremony at
     a time now weeks back.

So each category of Aboriginal ownership has its capacity for the generation and regeneration of sorts of debt. While profit and loss accounting is germane to Aboriginal business, the items taken into account are in definition and derivation quite unlike those that are registered by the programmer who punches the entries for a Western enterprise. My point is that for each category of Aboriginal ownership, there is a corresponding sort of debt. In the end, people of 'beat', 'line' and 'run' and Darwin people called Countrymen are linked to one another through a web of relationships that can be expressed roundly in terms of economic advantages and deficits. People come out of 'business' either as people owing something to their co-participants or as people who by their witnessed contribution to action have credit and are creditors. Either way, debtor and creditor reassert their bonding and ritual relevance to one another as people linked by ties that come of the action that produces debt. Aborigines, in short, are integrated in a system of exchange where the debts that are grounded in Aboriginal conceptions of ownership are totalized to be balanced one against the other to social, economic and political effect.

Dealing with ownership and debt, I have provided a rather abstract exposition. The trouble is that grounding it would require much space for illustration, explanation and detailed commentary. The culminating point I wish to make to cap my abstracted analysis is this: Aboriginal economizing requires people to enter into compacts of reliance with one another that, as contractual compacts of performance (completed, promised or merely proposed), are the units whose multiple contraction link people of a region in a web in which debt is derived from ownership where service rendered or accepted provides the coin for a system of exchange.

The parathetic relationship:

People called Countrymen and those of runs and beats and lines live in created worlds of Aboriginal identity and performance that stand in parathetic relationship to mainstream Australian society. The parathetic relationship is an inter-ethnic thing -- the relating of distinct cultures. Aborigines have adopted material goods, have taken to drink and use Toyotas or motor cars but they use these things their way. They have not appropriated Western modalities and values along with their take-over of ranges of provided goods. The camp Toyota is used as camp Toyota and its petrolling as much as its maintenance and use is modulated to Aboriginal allocations of value. The vehicle will be released to travel miles for a ceremony, but not given up to the young man who sees profit in a mooted buffalo shooting enterprise that is grounded in possession of a four wheel drive conveyance. This is not perversity. It is the assertion of value collectively determined and agreed. The Toyota is better as an available conveyance -- a potential ambulance if someone 'gets accident'. And the retention of the truck is related to the web of created indebtedness. The people who call for its reservation to domestic camping use can, if challenged, point to acts of helping and contribution. The bevy of people joined to oppose the conversion of the Toyota into a hunting vehicle whose use will yield profits, is made strong if its members can argue from what generally they are owed. They make the balance of accumulated credits over into a group demand that a battered but working group vehicle stay in camp and be available to serve their unknown and therefore unpredictable future needs.

Commonality and ethnogenesis:

Jones and Hill-Burnett (1982) have looked for but largely failed to find an Aboriginal ethnogenesis - the forging of a pan-Australian Aboriginal identity that can be politically asserted. The reason is not far to seek. The Aboriginal commonality of fellow feeling and similar understandings

contains the countervailing forces that would need to be overcome if a
pan-Aboriginal ethnogenesis were to be achieved. Traditional or 'modern',
Aboriginal society is small-scale. The Aboriginal conception of ownership
and consequent debt is possible to maintain in a consociate society of
known others. The interchange of personnel who belong to beats or lines
or runs or communities of Countrymen, is governed by a set of processes
that are comprehended within contained populations associated with specific
regions. There were few marriages between Condobolin and Euabalong in
'The Corner' of New South Wales. Then let us return to Barwick's cited
statements. She remarks that _individual_ Aborigines can move largely to
find themselves at home in Aboriginal communities removed from their
normal stamping grounds. In such distanced places they find unrelated
but socially created Aboriginal uncles and aunts who talk of place
and family and people in terms the visitor can readily understand. The
individual traveller finds himself at home away from his own country. The
trouble is that the Aboriginal commonality is posited on particularistic
manifestations, consociate experience and a conception of a closed set of
others who are truly and really one's Countrymen. Without such closure
and limitation the system for creating Aboriginal regional communities
would not work. It is posited on in-marriage, on regionalism, and above
all on the reachability of persons who owe one recompense or to whom one
owes acknowledged debt. The Aboriginal commonality has its genesis in the
repetitive reassertion of similar forms for social association on a
continental scale. The essential similarity of Aboriginal social
organization is reproduced across Australia. The similitude is centred
within social groupings that are defensively maintained against the
world. These are bordered communities of regions in which people hold
debts to one another, recognize mutual interests and arrange marriages.
The paradox is that the Aboriginal commonality has until now defeated

ethnogenesis writ large. This is because people who are 'all same' in the modalities of their social expression are 'different really' when their loyalties and ties of indebtedness are considred as bases for their association. The Aboriginal commonality is, at once, an extensive and distributed sharing in understandings and a limited and constricted vision of these others who may be admitted to one's own known world made up of trusted and genuinely established persons. This is to say that Aborigines limit their world to consociate involvement, and have no developed means for accommodating categorically defined contemporaries as figures who legitimately can have a place in a landscape that is more extensive than the country that the observer has himself walked and so can claim to know.

REFERENCES

Barwick, D. 1974 The Aboriginal family in south-eastern Australia. In The Family in Australia (J. Krupinsky and A. Stoller eds). Pergamon Press, Sydney.

Barwick, D.E. 1981 Writing Aboriginal history: comments on a book and its reviewers, Canberra Anthropology, Vol. 4.

Beckett, J. 1965 Kinship mobility and community among part-Aborigines in rural Australia, International Journal of Comparative Sociology, Vol. 6.

Berndt, R.M. and C.H. 1981 The World of the First Australians. Lansdowne Press, Sydney.

Decamp, D. 1971 The study of pidgin and creole languages. In Introduction to Pidginization and Creolization of Languages (D. Hymes ed.). Cambridge University Press, Cambridge.

Gale, F. 1972 Urban Aborigines. Australian National University Press, Canberra.

Jones, D.J. and J. Hill-Burnett 1982 The political context of ethnogenesis. In Aboriginal Power in Australian Society (M.C. Howard ed.). Queensland University Press, St. Lucia.

Keen, I. 1977 Yolngu sand sculptures in context. In Form in Indigenous Art (P.J. Ucko ed.). Australian Institute of Aboriginal Studies, Canberra.

Kolig, E. 1981 The Silent Revolution. Institute for the Study of Human Issues, Philadelphia.

Lear, E. 1947 The Complete Nonsense of Edward Lear. Faber and Faber, London.

Mauss, M. 1954 The Gift (Trans. I. Cunnison). Cohen and West, London.

Rowley, C.D. 1972 a Outcasts in White Society. Penguin, Harmondsworth.

Rowley, C.D. 1972 b The Remote Aborigines. Penguin, Harmondsworth.

Sansom, B. 1976 'Humpty Doo Land Claim'. Report submitted to the Northern Land Council, Darwin.

Sansom, B. 1980 The Camp at Wallaby Cross. Australian Institute of Aboriginal Studies, Canberra.

Sharp, L. 1968 Steel axes for stone-age Australians. In Economic Anthropology (E.E. LeClair and H.K. Schneider eds). Holt, Rinehart and Winston, New York.

Stanner, W.E.H. 1959-61 On Aboriginal Religion, Oceania, Vols. XXX-XXXIII.

Young, E. 1981 Tribal communities in rural areas: the Aboriginal component in the Australian economy. Development Studies Centre, Australian National University, Canberra.

A GOVERNMENT PERSPECTIVE

PETER BAUME

The federal government accepts and acknowledges the fact that
Aborigines have an important association with the land. It is an association
that is unique -- one that is not shared by European cultures. The government
recognizes and accepts the spiritual and cultural importance of certain
sites to Aborigines. But we also accept the need for ordered development of
resources. We seek to balance these needs. The government sees its role
as facilitating in this balancing process. Results so far have been mixed.
They have covered a wide spectrum. At one end, there was Noonkanbah --
where there were no winners: not the state or federal governments; nor
the Aborigines; nor the miners. At the other end, there are many successful
mining ventures -- the result of Aborigines and miners working in
consultation together.

The government wants the development of Australia's mineral resources,
which are essential for a resource hungry world, for Australia's welfare,
and for the benefit of Aboriginal communities. At the same time, the
government is determined to see protected those sites of importance to
Aboriginal people.

Just how the Commonwealth balances these two objectives is determined
to a large extent by our federal structure. The activities of the mining
industry take place largely within the context of state legislation and
regulations. Because of different conditions prevailing under Commonwealth
and under state jurisdiction, conflicts can and do arise. Noonkanbah was
an example of just such a situation. It is true that the states have primary
jurisdiction for land and mining matters within their own boundaries. It
is also true that the 1967 <u>Referendum</u> resulted in the deletion of the

reference to the Aboriginal race in the Constitution. This reference in Section 51(26) had prevented the Commonwealth parliament from passing laws for Aborigines in any state. Since 1967, it has generally been assumed that the deletion of the offending words has resulted in a grant of power to the Commonwealth to make laws for Aboriginal people. The Referendum did not remove the Commonwealth's discretion either to act or to choose not to act. The fact is that, since 1967, all governments both Labor and Liberal have chosen not to use Section 51(26) to impose land rights for Aborigines on a state government. There is an initial implementation question for the Commonwealth. It is: whether the Commonwealth power should be used as a first step, or whether the states should be encouraged to act, with Commonwealth power used only if needed.

In 1973, when confronted with these two options in relation to the granting of land rights for Palm Island, the then Labor Minister for Aboriginal Affairs, Gordon Bryant, chose the second option. He argued for persuasion first, and only if that failed should counteracting legislation be introduced. The events of Noonkanbah demonstrated to the Commonwealth that the interests of all parties will best be served, not by confrontation, but by pursuing a policy of negotiation and consultation.

Before the Commonwealth would use its powers, we would need to be convinced that intervention was the only realistic course open to us, that it was necessary, and that it would in fact result in Aborigines being better off in the long term. Persuasion has been effective in the past. We have seen significant advances where states have been encouraged to act independently: for example, the passing of the Pitjantjatjara Act by the South Australian government, and smaller but no less important steps that have been taken by the Victorian and Tasmanian state governments.

While independent state action is to be encouraged, at the end of the day, the Commonwealth may have to consider use of its powers under Section 51(26) of the Constitution; and here I recommend you to a discussion in a 1978 Report of the Senate Standing Committee on Constitutional Affairs. I do not propose to discuss at length how the Commonwealth could or might react, except to say that there are many options and many problems and many variations -- any of which would be developed only if a cooperative approach with the states had failed.

Given the constraints of our federal framework, the government aims to balance the legitimate interests of Aboriginal people with the need for ordered development of our resources. There are many ways in which the government fulfils this role:

1. We endeavour to ensure that Aboriginal sites are recorded and protected.

    (a) The Commonwealth funds the Australian Institute for Aborginal Studies, which conducts a site-recording programme.

    (b) Over 6,000 sites have so far been recorded by the Institute.

    (c) The Commonwealth funds the Heritage Commission, which has so far recorded 246 Aboriginal places and 3,000 sites.

    (d) Prior to 1965, there was no state legislation on Aboriginal sites (with the exception of some minor regulations relating to the Northern Territory).

    (e) In 1965 the South Australian government took the initiative, and now all other states have followed suit.

    (f) There are now many thousands of sites recorded by state authorities.

    (g) This represents a vast improvement on the situation of 10 years ago -- even though there may be room for improvement in some states.

2. Land Rights:

The Commonwealth aims for:

(a) Secure tenure of Aboriginal land.

(b) Management of Aboriginal land by Aborigines.

In the Northern Territory, the <u>Aboriginal Land Rights (N.T.) Act</u> is a practical example of the implementation of the Commonwealth's aims. In the Northern Territory, not only was title to existing reserves transferred; machinery was also established to deal with traditional claims to other land -- namely, vacant Crown land, or land held by or for Aborigines. In the case of a successful claim, a Lands Trust is set up to hold the land, which is then managed by the appropriate Land Council according to the wishes of the traditional owners.

Claims have been lodged over virtually all the vacant Crown land in the Northern Territory. Twelve have been successful, over 106,000 square kilometres. This represents 8 per cent of the Northern Territory. The accompanying maps of the Northern Territory will demonstrate the progress that has been achieved. Map 1 shows the area of land owned by Aborigines as at the proclamation of the Northern Territory <u>Land Rights Act</u>. Map 2 shows the area of land owned by Aborigines as at October 1981. Map 3 gives an indication, not only of the land held by Aborigines as at October 1981, but also of the areas that are subject to land claims not yet determined.

In all, Aboriginal freehold title now accounts for 27 per cent of the Northern Territory (or 362,700 square kilometres). Aborigines represent 25 per cent of the population of the Northern Territory.

The legislation also provides that minerals on Aboriginal land are the property of the Crown, but that (except in instances where the national interest is involved) the consent of Aborigines is necessary for exploration and mining of their land. As Minister, my role in the approving of any

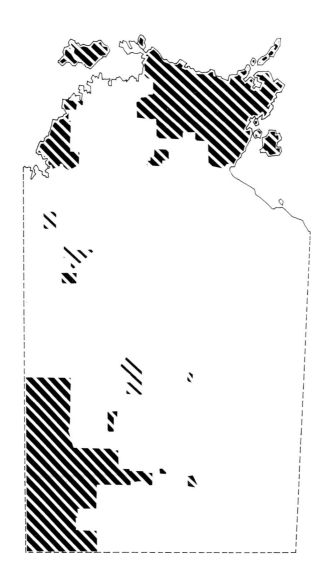

MAP 1: Aboriginal land ownership in the Northern Territory (Stage 1) as at
the proclamation of the Land Rights Act.

Land granted to Aboriginal Land Trusts under the Aboriginal Land
Rights (N.T.) Act 1976, Schedule 1.

Land purchased for Aborigines (areas larger than 10 hectares)
prior to the proclamation of the Act.

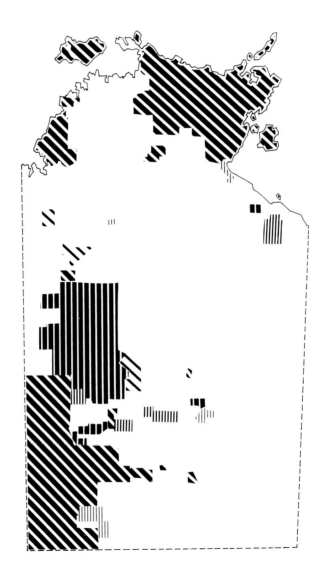

MAP 2: Aboriginal land ownership in the Northern Territory (Stage 2) as at October 1981.

Land granted to Aboriginal Land Trusts under the Aboriginal Land Rights (N.T.) Act 1976, Schedule 1.

Land purchased for Aborigines (areas larger than 10 hectares) prior to the proclamation of the Act.

Land claims concerning which the Minister has announced a decision: to 1 July 1981.

Land claims concerning which the Minister has announced a decision between July and October 1981.

Land purchased for Aborigines (areas larger than 10 hectares) since proclamation of the Act.

145

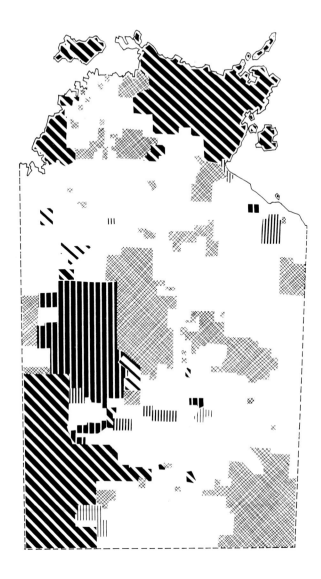

MAP 3: Aboriginal land ownership in the Northern Territory (Stage 3) as at October 1981, and land claims not yet determined.

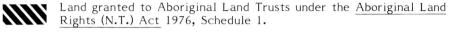

Land granted to Aboriginal Land Trusts under the Aboriginal Land Rights (N.T.) Act 1976, Schedule 1.

Land purchased for Aborigines (areas larger than 10 hectares) prior to the proclamation of the Act.

Land claims concerning which the Minister has announced a decision: to 1 July 1981.

Land claims concerning which the Minister has announced a decision between July and October 1981.

Land purchased for Aborigines (areas larger than 10 hectares) since proclamation of the Act.

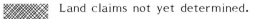

Land claims not yet determined.

agreement between Aborigines and mining interests is clearly defined. I must be quite certain when I give my approval to any agreement that it does in fact meet all the conditions of the Land Rights Act. I will not give my approval until that point is reached. In the past, I have felt compelled to hold up the Mereenie Agreement in the Centre for some time because I was not entirely satisfied.

In the state arena, South Australia has been the first state to take the initiative. In an exercise which has paralleled the Commonwealth experience, the Tonkin Liberal Government has enacted the Pitjantjatjara Act. This legislation gives the Pitjantjatjara people inalienable freehold over 100,000 square kilometres in the north-west of that state. Aborigines now have control over these areas, control over access, control over mining, and they receive a share of the royalties.

3. The government aims to ensure that Aboriginal people are able to exercise their right to be involved in any decision that concerns them. There are some people and even some governments who make light of the need to consult directly with Aborigines or their representatives. This is both shortsighted and counter-productive. It leads to misunderstanding and confrontation. Aborigines want to be involved in land-dealing which affects them. Negotiation with Aboriginal people or their own representatives is better for companies than are negotiations through governments acting on behalf of Aboriginal communities. What is more, Aborigines and mining companies together are proving that negotiation works.

The events of Noonkanbah showed that the interests of all parties will best be served, not by confrontation, but by pursuing a policy of negotiation and consultation. The government seeks agreed-upon solutions, not imposed solutions. We see our role as one of bringing different parties together to reach a reasonable accommodation of interests. For example, over

the four years the Northern Territory Land Rights Act has been in operation
we have come to know its strengths as well as its weaknesses. We have come
to see the areas which need to be attuned to meet today's conditions.
Mr Justice Woodward himself argued that the scheme of the legislation should
be flexible. At the same time, he spelt out that it was "important for
all concerned to be able to plan on the assumption that the broad basis of
arrangements will remain undisturbed". We have now called together
representatives of the Northern Land Council, the Central Land Council and
the Northern Territory government to discuss amendments to the Act. The
importance of these discussions should not be under-estimated. They are
proving that patience and a willingness to negotiate can be effective. The
Noonkanbah dispute highlighted the need to establish agreed and recognized
procedures to deal with existing and possible conflicts of interest between
mining companies and Aborigines. As Senator Chaney, the then Minister for
Aboriginal Affairs, stated in September last year: "We will continue to
work with Aborigines, with mining companies, and with state governments to
ensure that there are ground rules for the reasonable accommodation of all
interests".

To this end, Commonwealth ministers have already initiated serious and
wide-ranging discussions with the Australian Mining Industry Council
(AMIC) and with the Australian Petroleum Exploration Association (APEA).
Both have responded by issuing helpful booklets setting out guidelines that
could help to avoid another Noonkanbah. The government intends that these
discussions with AMIC and APEA will continue, and will be extended to
include also state governments and Aboriginal interests.

The Record:

Far from seeing endless confrontations, we are seeing most problems
being overcome. We are seeing that consultation can achieve results. And

Aborigines, mining companies and all Australians are receiving the
benefits.

For the Aborigines, there are:

(a) Established procedures for the protection of their sacred
    sites.

(b) Large areas of Australia to which they hold title. (As the map
    shows, 361,000 square kilometres of Aboriginal freehold in
    the Northern Territory and 106,000 square kilometres in South
    Australia.) See Map 4.

(c) Aborigines, representing 1.2 per cent of the population, now
    hold 9.6 per cent of the land area of Australia. The
    accompanying graph gives a detailed breakdown of Aboriginal
    land in Australia. See Table 1.

(d) Indications of great social and economic change arising from
    the granting of land rights. Aborigines now have new power,
    not only to control their own lives, but also to influence --
    in the best kind of way -- the future of the Territory. The
    Land Councils have shown that they are capable of tough
    bargaining and efficient negotiation on the most difficult
    issues.

For the mining companies there are:

(a) Two major projects proceeding on the basis of agreements
    negotiated under the Land Rights Act.

(b) A third agreement for an important oil and gas development in
    Central Australia which was negotiated with the Central Land
    Council in 1981.

(c) Progress is being made at Beagle Bay in Western Australia,
    where Esso have come to an agreement with the local Aboriginal

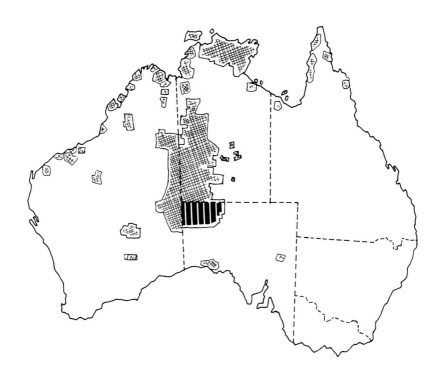

MAP 4: Major areas of Aboriginal land in Australia.

Aboriginal freehold 361,700 sq. kms, in the N.T.

Aboriginal freehold 106,763 sq. kms, in S.A.

Aboriginal land 738,032 sq. kms.

	ABORIGINAL FREEHOLD km²	ABORIGINAL LEASEHOLD km²	ABORIGINAL RESERVES km²	TOTAL ABORIGINAL LAND km²
N.S.W.	109	121	-	230
Vic.	20	-	-	20
Qld.	5	8,721	21,344	30,070
S.A.	106,763	506	-	107,269
W.A.	9	25,708	192,422	218,788
Tas.	1	-	-	1
N.T.	361,700	19,911	-	381,653
A.C.T.	-	-	1	1
TOTAL:	468,607	54,967	213,767	738,032

TABLE 1: Statistical chart showing Aboriginal freehold, leasehold and reserves in the states and territories with accompanying totals. (Note that totals include Aboriginal mission land involving 649 sq. kms in W.A. and 42 sq. kms in the N.T.)

community; and at Lake Argyle, where the Ashton Joint
Venture has made what is termed 'good neighbour' arrangements
which provide for substantial benefits for the two local
communities.

Previous problems such as undue cynicism about 'invented' sacred
sites by some mining companies with little anthropological background are
being resolved. Mining companies have come to recognize the importance of
certain sites to Aboriginal people. They are employing anthropologists;
and they are consulting with Aborigines.

The Comalco model, initiated by the Pitjantjatjara Council, is being
adopted elsewhere. The Comalco model is a process for appropriate
negotiations to ensure that exploration activities would not interfere
with significant sites. Mining representatives are advised in general
terms of the areas which are of sensitivity to the Aboriginal people.
Importantly, the sites themselves are not identified. By following this
model, companies such as Comalco and Getty Oil have proceeded on the basis
of support and agreement, rather than by way of confrontation and opposition.
It is encouraging to find that this process is now being seen by many
of the larger mining companies as representing a reasonable way of proceeding.
Both the Australian Mining Industry Council and the Australian Petroleum
Exploration Association have adopted a similar approach in their published
guidelines.

Whether it be for federal politicians, state ministers, for Aboriginal
leaders or for miners, the challenge is the same: to resolve difficult
problems, to balance conflicting interests, by dealing with each other as
mature adults. It is not merely a matter of asserting a legal right, or
of alleging Commonwealth or state sovereignty. The Commonwealth tries to
set the climate and the content, and to limit the extent to which one group
holds another to ransom in an improper, unreasonable, uncaring way. We are

certainly available as honest brokers, and we hope we can set a context in which reasonable people will work to find solutions -- not simply assert rights.

I believe, and my government believes, that Australia as a whole, including the states, Aboriginal communities and industry groups, can benefit from an atmosphere of cooperation which will permit exploration and mining to proceed in a manner which protects essential Aboriginal rights.

ECONOMIC IMPERATIVES AS FAR AS ABORIGINES ARE CONCERNED

CHARLES PERKINS

The subject of this paper is the economic imperatives which concern
Aborigines in this decade of the 1980s; and it is one which is crucial
to the advancement of Aboriginal Australians. Naturally, when I refer to
Aborigines, I include also the Torres Strait Island people. My objectives
here, then, will be to identify and define what I perceive as the
economic imperatives in this decade as far as Aborigines are concerned,
and in that context to discuss what we in the Aboriginal Development
Commission are doing to come to terms with these imperatives. I will
then make some concluding remarks which should be of interest to all of
us. I should mention that, for my purpose here, I interpret economic
imperatives to mean basically 'our most urgent economic priorities in
this decade among others as being to fight so as to ensure that
Aboriginal Australians do get a fair and just share in real terms of the
wealth and resources of Australia'.

In so far as Aboriginal Australians are concerned, I believe that
it is useful to relate these imperatives to the North-South Dialogue,
which has become topical all over the world and most recently in the
biggest international conference of world leaders that Australia has ever
hosted — the Melbourne Conference of the Commonwealth Heads of Governments.
As I understand it, this dialogue calls, among other things, for a more
equitable redistribution of wealth and income, an equitable transfer of
assets (both fixed and moveable) from the rich to the poor sectors of
society, and the recognition that a realistic restructuring of the
international economic system must be made in order to achieve these
goals.

In this decade of the 1980s, we all face the ever daunting and disconcerting fact that we are living in a world of the rich getting richer and the poor getting poorer. Therefore, there is a definite need for those who advocate the North-South Dialogue to make more commitments so that the dialogue becomes a reality instead of being a mere rhetoric in the jargon of diplomacy. Such a commitment necessarily calls for a global approach to rectify the enormous economic disparities between the rich and the poor, between the privileged and the under-privileged, and between the 'blacks' and the 'whites'. That concept should be applied, not only in relation to the developing Third World nations, but also in a very practical way within the Australian context, for it is becoming increasingly imperative that the enormous economic and social disparities which exist between Aborigines and other Australians can only be overcome if a serious commitment is made at the national, state and local levels.

Indeed, overcoming such problems must be made the main priorities of all Australian governments at the federal, state and local levels as well as the Australian people at large, if Australia is to achieve the status of a mature, responsible and just nation in the eyes of the world. For we can no longer ignore the fact that Australia's standing in the international community is judged by, among other things, its treatment of its Aboriginal minority. That minority is now generally recognized as the most disadvantaged and under-privileged sector of the Australian community, with the highest death rates, highest morbidity rates, the worst health and housing conditions and the lowest educational, occupational, economic, social and legal status of any community within the Australian society.

The appalling statistics of the general situation of Aboriginal people are well documented and confirmed in the 1975 Borrie Report, and more

recently in the Report of the World Council of Churches. There is no
need for me to elaborate here, except to say that we must regard the
1980s as the decade of producing results rather than more slogans and
promises. This is the decade of getting on with the job of eradicating
the glaring inequalities and disparities between Aborigines and other
Australians. The evidence in those reports should put to rest the often-
stated claim, particularly among people in northern Australia, that
Aborigines are living on 'hand-outs' and are advantageously placed when
compared with other sectors of the Australian population.

It should be noted that any special measures designed to overcome
these inequalities and injustices in our society, and successfully to
achieve a sound economic growth in this decade, must emphasize a
preventative rather than a curative approach. Only in that way can we
benefit positively in the long run. By this I mean that adequate
government expenditure now on the most pressing economic and social
programmes should eliminate the need for many others in the future; or,
at least, it should change positively the context of these initiatives
for the better.

It is equally important that all Aboriginal people must respond
positively to the challenges ahead. We must take up the cudgels and be
responsible ourselves both for our own decisions and for their
implementation. Naturally, this calls for the achievement of good
management and economic viability in Aboriginal programmes of an economic
nature, both in the short and in the long run. We must develop sound
economic and social infrastructures based primarily on self-management,
self-help, and self-sufficiency in order to control our own destiny.
In my experience, the achievement of such worthwhile goals is not
necessarily incompatible with most Aboriginal traditions, life-styles and

aspirations today. It is, therefore, with these considerations in mind, that I turn to consider what I believe are the major economic imperatives for Aboriginal people.

Economic imperatives:

Firstly, it is economically imperative for Aboriginal people that a more just and adequate distribution of wealth and resources is actively pursued as a top priority of all Australian governments, at the federal, state and local levels.

Secondly, Aboriginal people must be given a greater voice, and opportunities to participate more actively, in the process of achieving that distribution. This would, in the main, enable us to reappraise the resources and funds allocated, in the light of our most pressing priorities, together with the complexities involved in the generally fluid areas of Aboriginal affairs, our cultural differences, and our special needs as the most disadvantaged sector of the Australian community.

Thirdly, there must be more cooperation and coordination between all Australian governments and instrumentalities responsible for the advancement of Aboriginal Australians than exist today — especially in regard to administering the distribution of resources and funds to Aboriginal communities. A more coordinated, national approach in achieving this is integral to the positive advancement of Aborigines.

Fourthly, the federal government's present methods of allocating funds must be restructured so as to allow for a more rapid and flexible system of getting the funds and resources directly to where the real needs of the Aboriginal people are — a system that responds to these needs, rather than to those of the bureaucracy. A more responsive system of funding priority needs, and helping the needy and not the greedy, is central to any effective arrangements of allocating and distributing funds.

In my opinion, it is not unreasonable to suggest that the current financial arrangements of the Commonwealth Departments of Treasury and Finance are inappropriate when viewed in relation to the dynamics of Aboriginal affairs. The present financial rules and guidelines in the Aboriginal context are outmoded. For example, there should be an immediate re-evaluation of the Treasury/Finance funding levels of '10% annual increase'. This is necessary to get things moving in regard to achieving the economic and social priorities I have mentioned. Unfortunately, it is not uncommon to encounter in some government departments bureaucrats with 'blinkers on', divorced from the exigencies and realities of Aboriginal communities. Moreover, the present system does not allow satisfactorily for new and innovative projects that require more funds each year.

During the 1981/82 fiscal year, it has been estimated that the total Commonwealth expenditure on Aboriginal affairs amounts to some $228 million. This will benefit a total Aboriginal and Islander population of approximately 300,000, many of whom are not only users but also producers of goods and services as well as being taxpayers in the Australian economy. However, this is not good enough. There is room for improvement, when you take into account such factors as the special disadvantages and disparities faced by Aboriginal communities, and the fact that most of these receive much less in real cash income, goods and services as compared with the average citizen within other sectors of the Australian society.

It has been estimated that the per capita expenditure for all Aboriginal and Islander communities in the 1981/82 fiscal year is approximately $760. But most Aborigines still do not share equally with non-Aborigines in the normal distribution of funds and services. They remain, therefore, at a greater disadvantage. In addition, the above expenditure usually concerns the basic needs that the average Australian takes for granted. It is insignificant when compared with Australia's annual tariff bill of approximately $6,000 million, or more than $200 for every Australian household for tariff protection. And it is a small rent for the $4,700 million worth of minerals alone exported from Australia in the 1980/81 fiscal year.

It is also worth noting that, out of a total federal Budget of $40,000 million, the Department of Aboriginal Affairs receives only $148 million. In the 1980/81 fiscal year the gross domestic product (GDP) — the value of all goods and services in Australia — is estimated at a total of $125 billion. However, Aboriginal Australians would have received in the order of about 0.2% of the GDP, although the total Aboriginal population accounts for approximately 1.2% of the total Australian population. In the context of these comparisons, it is clear that the Aboriginal people's share of the wealth and resources of this great country of ours is far from satisfactory.

Aboriginal Development Commission:

I shall now turn to what we in the Aboriginal Development Commission are trying to do in the context of the economic imperatives that I have discussed so far. The Commission came into operation on 1 July 1980. Through its land, housing and enterprises function it is now instrumental in distributing funds and assets to Aboriginal communities throughout Australia. Its policy is, clearly, to distribute such assets, so that Aboriginal communities and individuals can own and control them.

The Commission has the broad practical purpose of advancing the economic and social well-being of Aboriginal and Torres Strait Islanders. Under the terms of the Aboriginal Development Commission Act 1980, it performs the following major functions:

1. to acquire land for Aboriginal communities and groups;

2. to lend and grant money to Aboriginal individuals and groups
for housing and other purposes; and

3. to lend and grant money to Aborigines for business enterprises.

As from 1 July 1981, the Commission took on the responsibility for
distributing the Grants-in-Aid Housing function from the Department of
Aboriginal Affairs.

It should be noted that the Commission's legislation sets out very
broad guidelines, and provides it with a large degree of power and
flexibility over its own affairs. However, the Commission has been careful
to develop responsible policies and guidelines to cater for the diverse
needs and circumstances of Aboriginal communities throughout Australia.
These policies are based on the fundamental principle of Aboriginal control
of their own affairs and assets, and as such they are vital to helping
overcome the disadvantaged position of Aborigines generally. In this
context, the Commission provides advice, finance and support for a wide
range of projects, including Aboriginal Housing Associations, cattle
stations, farms, cooperatives, community stores, fishing ventures and
home buyers.

During the 1980/81 fiscal year, the Commission received a total
allocation of $23.8 million from the Commonwealth government, with about
$9.4 million allocated to its Housing function, $2.3 million to its Land
function, and $3.78 million to its Enterprises function for grants and
loans. The 1981/82 fiscal year appropriation is $47.8 million in round
figures, of which $22.8 million will be expended on Housing grants-in-
aid, $12.6 million on Housing loans, $6.6 million on Enterprises grants
and loans, $3.5 million on Land acquisition, and the balance on

administration and salaries. The Commission also maintains a capital fund of $9 million in this financial year for the purpose of accumulating capital for investment projects.

The prior occupation and ownership of the Australian continent by Aboriginal people, together with their dispossession and dispersal, has created a need for positive policies which would lead to their reinstatement on their own land with adequate compensation. The role and function of the Commission are an integral part of this process. Also, a basic aim of the Commission is to provide some guide to the direction of Aboriginal economic and social development. Unlike previous governmental bodies, it does not wish to withhold assets from the people, as the Commission sees no useful purpose served in its being an asset-holding body. There is a clear intention to transfer assets such as land to Aboriginal communities, be they urban or rural.

Under its Land function, the Aboriginal Development Commission acquires land for Aboriginal communities, within the ambit of available resources, so as to guarantee their economic and social development. As I have already mentioned, its eventual aim is to transfer land and assets to the control of Aboriginal communities, instead of maintaining a landlord-tenant relationship. Ownership of land, caring for it, and having adequate resources to develop it, are crucial to the social and economic development of Aboriginal Australians. In this way, where Aboriginal communities have lost their land and need it restored in order to plan for the use of resources on that land, they have a secure base for future economic and social development; and this will maintain cohesion within the community as a distinct and viable cultural group.

In the Northern Territory and South Australia, Aboriginal land rights legislation is now in operation. Aborigines with traditional

links with otherwise vacant Crown land can make claims and be granted
title to areas of land. In Western Australia and New South Wales,
Aboriginal Lands Trusts now control some of the small areas set aside
for Aboriginal communities. For most of Australia, however, much of the
land is alienated, and the present forms of land rights legislation are
insufficient in terms of developing and extending Aboriginal ownership
of land throughout Australia. The development of suitable Aboriginal
land rights legislation throughout Australia, based on needs as well as
on traditional links, is fully supported by the Commission.

Examples of the Commission's land policy in action and in the
transference of assets include the vesting of title and ownership in
the Garawa tribe for the Robinson River pastoral lease in the Northern
Territory. This was purchased by the Commission for $670,000 in
December 1980. The Commission consented recently to surrender its title
to Kenmore Park pastoral lease, in South Australia, so that the
Pitjantjatjara people could have freehold title to this land, under the
terms of the Pitjantjatjara Land Rights Act, 1981. It consented also to
surrender its title to Utopia pastoral lease in Central Australia, so
that the Utopia Aboriginal community could have freehold title and
ownership, pursuant to the terms of the Aboriginal Land Rights (NT) Act,
1976.

Under its Housing Loans function, the Commission allocated
approximately $10 million during the 1980/81 fiscal year to provide
financial assistance for Aborigines, who are unable to obtain credit
facilities through conventional financial institutions for housing and
associated purposes. As a result, opportunities are created for
Aborigines to stabilize and enhance their living standards and take their
rightful place in the Australian community. With funds being provided

for houses which Aborigines own themselves, individual families can establish a sound economic basis, and thereby obtain a degree of stability and an opportunity to manage their own life-styles. With regular employment and a home, children should find more assurance in education. The family can settle in a community on an equal socio-economic footing with others. They then have a secure base from which to advance socially and economically.

Under its Housing grants-in-aid function, the Commission is expected to spend some $23 million in the 1981/82 fiscal year for Aboriginal Housing Associations, to provide suitable houses for Aboriginal communities throughout Australia. It has been estimated that the assets held by Aboriginal Housing Associations throughout Australia total some $100 million. As such, these provide an economic base which should be expanded by the expenditure of more funds until such time as each Aboriginal Housing Association can generate enough to give it a flow of funds over and above costs, so that it can become economically independent.

The Commission encourages the sale of houses held by such Associations to approved tenants. This is consistent with its policy of making assets available to provide the people, in this case families, with an economic base from which to increase their independence. It also recognizes that such Associations should own the houses purchased or built with funds provided under the Commission's Housing grants-in-aid. It will, therefore, develop policy with this important principle in mind. I must emphasize here that because of the continuing and considerable demand for housing for Aboriginal people throughout Australia, and with a huge housing backlog of some three years to catch up, a much greater appropriation of housing funds is required from the federal government each financial year — if we are to come to terms, effectively, with the Aboriginal housing crisis generally in this decade.

Under its Enterprises function, the Commission gives priority to those which will contribute to Aboriginal economic and/or social independence, especially where such enterprises involve the production of essential goods or services, which would otherwise have to be purchased. Under its Act, the Commission is charged with making available sume of money on terms and conditions considered appropriate by the Commissioners, the funds to be applied toward the economic and social development of Aborigines. Applicants must satisfy the Commission that they are capable of engaging in, among other things, the proposed enterprise. Under the Act, individuals and partnerships can receive assistance only in the form of loan funds, while Aboriginal communities or groups can receive assistance by way of grants, as well as loans.

Grants to business enterprises are categorized as viable or potentially viable ventures, and non-viable ventures. The benefits of either can be economic or social, although there is special provision of enterprise grant funds for social purposes. Profitability, management, Aboriginal employment and self-sufficiency are some of the key criteria taken into account by the Commission when considering such proposals. For this type of proposal it is possible that budgeted projections will show that the project may sustain a loan rather than grant funds. Thus, in these cases, a loan is preferred. In cases where an injection of grant funds is necessary, it is preferable to consider the grant as a substitute for the group's injection of its own capital or equity.

When considering non-viable business enterprises for grant funding, the Commission takes into account such factors as cohesiveness of the group, worthwhile social benefits accruing to the group, training potential, and whether the production of the goods or services will have a direct cost-saving or economic benefit for the community. Aboriginal individuals and organizations are usually required to contribute some cash equity to the proposed enterprise, unless very special considerations apply. Past equity requirements have been based on a contribution of not less than 5 per cent of the estimated total capital requirements of the project. This assessment is influenced by the amount that can be offered from the applicant's own resources, including assets used in the enterprise, the amount of loan funds required, and the degree of risk associated with the enterprise. In determining interest charges, the Commission is primarily concerned with the applicant's personal circumstances and with the capacity of the proposed business to service loan repayments. In the past, this has resulted in reducible interest rates, varying between 1.5% and 10%, the median average being 5%. The Commission has recently decided that a standard reducible interest rate of 5% would be struck on all loans.

It should be noted, therefore, that the Aboriginal Development Commission is a catalyst for economic and social development on a broad scale. Through it, significant financial assistance has been directed toward acquiring land for economic or social purposes, establishing viable economic ventures, and providing low-cost housing finance. During the 1980/81 fiscal year, this has resulted in the programmed re-establishment of firm social, economic and cultural foundations for many Aborigines throughout Australia.

Conclusion:

In conclusion, let me say again that Aborigines and Torres Strait Islanders must achieve economic independence and self-sufficiency through self-management of a greater share of Australia's wealth and resources. This is an important part of the process of reinstatement through adequate

and proper compensation for past dispossession and dispersal of
Aboriginal people.

Because of initiatives such as the Commission, the future is becoming
ours to decide in this decade. The range of functions now performed by
it has never before been so effectively in the hands of a national
Aboriginal body. Such direct responsibility is unique in the context of
Aboriginal struggles for a fair and just share of Australia's wealth and
resources. Indeed, the Commission is an important instrument, not only
for achieving Aboriginal self-management and self-sufficiency, but also
for facilitating the equitable transfer of funds and assets, both fixed
and moveable, to the ownership and control of Aboriginal communities
throughout Australia. Such a role is in accordance with Aboriginal needs
and aspirations.

Greater government financial assistance for the Commission now would
assist considerably in eliminating the economic and social disparities
between Aborigines and other Australians. Apart from federal and
state instrumentalities, the Commission is just one of many which is
endeavouring to provide such services within the limits of the functions
and finance entrusted to it by the federal government. A sound economic
basis will help us to cut the welfare umbilical cord that binds us.
Increasingly, we must become active producers, instead of passive users,
in the context of the Australian economy. We must develop sound economic
and social infrastructures in the terms I have discussed, in order to take
control of our own destiny. Unless these imperatives are achieved,
Aborigines will continue to be gripped by a counter-productive 'hand-out
mentality' and destined to be a race of economic cripples and perpetual
dependants.

APPENDIX

[The following is an extract from a paper by Mr Charles Perkins
distributed at the symposium as being complementary to his address.
The full version was given by Mr Perkins at the 8th Annual Conference
of the Aboriginal and Islander Catholic Council in Townsville,
January 5th 1981. Some minor editorial amendments have been made to it,
including a small reduction in size.   R.M. Berndt.]

A measure of Aboriginal advancement:

Although there had been assistance programmes since the 1800s, the
late 1960s saw an acceptance for a national approach to help the
Aboriginal people develop. Since that time the Commonwealth government
has had major programmes in the field of Aboriginal affairs. There are
still bad statistics, but there are also real and measurable improvements.
What Australia is currently witnessing may be the time lag between the
introduction of positive programmes and the point at which the benefits
affect the overall statistics.

The Australian government has recognized that Aboriginal people
have the right to opportunities and the access to services equal to those
of other Australians. Its job now (in conjunction with the states) is
to lessen that time lag.

It is worth noting that since 1967 (when a Referendum overwhelmingly
agreed to a Commonwealth approach), and particularly during the last
decade, Australia has seen:

(1) A most significant development in the '70s with the emergence of
     the National Aboriginal Conference, now chaired by a most competent
     person, Mr Jim Hagen. The emergence of this Aboriginal organization
     into the public arena in the last few years has meant that

Aboriginal people now have a new political voice in Australian society. The Conference is funded and promoted by the Australian government, but is independent in its deliberations and actions. Its delegation in late 1980 to a United Nations' forum in Geneva over the Noonkanbah question has demonstrated its determination to be a voice for the Aboriginal community. Members of the delegation did great credit to our race.

(2) Education grants were introduced. In mid-1979 there were over 17,000 Aboriginal children studying at secondary schools (compared with 3,600 in 1967), and a further 4,500 at technical and tertiary institutions.

(3) The Aboriginal Development Commission:

(a) The purchase of land for Aborigines. Aborigines now operate nearly 60 properties throughout the country bought for them by the Commonwealth government.

(b) Funding of Aboriginal enterprises. A variety of individual and community enterprises have been established through the Commission's funding arrangements.

(c) Through the Commission, more than 1,400 low-interest loans were made available to Aboriginal families for housing.

(4) Under the Department of Aboriginal Affairs programmes, more than 7,000 houses were purchased or constructed.

(5) Aboriginal Hostels Ltd. provide through their 104 nationally based hostels, over 3,000 beds per night to every category of Aboriginal in need. Such needs include medical, educational and transient help for young and old. This gives us a total of well over 600,000 beds per year.

(6) Eleven independent Aboriginal Legal Services were established throughout Australia, funded by the federal government, operating through 38 offices.

(7) Fifteen Aboriginal Medical Services were established in urban areas, and another three community-based Health Services operating in remote areas of Central Australia.

(8) Legislation granting Land Rights to Aborigines in the Northern Territory, resulting in 345,833 sq. km — that is, approximately 25% of the Northern Territory — being transferred to them freehold.

(9) A national employment strategy aimed at creating better training and job opportunities for Aborigines in the public and private sectors. It should be noted that over 10,000 Aboriginal persons are funded for employment through various schemes such as NEAT, SWP, CDEP, and by virtue of employment in semi-government or Aboriginal-controlled organizations: included in this are over 2,800 under the NEAT scheme.

(10) Support — both financial and moral — has been given to the outstation movement, where Aborigines (in pursuit of their own life-style) can move back to traditional lands into small communities. Over 160 communities of this kind are involved.

(11) Aboriginal Arts and Crafts Pty Ltd. was established to promote and sell the work of Aboriginal artists and craftspersons, and the Aboriginal Artists Agency to protect their interests and copyrights.

(12) Aboriginal participation in the formulation of policies at all levels has been encouraged through groups such as the National Aboriginal Conference, the Council for Aboriginal Development, the National Aboriginal Education Committee, the National Aboriginal Employment Development Committee, and more recently the Aboriginal

Development Commission (mentioned above and in the main body of
this Chapter).

(13) In terms of money, since the creation of the federal Department
of Aboriginal Affairs in 1972, greatly increased funds have been
available and more than $1,000 million has been spent by the
Commonwealth government on Aboriginal development programmes (i.e.,
in the last five years alone).

(14) New South Wales and Victoria several years ago passed reserve lands
to Aboriginal ownership under the control of an Aboriginal Lands
Trust.

(15) The South Australian government has now granted reserve lands to
the Pitjantjatjara people living in the north-west of that state.
(See main body of this Chapter.) An important part of this is the
right of these Aboriginal people to negotiate directly with
companies for royalties or compensation for mining on their land.

(16) In New South Wales, an all-party parliamentary committee unanimously
recommended a new approach, of making substantial land purchases
to meet Aboriginal social and economic needs.

(17) Against a background of government policies to encourage Aboriginal
people to live their lives independently and to have a greater
responsibility for their own affairs, one of the most significant
developments was in fact the creation of the Aboriginal Development
Commission (ADC), which began operations on 1 July 1980. The ADC
replaced the Aboriginal Land Fund Commission and the Aboriginal
Loans Commission, took over the Aboriginal Enterprise programme from
the Department of Aboriginal Affairs, and more recently took over
responsibility for the Commonwealth government's Aboriginal Housing
Association grants-in-aid function. Legislation to establish the

ADC was introduced into federal parliament on 21 November 1979 by Senator Neville Bonner. In presenting the Bill, he said it was a positive move toward meeting major policy commitments to the Aboriginal people. It placed in their hands important instruments for their own advancement, and was a further step in the implementation of the policies of self-management. A sub-committee of the National Aboriginal Conference visited most communities throughout Australia, and advised generally on Aboriginal views. The Bill was proclaimed on 1 July 1980, and was extensively debated through Australia. Over 40 amendments were made to the original draft.

(18) The Makarrata. As most people probably know, the National Aboriginal Conference accepted the responsibility for formulating in detail proposals for a Makarrata (Treaty) on behalf of the Aboriginal people of Australia. During 1980, it discussed this with most Aboriginal communities throughout Australia. The Makarrata is a most significant development and has been recognized as such by the federal government (particularly by the Prime Minister, who indicated his willingness at that time to hold discussions with members of the National Aboriginal Conference).

What of the future then?

The simple solution is that the future is basically ours to create. We have today the people, the knowledge and, albeit limited, resources to create our own destiny.

The media:

There is no doubt that the media in their various forms can be of assistance in helping a minority. But they can also construct a particular perspective on race relations that can, in the short- and in the long-term, act to the detriment of a minority group. This has often been the case in Australia. Certain journalists and newspapers, particularly, have found it worthwhile to sensationalize some of the more unsavoury aspects of Aboriginal affairs. Such reporting denigrates Aboriginal people, confirms stereotypes, and develops an unbalanced attitude in the relations between Aborigines and non-Aborigines — particularly where young people are concerned. The nation's media should realize that they have a responsibility to present a balanced view of Aboriginal affairs that will in the long term facilitate good relationships. Race relations is the razor edge, and much good effort by many people can be virtually destroyed by one or two negative articles.

Stereotyping:

People in Australia have got to get out of the bad habit of literally indicating every Aboriginal person as 'a drunk' who refuses to work. There is no basis for the belief that Aborigines, in the majority of cases, are alcoholics. It should be noted there are, unfortunately, over 600,000 European alcoholics in Australia, and a rapidly increasing number of drug users. Aboriginal people in known areas drink, not as alcoholics but generally as abusers of social drinking practices, and then mostly in customary groups. European-Australians should look to their own bad drinking and drug situation, and not try to rationalize their way out of such consideration by reflecting on Aboriginal difficulties in this area. Obviously, something should be done for the drink and drug problem in Australia as it affects everyone.

Reconstruction of the physical environment:

The objective is to build an environment which will make it possible for Aboriginal people to move toward self-management. Adequate funds

must be made available, to enable specific, integrated and time-scaled
programmes in the major areas of housing, health, employment and
essential services to become a reality in the current life-span of all
Aborigines. There should be no tolerance of sub-standard dwellings and
poor health. Aborigines must be given the chance to begin life free
from unnecessary disadvantage. Together with this reconstruction, must
obviously go suitable wide-ranging training programmes which will allow
Aborigines to grasp and hold the new opportunities, and assert effective
control over their environment both in the physical and in the social
contexts.

Socio-cultural and psychological environment:

Aborigines and Europeans have much to offer each other. It has been
this way since the Europeans first arrived, but the value that both
groups could gain from fruitful interaction remains a potential value
at best. Improved race relations could be brought about quite quickly
and an atmosphere of cooperation and goodwill between Aborigines and
non-Aborigines could be created. To build this, calls for an understanding
in the wider society of the wide range of problems Aborigines have had to
face following the coming of Europeans, and an understanding within the
Aboriginal community of the problems non-Aborigines often seem to face
in communicating with people of other cultures. A determined national
public relations programme could be helpful here. The comprehensive
information and public relations document prepared in 1978 by the Department
of Aboriginal Affairs points out where that department, the government
and the general public, including Aborigines, can make a major contribution.
This document is available: its recommendations need to be implemented.
It is mainly a clear-thinking commitment and a positive approach that are

required. Such a programme is important, because in the past many of
our efforts have been subject to 'white backlash', criticism, and general
undermining by sections of the Australian community — some parliamentarians
included. Such people need to be fully informed of the objectives of
our programmes and projects, and thus help to create a situation for
their more effective implementation.

Aboriginal participation:

Aboriginal people would do well to consider that in this decade
benefits can be gained for themselves and the nation by projecting into
other areas of concern. By this I refer to comment and involvement in
general issues within the Australian society at the local, state and
national levels. Our participation in these areas would be welcome and,
as I have said, beneficial. We should not be dependent on the initiative
of others, or fall into the trap of previous years of being role-cast
in such a way as to have people ignore our contribution and give us
consideration only when Aboriginal affairs are mentioned. We should
remember our cultural foundation, but also not forget our national
allegiance and obligations.

Having been brought up in an Aboriginal Boys Home on strict Christian
lines, it has always been my belief, but not my understanding, that
heaven is yet to come and is located in some mythical place. I cannot
today really agree with this. My firm conviction is that heaven is on
earth and with us in our daily life. There is no real heaven, no real
hell. Life itself can be either, depending on circumstances and on the
individual person's nature, needs and wants. In most cases we can make it
what we want. The pursuit and obtaining of reasonable happiness despite
other influences is the most one can ask for or claim. Although this is

rather simplistic, I would think Aboriginal affairs can be considered in much the same light.

We Aboriginal people in this nation of ours with other Australian people can create — despite lack of essential elements, such as adequate funds, education, and political power, plus overt racism and such — our own form of heaven or existence which will satisfy our needs and expectations to a greater degree than ever before. We have our destiny in our hands, and it is up to us to achieve the results we so desperately seek. We can make things happen, to overcome disadvantages. The plain fact is, we have nothing to lose. There is only disadvantage, if we don't grasp the fundamental fact staring us in the face today: that is, life is what you, we, make it. Our own rehabilitation, to find ourselves once again as a nation of people within a nation, begins and ends with ourselves. We must individually and collectively make the effort to overcome our own feeling of no confidence, lack of dignity and purpose. We must develop the 'inner' Aboriginal to accept the challenge and responsibility. Europeans, and the difficult system that encompasses us, can no longer be used as a rationale for inaction on our part.

We cannot, quite frankly, blame either the churches, or governments of whatever political colour. Even in Queensland, the land of my father and his people, the present and future for Aborigines and Torres Strait Islanders lies in their own hands. The struggle for human dignity and rights in that state can be won if the people want it, and more so if they need it. They must realize now that only they, in unity with organization and clear objectives, can obtain justice for themselves, the next generation and, subsequently, our nation. An outstanding current example is the Queensland government's obstinate stand on Land Rights, which must be faced by the people in that state. It is not right that the federal government or anybody else outside the state should necessarily fight the case for us. The federal government may have the constitutional power, but it is for us to bear the experience. The struggle for land rights legitimizes eventual victory, and preserves the reality in every way and for the future.

The future is for us to decide. Injustice can be a continuing reality, or a figment of our imagination. The main factor is that we must act to influence this future. We cannot leave it to churches, government, international pressures, the goodwill of others, or to dreams. The cold facts must be faced, and responsibility must be exercized with authority. We must carry responsibility for decisions made, and with that we can savour the new experience of confidence, self-respect and respect for others. If we fail to grasp this opportunity in this decade, there is no future. This is the challenge to us. We must re-organize ourselves within ourselves. Our main problem today is we, you, me, us — in other words ourselves.

There is a majority of non-Aboriginal people in this country who will see that justice is done toward Aboriginal people — if only we can give them the constructive leadership they require, and clear ethical objectives. We must be seen to make the effort, and thus give them the opportunity to respond.

We, the Aboriginal and Island people, can give this nation a fundamental element it lacks at the present time — a soul. Without Aboriginal people as part of this nation, Australia exists only in name and has no real future. Aboriginal people have the power to unite this nation and give it a real reason for living, and provide it with a social and cultural uniqueness. We must struggle, not only for our own dignity and self-respect, but also for the nation. Our country needs us, and we need it. If we find ourselves, we find a nation — and what a great nation it can be.

THE MINING INDUSTRY AND ABORIGINES

H.M. MORGAN

I must admit to a sense of trepidation when I first discovered from the programme that in a symposium dealing with the impact of resource development on Aboriginal rights and sites I was to be the only miner among the speakers. Nevertheless, the fact that you did ask a representative of my industry to talk to you indicates a willingness to hear our views on this important subject and I hope that when I have finished you will agree that our views are positive, and perhaps closer to those of yourselves, than might be gathered from the impression created by the normal media presentation of the issues involved in this theme.

Throughout its history in this country, the mining industry has been in the forefront of most major moves for beneficial economic, social and political change. The initial discoveries of coal near Newcastle about a decade after the arrival of the First Fleet, of copper in South Australia and later of gold in other states each had great social and political impacts on the development of Australia as well as in providing a broader economic base. From a demographic perpsective alone, the trebling of the total colonial population during the gold rush period was the first experience of the multi-cultural Australia we know today. The results of the Eureka rebellion, despite the lessons which conservatives, republicans, liberals and radicals now wish, in their own ways, to draw from it, established the basis for most mineral legislation since that time and thus fostered the orderly development of the industry and the benefits which have flowed from it.

At the outset let me state quite clearly that the mining industry
has consistently supported the desire of the Aboriginal community to
have access to traditional areas of land and that the industry has no
desire to destroy either wilfully, or unwittingly, traditional sites
of cultural importance. Paralleling that support, expressed now for
many years, is our wish to avoid confrontation with Aboriginal
interests over these matters despite the attempts of some within both
the Aboriginal and non-Aboriginal communities to create the impression
that the industry does.

The industry also recognizes and supports the Aborigines' desire for
freedom to choose their way of life, be it traditional or otherwise;
to have a say in their own affairs;   to protect important archaeological,
anthropological and cultural sites;   and to have less reliance on others.

(a) Mining companies:

    (i)   operate in diverse geological, geographic and political
environments in Australia and have to consider many
different interests when exploring such ground;

    (ii)   operate under widely different and sometimes contradictory
laws including Mining, Heritage, Environmental Planning,
Protection of Sites and National Parks Acts;

    (iii)   encounter Aborigines of differing life-styles, associations
with land, aspirations, attachment to tradition, and
understanding of business in general and mining in
particular;   and

    (iv)   do not profess to be experts in Aboriginal affairs, culture,
history, Archaeology or Anthropology. But many
explorationists have a better appreciation of some of those
aspects than the average city-dweller.

(b)   Australian Mining Industry Council (AMIC) companies working in remote areas have established sound principles for contact with Aboriginal communities.

(c)   Most exploration in remote areas is carried on quietly and efficiently by companies in accordance with the law and without disturbing Aboriginal culture, way of life or traditional and important sites. However, as with other occupiers of land, it does sometimes disturb their expectations.

Companies encounter Aborigines or evidence of their past habitation on land not only claimed by or granted to Aborigines, as in the Northern Territory and the Pitjantjatjara lands, but also:

(a)   in Aboriginal reserves where strict conditions of entry apply;

(b)   on land leased by Aborigines or held in trust for Aborigines (as for example by the Western Australian Aboriginal Lands Trust);

(c)   on land in which Aborigines have no legal rights but in which they maintain a traditional and close association with the land; and

(d)   on land with which Aborigines no longer have any close associations, but in which archaeological sites are found. (The sum of (a) and (d) probably covers the greater part of Australia.)

Those who had read what the industry's leaders and its national organization, the Australian Mining Industry Council, have been saying over the past decade would have recognized that it has been following a positive course. In its annual Declaration of Policy, AMIC has consistently pointed out that:

1.   the industry is aware of the special problems facing Aboriginal people and shares the community objective of improving their

position, especially through increased responsibility for their own affairs;

2. the industry is one of the few which has the potential, mainly in the development and mining stages, to provide employment and training in industrial skills in remote areas where there are scant employment opportunities;

3. the industry is aware of the need for special efforts to accommodate its training and working procedures to allow for Aboriginal cultural differences;

4. it is a national responsibility to assist and foster the development and welfare of the Aboriginal people, not simply a matter for the industry alone;

5. special efforts are necessary by all concerned in the education, training and employment fields to enable those Aborigines who so elect to compete on equal terms in the wider Australian community;

6. while the responsibility for Aboriginal community development rests with governments and with the communities themselves, mining companies should encourage and cooperate with any traditional Aboriginal community within its operational area should it wish to undertake development projects;

7. the industry supports measures designed to provide Aboriginal communities with access to their own traditional lands and to protect important traditional sites; and

8. Aboriginal owners and occupiers should be treated with the same consideration as other owners and occupiers.

In addition, the Declaration of Policy includes special guidelines for mineral exploration companies engaged in communication with Aboriginal communities. While the guidelines codify the common sense approach which many companies already pursue, they are an indication

of the importance the industry attaches to communication with

Aboriginal communities. Briefly, the guidelines:

(i)   stress the importance of obtaining early approval to hold

        discussions directly with the relevant traditional community

        or their appointed representatives or agents;

(ii)   remind companies that Aboriginal communities will be concerned

        particularly with the protection of the communities'

        interests and sites of significance;

(iii)   suggest early explanations of exploration programmes, including

        techniques to be used and the locality of the work;

(iv)   advise companies and contractors to keep their employees fully

        informed about any understanding reached with Aboriginal

        communities and suggest that failure to comply should result

        in dismissal;

(v)   advise that one experienced person should be nominated as

        liaison officer for the company; that the privacy of communities

        must be respected; that reasonable notice should be given of

        visits, and that where possible these should coincide with

        community council days;

(vi)   recommend that company personnel and contractors should be

        advised not to show disrespect for Aboriginal customs or

        beliefs;

(vii)   remind companies that any understanding reached with Aborigines

        regarding exploration or mining activities may or may not be

        legally binding, but in any case should be recorded in writing

        and signed by the parties or their representatives; and

(viii) suggest that compensation for damage to the land surface and

loss of its use directly caused by the mining company should

be negotiated.

Because of the need to inform Aborigines adequately about mining

and staff about Aborigines, dealing with Aborigines is usually slow.

The industry has no power to force companies to observe these

guidelines, but I doubt that any responsible organization would allow

its employees to pursue any course other than that suggested by them.

Together with our broader policy, the guidelines indicate an

appreciation of the position of Aborigines and a positive approach to

meeting and solving the issues which can be raised by proposals for

exploration and other mineral activity on Aboriginal land.

Several measures have been taken by member companies to facilitate

communication on Aboriginal matters. These are:

(a) The AMIC has established an Aboriginal Affairs Committee and

AMIC liaises with similar committees formed by the Chamber of

Mines in the various states and the Northern Territory, with a

view to informing other companies of procedures for consulting

with the relevant Aborigines. This is important because of the

range of Aborigines encountered in different areas, with

differing needs and aspirations and attachment to tradition.

It is also important on account of the different laws which the

companies must comply with in different areas.

(b) Member companies are making genuine efforts to consult with all

occupiers of land on which they are active, and in particular

with Aborigines.

(c) The Council has established a dialogue with the various government

departments concerned with Aborigines and protection of their

important anthropological and archaeological sites and their
quiet enjoyment of land (e.g. Department of Aboriginal Affairs,
Aboriginal Lands Trust, administrators of the various Heritage
Acts, e.g. the Western Australian Museum).

(d) Employment of anthropologists and archaeologists to conduct
limited site surveys where appropriate.

(e) Members of the Northern Territory Chamber of Mines and companies
operating in other areas have arranged to put on, for Aboriginal
communities, displays of typical exploration procedures and
equipment used.

(f) Appointment of liaison officers to provide continuity of
communication with Aborigines.

Employment of Aborigines:

It is expected that companies with sufficient resources, and which
are managing resource developments on land occupied by Aborigines,
will offer to train and employ them on the same terms and conditions
as other employees in comparable jobs. In respect of employment it
should be noted, however, that the ability of companies to offer
employment at the exploration stage is quite small due to the low
manpower requirements of individual exploration projects. Aborigines
are employed by companies to assist companies to avoid archaeological
and anthropological sites during roadmaking, shifting of camp and
other activities, or to act as guides.

The mining industry, in talking to Aborigines or their
representatives and advisers about exploration and mining activities
and preservation or protection of Aboriginal sites, is generally
dealing with people with little or no understanding of mining. The
onus is on the mining industry to explain its business to these

people. That takes time. While the industry is genuine in its desire to proceed quietly with its business with the cooperation and goodwill of all land users and occupiers, including Aborigines, it recognizes that it has a long way to go before its methods and objectives will be understood by many outside the industry.

It should be stressed, as I am sure you all recognize, that Australia is one nation — but one which, nevertheless, comprises different interests, all striving to ensure that the benefits of hard work and enterprise are spread equitably; that no one section of the community advances to the detriment of others, and that all points of view are given a fair go. All thinking members of our community recognize that efforts must be made to make up for almost 200 years of neglect and ignorance of Aboriginal interests. The overwhelming approval for the constitutional amendment in May 1967 is indicative of the support which the national community has given to the Aboriginal cause. But we make a grave mistake if we believe that the high principles embodied in the sentiments of that amendment can be pursued without proper consideration being given to the equally important overall national interest. It is a matter of some concern to my industry that we, more than any other, are expected to bear the cost of the legislation designed to implement those principles, and the mining industry is often expected to bear the whole community's welfare obligations.

The mining industry is one of Australia's most efficient and productive industries. But there is a tendency for many in the community to view it in a 'cargo-cult' manner and forget that the principles of business apply. The industry cannot and should not be asked to bear alone the obligations of funding Aboriginal welfare.

The industry already pays substantial taxes in the form of royalty
taxes, company taxes, freight 'taxes' and taxation of employees,
and also contributes many other benefits to communities in the form
of services. The more the industry has to bear those financial loads,
the less money it has available to invest in exploration and production,
and in consequence less income will be available for future
disbursement to governments, shareholders, employees and service
industries.

Mining can benefit the whole Australian community, including
Aborigines, by providing:

(a)   increased services including medical, education, housing,
      cultural recognition;

(b)   increased infrastructure and communication in remote areas; and

(c)   increased taxation paid which is spread throughout the community.

Taxation is the prime source of Aboriginal welfare benefits.
The industry requires that maximum access to land must be maintained
for exploration and mining purposes.

It is imperative that exploration, which is essential to the
survival of the mining industry and indirectly of most other industries,
is conducted where we consider the geological potential for the
existence of minerals is the best. That can be on land occupied by
Aborigines or where Aborigines have had an historical association.
Minerals are found only where they exist, not where we would like them
to be. If the unfettered right is given to owners or occupiers of
land, including Aborigines, to refuse entry or to impose open-ended
and unreasonable conditions of entry on mining companies, then the
welfare of that state or territory and the whole nation could suffer
in the long term. The Northern Territory Land Rights Act falls down

badly in those respects, and represents an unreasonable impediment to exploration in the Northern Territory. Where Aborigines have been granted land rights (as in the Northern Territory, and the Pitjantjatjara lands in South Australia), they have a wide choice of usage of the land, most of which usage has little to do with exploration or mining. At the exploration stage, and particularly in the earliest phases, the mining industry generally needs access to large areas in order to evaluate the ground for potential mineralization. In the mining and development stages, the area utilized by a company is generally much smaller. I should point out here that most exploration is not blessed with success.

Aboriginal Sites:

(a)   Geologists as trained observers (and the first sector of the mining industry to encounter Aborigines in remote areas) often are the first to bring the presence of archaeological sites to the notice of Aborigines who claim a traditional association or custodianship over a particular traditional area. Some of these sites were previously unknown or were forgotten by those Aborigines.

(b)   Some legislation obliges a company to report the discovery of Aboriginal sites or relics to a statutory authority. On the other hand, some Aborigines or their agents prefer not to divulge the locality of traditional cultural or archaeological sites.

(c)   It is a paradox that, the larger the area in which a company is exploring, the less likely it is to disturb the ground surface during those reconnaissance phases.

In the early stages of exploration when the work involved does not disturb the land surface, and during the reconnaissance phases when the exploration areas covered can be hundreds or thousands of square kilometres, it would be both prohibitively time consuming and logistically impractical to survey the full area or exploration tenement for Aboriginal sites even if anthropologists and archaeologists could be hired to complete such a survey. At this stage a company usually has a reasonable degree of flexibility as to location of measurement or observation points, and can vary the locations so as to avoid certain areas in response to legitimate wishes and concerns of the relevant Aborigines. However, as the exploration programmes progress and the results of the observations are assessed, the areas are reduced as a company narrows down its areas of interest. It might be more feasible to carry out comprehensive archaeological and anthropological surveys when smaller tenements are secured, and when the greater intensity and density of the work is more likely to disturb the ground surface. With intense exploration, or at the mining stage or feasibility study stage, the ability of a company to vary the location of its sampling or observation sites is limited. Consequently, a mining company needs to know in advance where important sites are so that it can avoid them or adequately protect them as appropriate.

A company must know the ground rules before committing itself to large development expenditures, and accordingly would require to know the location of important Aboriginal sites so as to plan developments to avoid them. Important Aboriginal sites should not be 'discovered' after the discovery of the orebody. Exploration in the reconnaissance phase is a competitive business, and particularly when tenements have not been secured. In <u>those</u> circumstances secrecy of purpose and location of work is of utmost importance to a company. While companies usually inform occupiers of the type and extent of work they intend to carry out, they are reluctant to do so when the company does not hold tenements over the ground. That might be a reason for some companies being reluctant to talk to Aborigines or their representatives in advance of the earliest exploration activities, before tenements have been secured.

It would be useful to consider some typical problems encountered by the mining industry.

(a)   Aboriginal sites

Firstly, on land <u>not</u> granted to or held by, or on behalf of, Aborigines:

(i)   Identifying whether or not one is exploring on land where Aborigines retain a traditional and active association with the land. There is no national or state register to which one might refer.

(ii)   Identifying and locating traditional owners for the purposes of explaining the general exploration approach. Where land councils and traditional owners are in disagreement, a company must carefully determine who represents the traditional owners. Statutory obligations imposed on holders of tenements are usually designed to encourage companies to explore and work areas at a minimum rate. Exploration below that rate could risk cancellation of the tenements by the government concerned. In most areas (excepting Pitjantjatjara lands where time limits for negotiations are imposed) lawyers and anthropologists as

advisers to Aborigines are under no urgency to expedite
arrangements between Aborigines and the companies. Time
has little significance to many Aborigines. Therefore,
any discussions or understanding reached with them will be
slow.

(iii) The extent of time taken to reach agreements.

(iv) Conflicting advice from different government departments
concerned with the industry, and Aboriginal interests.

Secondly,

(b) Aboriginal sites

on land granted to or held by or on behalf of Aborigines (e.g.
Northern Territory, and Pitjantjatjara lands).

The Eureka rebellion led to the enactment of legislation both to
foster and to regulate the mining industry. Today, the mining industry
operates under legislation which means that elected governments, rather
than individuals, control mineral development as agents of the whole
community. You may not agree that that control is exercised as you
personally would like to see it exercised, but control exists and,
as any exploration or mining company can testify, it has an impact on
almost every aspect of the industry's activities. This legislative
framework is primarily a state one, but the federal government,
principally through its taxing and foreign trade powers, also has a
role.

Whether we like it or not, British settlement on this continent
brought with it a commitment to the British tradition of government.
Part of that tradition is the constitutional practice of reserving,
except in a few minor cases, ownership of minerals to the Crown, which
essentially means for the benefit of the community as a whole. Unlike

the United States, where minerals are generally privately owned, the Crown ownership principle means that it is the state which grants approval to explore for and mine minerals, in return for the payment of monies.

According to some interesting figures taken from The News (28/10/81, Adelaide), federal government figures show Aboriginal land extends over 738,032 square kilometers of the 7,685,854 square kilometers of land area of Australia. That is, 9.6% of Australia's land has been vested in 1.2% of the population. It includes leasehold, reserve and mission land. Freehold accounts for the largest part, of which 361,700 square kilometers are in the Northern Territory; and 101,900 square kilometers are in north-west of South Australia. This last parcel of land is vested in the Pitjantjatjara Council through the Pitjantjatjara Land Rights Act, which was proclaimed in October 1981. This amount of land represents about 10% of South Australia, or is equivalent to about twice the area of Tasmania.

Some companies which have been approved under the provisions of the Act as eligible to apply for exploration tenements have begun negotiations with the body corporate which represents the Aborigines in whom the land is vested. Exploration and mining tenements cannot be granted pursuant to the Mining Act until agreement concerning terms and conditions of entry and operations is reached between a company and the body corporate which must consult with and carry out the wishes of the traditional owners. Companies are specifically precluded from making any payment to the body corporate (Anangu Pitjantjatjaraku) other than compensation for disturbances to the land surface and to their way of life. The legislation also forbids any demand by the Pitjantjatjaraku for such payments other than compensation. The Act

is imperfect and might need amendment in the future, but is a
considerable improvement on the ill-conceived and substantially
impractical Northern Territory Land Rights Act.

Aboriginal Land Rights (Northern Territory) Act:

Having regard to the extremely large areas of Aboriginal land in
the Northern Territory and the relatively small numbers of Aborigines
living on them, as well as the fact that, statistically, mining
activity in Australia affects only a minute fraction of the land
surface, mining pursuits and Aboriginal landholdings can co-exist
harmoniously. However, to date there has been little opportunity to
display this co-existence in the Northern Territory. Despite the fact
that the federal Land Rights Act has been in force now for five years,
the Act has proven to be substantially impractical. Only two or three
agreements have so far been entered into between the Aboriginal Land
Councils and mining companies in the Northern Territory. Long delays
were experienced in negotiating these agreements, and similar delays
are now being encountered by the few other mining companies which have
been able to begin meaningful negotiations with a Land Council.
Despite the large backlog of applications for exploration or mining
titles on Aboriginal land, most companies have not been able to begin
such negotiations, and it must be questioned whether the Aboriginal
Land Councils will ever be able to exercise effectively the powers they
have been given under the legislation.

Many of the problems with the Act have stemmed from the narrow
approach to such issues adopted by the federal government when the
legislation was framed. Insufficient attention was given to
fundamental matters and to the workability of the Act. I do not

believe that this situation will help Aboriginal interests, exploration and mining companies, or the total community.

In introducing the Aboriginal Land Rights (Northern Territory) Act into the House of Representatives on 4th June 1976, the then Minister for Aboriginal Affairs, Mr. Viner, described it as a complex piece of legislation. It certainly is, but many of the provisions were vaguely written and open to more than one interpretation. In order to maximize its chances to discover mineral deposits, a mining company requires that it spends as much as possible of its exploration budget directly on the ground. Payments for permission to enter freehold or leasehold land reduce the effective budget of the explorer and lessen its chances to discover a deposit.

Inconsistency in respect of the Crown ownership principle is avoided in the states' Mining Acts by way of provisions either setting definite parameters for assessing compensation only on the basis of disturbance to the land surface, or specifically stating that, in determining compensation payments, no allowance should be made for any Crown minerals known or believed to be within the land concerned. The rental fees are set at a level designed to inhibit non-productive trading in mineral tenements and to maximize bona-fide exploration and mining on the ground. However, to the annoyance of both the Northern Territory government and the mining industry, the federal Land Rights Act applying to the Northern Territory is open-ended with regard to royalties and other payments to Aborigines for the right to enter and conduct legitimate activities on Aboriginal land. Indeed, an impasse has developed whereby the Northern Territory government has informed companies that any agreements reached between them and the Land Councils as representatives of the traditional owners cannot provide production royalties or payments to those Aborigines. The Northern Territory government has argued that such payments would usurp the principle of Crown ownership of minerals.

The Land Rights Act does provide, of course, that the government may override an Aboriginal veto in the national interest. But that provision does not have much practical meaning, particularly where mineral exploration is concerned. The national interest, in the sense envisaged by the Act, is quite impossible to measure at the stage where minerals have yet to be discovered.

Most Australians would have no quarrel with a process which allows adequate areas of land to be set aside to provide Aboriginal communities with the opportunity to enjoy their own traditional way of life. Nevertheless, there is a growing concern in the wider community about the manner in which land is being claimed by and granted to Aborigines in the Northern Territory under the federal Land Rights Act, especially the inordinately large amount of land in relation to the relatively small numbers of Aborigines with traditional interests in the land which is involved. It is this consequence of the Northern Territory Act which is largely behind the state governments' reluctance, both outspoken and implied, to incorporate the provisions of that legislation into their own laws.

In a brochure issued in 1979, entitled 'Aboriginal Land Rights Legislation: What do you know about it?' the federal Department of Aboriginal Affairs stated: 'If all claims were granted — and this is unlikely — approximately 30% of the Territory at the most would be given over to Aboriginal ownership'. It now appears that the Department's estimate will prove to be much too low. Nearly 25% of the Northern Territory has already been designated Aboriginal land under the Land Rights Act, while another 25% is now under claim. As pastoral leases, which comprise most of the balance of the Territory, either expire or become acquired by Aboriginal interests, it is likely that many of these will be subject to land claims as well. However, no longer are land claims based only on areas in which Aborigines wish to live. In several land claim hearings, although arguing they are the traditional owners of the land, the Aboriginal claimants have not expressed any wish whatsoever to live on the land in question. Nevertheless, the Aboriginal Land Commissioner (at that time Mr. Justice Toohey) has recommended such land be granted to the claimants, notwithstanding the interests of others in that land.

It is not merely the extensive size of the existing and possible land grants which is basic to the problem with the federal Land Rights Act, and the cause of growing opposition to its wider application. Just as alarming has been the realization that, under that legislation, the interests of other Australians, including the overall national interest, would appear to have been completely disregarded. In short, major emphasis has been placed on the rights of one section of the community, without any corresponding emphasis on either the obligations which must necessarily go with such rights, or the checks and balances which would ensure a compatibility with the rights of the community as a whole.

It is AMIC's view that all future grants of land to Aboriginal communities should involve much more than the consideration of their traditional links with that land. A whole range of other matters relating to the national and individual interests need to be given at least equal consideration. In this regard, a measure of retrospective action should also be taken in relation to land grants already made.

Where Crown ownership of minerals applies in Australia, owners or occupiers of land do not have any ownership rights in respect of the minerals in their land. Nor do they have rights to extract minerals from their land unless they have specifically acquired mining titles for that purpose. They naturally have rights to the surface use of their land, and these rights are protected. Where minerals are concerned, Australian mining laws endeavour to provide for the rationalization of the various interests involved, on the basis of the simple adage that minerals can be mined only where they are found, whereas other pursuits of man such as farming, forestry and real estate development have some degree of flexibility as to location. The 'Crown ownership of minerals' principle has worked well for Australia since the turn of the century. In some other countries, mineral potential similar to that which Australia now enjoys has long ago become virtually sterilized as a result of the vetoes and self-defeating 'bidding-up' processes associated with general mineral ownership vested in individuals. Exploration for and, where appropriate, the mining of minerals are not necessarily incompatible with other uses of land. Crown ownership of minerals entails a responsibility for the government concerned to ensure that it alone assumes the right to make decisions in respect of those minerals, and that such decisions are made in the best interests of the community as a whole. The rights of other affected parties, particularly those of landholders in respect of the surface use of their land, must naturally be given full consideration whenever decisions regarding minerals within such land are to be made.

There are further problems with the Land Rights Act (N.T.). The Aboriginal Sacred Sites Act provides for setting up a register of sacred sites which is to be available for inspection by exploration lease-holders. However, the Aboriginal Sacred Sites Protection Authority (responsible for establishing and maintaining the register) has not yet been constituted.

If the laws governing exploration on land held by or on behalf of Aborigines require a company to obtain the permission of the Aborigines (as owners or occupiers) to enter and carry out work, the industry suggests that the conditions governing such permission should be known in advance and should provide that:

(i)   Permission to enter land should not be unreasonably withheld by the owner or occupier. If, after a defined time, a company considers it has been so withheld or the requested terms are unreasonable, there should be a mechanism which takes into account the company's, the community's, and Aboriginal interests in order to resolve the issue. For example, there is a time limit of 120 days in the Pitjantjatjara Land Rights Act, but there are no time limits in the N.T. Land Rights Act, where delaying tactics can readily be used to frustrate the search for minerals belonging to the Crown. Time is usually unimportant to Aborigines living in remote areas; and, in the absence of statutory time limits, anthropologists, archaeologists and lawyers assisting an Aboriginal organization are usually under no pressure to expedite arrangements between Aborigines and companies.

(ii)   Where the Crown owns the minerals, any payments relating to such permission should be restricted to compensation for damage to the land surface and loss of the use of the surface area of the land directly used by the mining company. Payments in advance of exploration reduce the amount of money spent on bona-fide exploration, because the amount or number of discoveries is directly proportional to the amount of money spent on field work. Royalties related to the production or value of minerals should be paid only to the Crown as owner of the minerals. It is up to the Crown to utilize the royalty revenue as it sees fit, and for the benefit of the whole community.

(iii)   Subject to the relevant provision of the Mining Act, permission of the owner or occupier to enter and explore should include the owner or occupier's permission to apply for subsequent titles and to proceed to the mining and development stages, subject to the normal environmental and other governmental approvals.

(iv)   Payments to Aborigines should not be considered by governments to be the principal means of financing Aboriginal welfare programmes, which should be shared by all Australians.

(v)   Entry for scientific purposes, or for reconnaissance visits of short duration involving no disturbance to the ground, should not be prohibited.

(vi)   In other respects, the integrity of the relevant Mining Act should be preserved.

(vii)   Once permission is given, a company should be able to assign a portion of its interest in a tenement to secure finance against the asset represented by its tenement without any further permission of the owners or occupiers being required.

All future agreements with mining companies should be negotiated in a form similar to those compensation agreements for disturbance to the land surface which are regularly entered into by mining companies with non-Aboriginal landholders elsewhere in Australia. However, matters of particular concern to Aborigines such as provision of employment, control of alcohol, protection of significant sites, etc., would also need to be considered. In the event of any failure to reach agreement, an arbitrator could readily settle the matter, again according to normal procedures.

Put at its simplest, the whole issue of resource development and Aboriginal rights and sites over the past decade or so has changed from one of a disadvantaged group within the community seeking to redress that position, to one of economics. I do not ignore the fact that social problems for Aboriginal communities are created with developments — whether by mining companies, farmers, tourist undertakings or whatever. These problems are broadly matters of retaining for Aborigines a special identity, of protecting traditional life-styles and, where people wish to pursue them, preserving a unique culture. We should be honest enough to accept that, notwithstanding those concerns the negotiation of agreements between mining companies and Aboriginal communities has been predicated on the basis of maximizing the economic benefits to those communities. As a businessman, I understand and accept that. But associated with that approach there has been too much attention given to the efforts of a minority to create political advantage from proposals to explore for minerals on land to which Aboriginal communities may lay claim. I do not believe, for example, that the situation over Noonkanbah served anyone's best interests, especially as much of the debate was ill-informed and at times quite misleading. Not nearly enough credit has been given to those companies and Aboriginal communities who have worked out positive agreements and, through cooperation, managed to protect the community's interests _and_ pursue mineral activity.

These successful experiences should provide a lead to all of us as we seek to build a better Australia for future generations. Our grandchildren will not thank us if we allow the scepticism, to which I earlier referred, to build division and resentment. Our task should be to find legislative mechanisms through which the important national interests of Aboriginal sites, and access to traditional lands and resource development, can be harmoniously achieved. We cannot afford to advance one at the expense of the other, but we can reach a national consensus on the issues discussed in this symposium. The search for that consensus will include frank and open debate. But it should be free of political point-scoring, and directed at ensuring that the Australia of future generations is not left with the legacy of a divided community. The challenge to reach that consensus is clearly ours. I hope we can achieve it.

THE RECOVERY AND DISCOVERY OF RIGHTS: AN OVERVIEW

OF ABORIGINES, POLITICS AND LAW

COLIN TATZ

1. Aborigines and Political Science:

The interests of this symposium go beyond Aboriginal sites and rights,
and take into account the severe and traumatic impact of intrusion of
mining into the Aboriginal domain. This is a discussion and debate about
reality -- and in this context what permeates the realities for
Aborigines is politics.

Like sex, the word politics produces an infinite array of reactions
in its readers and hearers. Sex, for so many, is in the dark, under the
blankets, something hidden, often even from the doctor. Politics is also
seen as being confined, at least to places called parliament, by peculiar
people who constitute parties and then only for particular periods per annum.

For what I wrote in a paper on 'Aborigines and Uranium' last year I
received a not-so-gentle reprimand. The knee-jerk reaction was this
sentence about the uranium social impact monitoring project: 'Implicitly
or explicitly, we (and the Institute [of Aboriginal Studies]) have a
political commitment ...' Most reactionaries, that is, people who reacted,
stopped at the mentally projected dots that didn't appear after 'commitment'.
The rest of the sentence read: 'in the widest and best sense of that word:
a commitment which recognizes that there are different visions of society
and man, different notions of a good society and what is good for man'.

It can be argued that politics -- as a discipline and as that activity
which allocates and regulates the available values in society -- has
abdicated in the Aboriginal context. How much political analysis has
been applied to Aboriginal affairs, or to this symposium agenda in
particular? The writings of Charles Rowley and myself notwithstanding,

or even withstanding, the literature to date is hardly rich, or substantial enough to derive strong conclusions with which to sway those who make decisions and exercise **their** will over or on behalf of Aborigines. Rowley, Tatz, Christine Jennett and very latterly, Peter Loveday, Dean Jaensch, Alistair Heatley and Rolf Gerritsen constitute a very small band, given the prominence of Aboriginal affairs these past 20 years. For the moment I leave out the handful of anthropologists who have expressed an interest in political aspects. Basically I am talking about the men and women steeped in the tradition of political thought, as Berki (1977: 11-13) explains it:

> The stuff of political thought is made up of the
> visions of political writers ... (and these visions)
> ... are not only descriptions or explanations of the
> state in the restricted, 'neutral' sense, but they are
> also - and by the same token - evaluations and
> advocacies. They are factual statements, philosophical
> arguments and value judgments all at the same time.
> They are consequential: their import reaches into the
> realm of future alternatives. They pronounce on the
> morality, the rights and wrongs of actions connected
> with changing or maintaining the character of the state.

Whether I have 'visions' as a political thinker is another matter. But the few political scientists who have studied the Aboriginal experience have certainly engaged in evaluations and advocacies and pronounced pretty strongly on the moral and ethical content of political decisions and actions. The core of politics is ethics. The very vigour of the intellectual study of politics can be attributed largely to its focus on the elaboration and consideration of varying visions of the nature of the 'good' polity.

There is another important attribute of the political science tradition, one put so well by Schall (1978:97): 'One of the major tasks of political theory as an intellectual discipline, as Socrates taught it from the beginning, has consisted in distinguishing between proclaimed form and actual conduct as compared to some normative standard'. Rowley

and I have spent a great deal of time, energy and space talking about
policy and practice, about measuring policy aims and governmental
claims against reality, between 'proclaimed form' and 'actual conduct'.
But even so, those sets of books and writings don't constitute a
'literature' in the usual sense.

One can understand political scientists not becoming involved
in Aboriginal issues per se. But studies of those topics and problems
can tell us a great deal about Australia's political and civic culture.
What has been written about Aborigines surely tells us something about
the Australian ethos: as it views human rights, racial and sexual
discrimination and remedies for such behaviour; as it shows how
those with power and influence treat those with neither; as it handles
the conflicts inherent in Progress and technology as against
tradition and a desire for a status quo; as it tries to assert, or
even enforce unity and homogeneity in a continent of diversity.

A great many aspects of both political theory and practical
politics need urgent examination. For example, one of the very
foundations of democratic theory is that a high level of public
participation, at many levels of government, is both an indication and
a method of democracy. The consequence of high levels of political
liberty, political equality and political fraternity is necessarily a
high level of participation. The role of political liberty, equality
and fraternity in a democratic polity is to ensure that effective and
continuing political action is open to all. But what we have in
Aboriginal affairs is a set of catch-cries and slogans that revolve
around the policy and practice of consultation. And consultation is not
and never has been a synonym for participation in the democratic
tradition of political process. As Mary Parker Follett (1940) would

have said of the consultation process: it is but a mere gesture

of agreement (or non-agreement).

Ignorance of politics and its vocabulary creates serious consequences

for Aborigines. One example relevant to this symposium context comes to

mind: the Plan of Management for Kakadu National Park as drawn up by the

Australian National Parks and Wildlife Service (ANPWS). When the Plan

was first published for public consideration, the Australian Institute

of Aboriginal Studies (AIAS), through its uranium social impact steering

committee, strongly criticized the absence of any executive role for

Aborigines in Park decision-making. The ANPWS insisted it was including

Aborigines in management. The AIAS then took the unusual step of writing

to every member of federal parliament, seeking support for a debate

on the Plan before it lay, tabled but undebated, for the 21 days it

needed to become 'law', at least for five years initially. Amid this,

I happened to hear an ANPWS officer in Darwin explaining to a

radio reporter how that Service involves Aborigines in management: as

trainee rangers culling out feral creatures, making fire-breaks, handling

potential erosion and the like. Voila! They manage the land of which

they are the landlords. We meant, and still mean, direct participation

as an exercise in power and influence; in what Dahl (1970: 17, 32)

calls influence: 'a relationship between actors in which one actor induces

other actors to act in some way they would not otherwise act' and power:

as 'a special case of influence involving severe losses for

non-compliance'. On power, Weber said it best of all perhaps: 'the

chance of a man or of a number of men to realise their own will in a communal

action even against the resistance of others who are participating in the

action'.

Why has there been so little study of Aborigines and politics? A

partial answer is that the social scientists who have been interested in

Aborigines have viewed political activity, if they have viewed it at all, as something happening within or between Aboriginal groups, not between Aborigines and what they perceive, often naively, as those formal governmental institutions they equate with politics. Political analysis, even 20 years ago when I began a Ph.D. at the Australian National University, was a no-no. The admonition was not to touch policy, legislation, administration, the 'welfare' field generally: for to do so was (a) to get 'involved' in politics which was none of the business of true scientists; and (b) probably to impede and inhibit fieldwork possibilities for scholars to come. Study the history of Queensland Aboriginal policy till 1910 -- and not a year beyond that -- was the advice of the A.N.U.'s Anthropology Department. In my day, said Sir Paul Hasluck, having digested my thesis on Aboriginal administration in the Territory from 1954 to 1964, we touched only those topics with which all the people concerned were duly dead and buried. The injunction to keep away from evaluations and advocacies is interesting because, while the anthropological tradition may well have been 'neutrality', 'objective' reporting and recording, we do have two pronouncers on the 'good' polity from the discipline: A.P. Elkin and Donald Thomson.

I do not wish to discuss what anthropologists do now. I want to say that much ethnography is useless for political theory analysis because it doesn't examine, explain or articulate political processes as political scientists understand them. Further, Australian Sociology has evidenced almost no interest in Aboriginal affairs, and legal studies are only now coming to fruition. Psychology that is concerned with Aboriginal education is of little value here; ethnopsychiatry I simply ignore. The attention of economists has been meagre, to say the least.

What is left? Basically we have the analyses of Rowley and myself, sometimes historical, often legal in emphasis, with much attention to the policy-administration problem. What we lack, and perhaps what this Academy can help to inspire, is analyses of Aboriginal political development. T.R. Gurr -- an eminent political scientist from Northwestern University in Illinois -- has provided us with a critique of what is missing in terms of both a research agenda and theoretical considerations.[1] In brief, his fresh view points to enormous gaps in the area of Aboriginal political development. 'All Australians', he writes, 'would be the better served if the general trajectory of Aboriginal political development were better understood and alternative goals clearly articulated'. He sees eight areas in need of serious attention: the role of political action in creating conditions for change; the institutionalization of Aboriginal participation in the growing number of institutions for their affairs; political responsiveness to Aboriginal demands, both positive and negative; the scope and content of government programmes and evaluations thereof; changes in Aboriginal welfare, that is, measurement in statistical terms of progress made and still required; the objectives of Aboriginal political development, through any statement -- if one can be found -- of 'explicit images of what Aboriginal political society might be or should be like'; the need to assess the number, nature, dynamics and effectiveness of the new political institutions; and finally, and astutely, he suggests we study the role of those who manage and 'broker' Aboriginal affairs, those of us (self included) who in political science terms are an 'interest group' in their own right.

II. Aborigines and politics:

Earlier I said that politics -- as an activity, system and process --
had abdicated. We need then to look, very briefly, at whether the
political system has given Aborigines rights, or allowed them to recover
rights. By political system I mean, for the moment, the _formal_ political
or politico-legal institutions, activities and processes of conventional
politics -- voting, parliamentary representation, political parties,
pressure group activity etc. -- that most people see as constituting
politics.

Are Aborigines as powerless as I have often said they are,
suffering all the imaginable consequences of that condition? How, I have
asked, does this disparate, scattered, fragmented minority -- about
one per cent of the population -- raise a voice, gain a hearing, excite
action and change their condition or, at least, some of their specific
conditions? My argument has been that the Australian political system has
nothing to offer Aborigines, that they will remain largely ignored and
unheeded (even if heard) so long as they abide by the _formal_ rules of
our political life. The contention has been that Aborigines can win legally
what they cannot win politically; that law and legal process are a
more effective means of asserting and recovering rights than conventional
politics.

The Aboriginal relationship to the political system is detailed in
C. Tatz (1979: 6-48): a short (and selective) résumé therefore suffices
here. With the possible exception of a handful of electorates in the
Northern Territory, it can be said that the Aboriginal vote is without
power and influence. In their case, voting is compulsory only if they seek
registration as voters. Non-compulsion is said to be a boon in their favour.
In only a few electorates do Aboriginal (potential) voters outnumber

'whites'. In one such -- the Western Australian (WA) seat of Kimberley --
the ruling Liberal Party did all it could to diminish the Aboriginal
vote: first, by resorting to a 'dirty tricks' campaign in the 1977 state
election which, ruled the Court of Disputed Returns, nullified sufficient
Aboriginal votes to 'win' the Liberals the seat; second, by amending
the Electoral Act, as a direct response to that verdict, to make
Aboriginal first-time registration and postal voting much more
difficult. An earlier amendment, defeated by the Speaker's casting
vote, would have disfranchised all non-literate Aboriginal voters.
Mere possession of a vote does not make Aborigines political participants.

As a representation, to date only five Aborigines have been
elected to legislatures: two to the Northern Territory (NT) Legislative
Assembly, one to the Queensland parliament, one to the WA parliament
and one, Neville Bonner as a Liberal, to the federal Senate.[2] Aboriginal
members do, can or may have strong symbolic meaning for them and for
us; even 'white' MPs reliant on an Aboriginal vote could mean the
useful airing of Aboriginal interests and grievances. But as a
political scientist I simply do not believe in legislature power, or that
legislatures any longer represent the people, 'watchdog' for them,
initiate laws and oversee their administration and consequences.

Until 1970 the lament was the lack of Aboriginal leaders, of their
standing up and speaking out. But with their emergence came the retreat,
the defence tactic of denying the representativeness of those who
articulated and criticized. The reaction now to Aboriginal voices is to
demand of each: 'how representative are you of Aborigines?' (as we define
them). Unless they can show, and clearly they cannot, that each has been
given a unanimous mandate, that each has been authorized, is accountable
for his actions, is truly symbolic of and each is acting for the total

'grassroots' community, then they are denigrated and negated as leaders
or spokesmen. The campaign to isolate Senator Bonner, particularly by
fellow party members, has been particularly vitriolic and venomous.

Neither state nor federal party politics has rated or treated
Aborigines as a political issue. Very briefly -- between the December 1972
and May 1974 federal elections, both won by Labor -- the Whitlam
government raised Aborigines to the status of a political problem, the
resolution of which, declaimed the Prime Minister, would be the yardstick
by which Australia's civilization would be measured in the perspective
of history. In 18 months the rhetoric and the euphoria ended, with
Aborigines relegated to what they have been -- at least consciously --
for the past 30 years: a social problem, within a generic species
that embraces (pejoratively) the aged, the doped, the drunk, the
criminal, the sick, the jobless and the retarded, for all of whom
there is need only of more money for more officers, for more programmes.

Political pressure by 'advancement leagues',[3] working within a civil
rights framework, did gain something for Aborigines. Established by
European middle-class liberals in the late 1950s, they were taken over
by Aborigines in the last 1960s and were politically 'dead' by the late
1970s. Broadly, they sought the right of Aborigines to normal
citizenship rights (as they saw them). They campaigned for equal wages,
free and compulsory education and later for retention of reserves and
land rights. They fought the prohibition on Aboriginal drinking, the
forced removal of people from reserves, and mining on such land, as well
as for a federal franchise (given in 1962), and for the successful 1967
Referendum which gave the federal government concurrent power to make laws
for Aborigines in the states. Despite a few wins and some notable draws,

two factors led to the general demise of these pressure groups. The
first was the ease with which these organizations were put down because
of alleged manipulation or infiltration by communists and fellow-travellers.
Communism as a menace is, for the most part, now passé, except in
Queensland and Western Australia. (Generally, the major tactic of
dismissal nowadays is to blame all criticism on academics, the legion
of people branded as 'do-gooders', and that unidentified, unidentifiable
mass known as 'southern stirrers'.) In the 1970s Aborigines took
control of the leagues and argued for Aboriginal rights in their terms.
But herein lay the other factor in their decline: their belief that sheer,
or mere, existence as Aboriginal organizations was more important than
exerting effective pressure, where it hurts, with professional skill.

Aboriginal councils on government settlements and church missions
may possibly come to exercise some authority-autonomy. Certainly this is
so at Yirrkala. As they became legal incorporations, and begin to seek
the aid of lawyers and other professionals on a contract basis rather than
rely on government and church welfare officers, so they start to exert
some muscle. All this is very recent, and these councils have yet to
show political impact. Until no more than three years ago they were
commonly subject to government and mission veto, with powers -- in a number
of instances -- limited to spending canteen profits and the like.

In 1978 the Queensland government bulldozed the Aurukun Council
when that body objected to the announced governmental takeover of the
mission from the Uniting Church. When Aurukun was then brought under the
Local Government Act (as opposed to the Aborigines Act 1971) and its
ruling body became a fully-fledged shire council, Russell Hinze as Minister
simply dismissed the entire council. In 1978 the federal government

suspended the council at Maningrida settlement in the Northern Territory
and terminated the services of all council employees. Eight European
workers were dismissed, six of whom promptly filed suit in the Supreme Court.
Government revocation of their permits to reside on Maningrida and the
unilateral termination of their employment was ruled invalid in that
natural justice was not accorded the plaintiffs.[4]

Recognizing the failure of our political rules and institutions
for Aboriginal progress, the federal government in 1973 created a new
political institution, the National Aboriginal Consultative Committee (NACC).
Without consulting Aborigines as to shape, nature and function, or
examining similar bodies in other countries created for similar motives
and purposes, it established an elected 40-member consultative body to
advise the Minister for Aboriginal Affairs. Simultaneously, Ministers
made speeches about 'transfer of power', about movement away from policies
of guardianship and protection, about 'self-determination'. Aboriginal
reaction to this was to seek a National Aboriginal Congress, with all the
attendant implications of that term. The then Minister, backed by a new
Department of Aboriginal Affairs eager to expand its staff, budget,
jurisdiction and authority, soon put paid to any of these ambitions.
Following Labor's defeat in 1975, the Liberal-Country Party coalition
government enquired into the NACC's future. Recommendations for a
policy-making role for a new Congress were rejected. The new National
Aboriginal Conference has become, as nomenclature suggests, 'a forum in
which Aboriginal views will be expressed 'on matters referred to it'.
The new National Aboriginal Conference is stillborn. The lesson of the
New Zealand Maori Council, the Joint Cabinet-National Indian Brotherhood
body in Canada and the Natives' Representative Council in South Africa,

together with the dismal history of the NACC, is that these political

devices seldom serve the interests of those for whom they are intended.

They are, in Paul Mosaka's words,[5] toy telephones: instruments into which

they can speak but at the other end of which there is no one to listen.

The 'White Australia' immigration policy has its own special

history, reputation, literature and responses. But one can only guess at

why Australia's brand of discrimination against Aborigines has escaped the

international spotlight.[6] Several speculations come to mind. There

is an historical vacuum, an absence of academic analyses of 'black-white'

relations.[7] There are no biographies, in English, of the equivalents

of Geronimo and Red Cloud. The Wounded Knees have been ignored. There

is no strident Luthuli-like Let My People Go, not even a 'white' Cry for

his Beloved Country. Certainly there has been a reluctance by 'black'

and 'white' proponents of Aboriginal interests to go abroad with

their grievances. Only in the past three or four years have Aborigines

begun to seek contacts in Europe, with Third World leaders and their

governments and organizations. Much of this activity appears to be

ineffective, as witness the inability of Aborigines to convince

Third World leaders of the need to raise the Aboriginal issue formally

at the September 1982 Commonwealth Heads of Government Meeting in Melbourne.

Aboriginal pressure abroad mounted following the Noonkanbah affair and as

the 1982 Commonwealth Games approached. The absence of violence has

doubtless contributed to the invisibility of Aborigines in international

politics. The techniques of politicizing Aboriginal problems have been

extraordinarily polite: petitions drawn on bark paintings, courteous

pleas to Ministers, open letters to newspapers, placard-waving marches

in Brisbane when such were once allowed, the civility of parliamentary

questions, and the erection of an Aboriginal 'Tent Embassy' on
the lawns of federal Parliament. (Denis Walker's incipient Black
Panther group was an exception to the general politeness.)

In _formal_ terms, however, there is no ballot power, no representative
power to balance European power, no credence to Aboriginal leadership, with
usually only moral pressure to bear, with basically only reparation and
restitution to seek. Land rights are avowedly not granted in two states
of major Aboriginal population and New South Wales is only now
beginning to think about ways and means of granting them. Except in the
Territory, where some power arises from their title to land, Aborigines
generally have no weapons. They have no capital to withdraw. Excepting
the Northern Territory and Kimberley pastoral industries, they have
no labour to withhold. They have toy telephones to play with and as yet
no real international boost or uplift.

So much for formal politics. But some commentators do see politics
as having achieved real change for Aborigines. They point to the
increasing political muscle of the new Aboriginal associations rather
than councils. The various housing associations or bodies like the
Gagudju Association in western Arnhem Land could well mean the chance
of Aborigines, in Weberian terms, 'to realize their will in a
communal action even against the resistance of others who are participating
in the action'.

T. Gurr (see Note 1) said to me that in democratic politics
publicized injustice is a powerful weapon, more powerful than any
minority's use of the ballot box or even disruptive protest, and that
this power has been used effectively by Aborigines and their supporters.
He rightly points out that there has been no systematic study of such new
political (often legal) institutions which administer Aboriginal affairs.

There is no inventory of them, let alone examination of their Aboriginal involvement, factionalism, relationships with government, their economies, dynamics, autonomy or their effectiveness. He takes heart from those he has seen -- through the spectrum ranging from the National Aboriginal Conference to the legal services to the land councils. They want to change their order of things, Gurr said, and they 'can do quite a bit within the system'. He believes -- and I am now more inclined to share his fresh, outside view -- that the Australian political system in practice has something to offer Aborigines, including the institutional means to keep the pressure on.

How then do Aborigines assert rights? One answer may well lie in these new politico-legal institutions, in the pressures brought by men like Foley, activists who seem accomplished at working both within and outside the system. Foley says Aborigines now have more highly skilled political leaders than ever before and they will use them to develop long-term strategies. If the Aboriginal issue had been raised once during a formal session of the Commonwealth Heads of Government Meeting in Melbourne in 1981, that (he is reported to have said) would have been 'a major victory for us and a major defeat for Malcolm Fraser'.[8] Foley and his supporters then expressed sharp disappointment at the failure of Robert Mugabe and others to introduce the Aboriginal question at CHOGM.[9] But Foley is optimistic: 'For the first time in 200 years we are winning the war. The white wall is starting to crack'. He may be right. But as I look at progress, at examples of winning, I also see some abysmal regression. There is the emergence of open hostility to nearly all things Aboriginal by the Queensland and Western Australian governments. There is retreat by the Commonwealth on several major issues for the sake of short-term political party considerations. There are short-sighted expediencies by the Northern Territory government, many of which are detrimental to Aboriginal interests. These are regular pronouncements by Queensland and Western Australian ministers of racial beliefs (sometimes acted upon) which are so bizarre and outrageous as to be beyond reporting for fear of disbelief. And then there are the pontifications of two Australian 'giant' public figures in their way: Sir Mark Oliphant, who didn't want Sir Doug Nicholls and his 'black' relatives in Adelaide's gubernatorial White House, and Mr Lang Hancock who wants the drinking water of part-Aborigines doped so that they become sterile and disappear from this earth.

But what of the rights of those Aborigines who are not under the umbrella of such relatively united and cohesive/cohering bodies? A traditional answer -- in societies of similar demographic, social and racial structure, of similar civic culture -- is that the weak either suffer what they must, or they engage in civil disobedience such as not paying rent, committing crimes, civic disruption, withdrawing from legal and moral participation in society, threatening violence or actually getting to the stage of committing it. One traditional reality is already with us: what E. Marx (1976: 2) calls _appealing_ violence, where damage to property, to friends, to wife, to self is a result of [Aboriginal] man at the end of his tether, unable to achieve a social aim unaided by others, 'a cry for help'. We may yet see Marx's _coercive_ violence, used rationally 'and in a premeditated and controlled manner, as an extreme but often effective means' toward achieving a social or political objective.

Reflection on all this leaves me with a greater sense of pessimism than of optimism about Aborigines and politics, about politics _for_

Aborigines. But it has made me modify an earlier position. It is <u>not</u>

that politics achieves nothing and that law is the only way left. Rather

it is that the legal route and the political one, followed simultaneously,

should achieve more than either followed exclusively.

III. <u>Aborigines and Law</u>:

There is indeed some optimism in the legal arena, in the belief

that resort and recourse to law can win for Aborigines what they

can't win politically: namely, a way of being heard (even if not

listened to), a way of asserting rights (even if not granted), of

effecting some changes (even if begrudged), a way in which to become

people of account (<u>Menschen</u>), to be taken into account (even if society

tries to dismiss them as <u>Nicht-Menschen</u>).

Law, it must be admitted, has been the creator of the Aboriginal

condition and the impediment to their aspirations. Aborigines are

engaged in a struggle for law and liberty. Several inimical roles of

law come to mind: law as the creator and perpetuator of a special,

inferior legal class of persons; law which ascribes, for generations,

immutable negative traits to that legal class; that brands as

criminal (for that class) behaviour which is acceptable in society

at large; law which controls Aborigines physically, mentally,

geographically; which predicates the negative Aboriginal image in

European eyes and fashions official stereotypes. There is law which can

be manipulated to their disadvantage; which excludes, or allows to be

excluded, Aborigines from its benefits. To claim that many of these

kinds of laws are now repealed is futile and witless. Their absence may

be a boon to the future of today's five-year olds; the reality is that

their operation has deeply scarred Aboriginal Australians. Minorities

repressed by law can forgive but they can't forget.

If such is the reality of negative law, how can it be reconciled
with the contention that for Aborigines there is more hope in the legal
than in the political arena? Here we need to look at the ways in which
law or legal processes can be positive. In an essay entitled 'Aboriginality
and Human Rights' (C. Tatz 1982 : 26-56), I discuss several possible
mechanisms: a Bill of Rights in the Constitution; the enactment of
specific civil rights and what I call 'giving' legislation; resort
to anti-discrimination legislation and, finally, recourse to the
solution offered by positive discrimination or affirmative action.
What I haven't discussed anywhere is the makarrata notion, about which
I have a number of reservations. Here I want to touch on only two
relevant legal avenues. The first is legal incorporation; the second,
recourse to civil law processes and procedures as a way of recovering
rights.

Legal incorporation is a device which can protect by redressing
(to some extent) the unequal contests which pit the 'naked'
Aboriginal against 'white' organization man. With no internal welfare
or social structures, without the institutional support most of us can
rely on when in trouble, the lone individual is up against the weight of
the police force, the Housing Commission, the Department of Aboriginal
Affairs. A misbegotten value in our society is the according of greater
respect to organization, any organization, than to individuals.
The legal cocoon or umbrella of incorporation has now given Aborigines
an organizational framework with which to meet other corporate men, a
vehicle of and for respect, an affiliation which can convey an outward
sense of power, of security and continuity even if those attributes are
lacking within. Only in this narrow but important context is organization
per se a weapon for the weak.

The Land Councils in the Northern Territory prove this point.
Their functions, stated clearly in law, are to express Aboriginal
views on land, to protect the interests of traditional owners, to assist
Aborigines with land claims; their powers are to acquire, hold and dispose
of real and personal property and to negotiate, on behalf of the
traditional owners, with those who want to use or exploit the land.
A mining interest on Aboriginal land (in the Northern Territory) cannot
be granted unless the Minister and the Land Council consent in
writing, or the Governor-General declares that the grant should be
made 'in the national interest'. During 1978, the Northern Land Council
(NLC), despite some grim obstacles, successfully negotiated mining rights
and conditions, together with royalty and compensation payments, with
Ranger Uranium and with Queensland Mines Limited for mining at
Nabarlek, both near (former mission) Oenpelli in western Arnhem Land.

The Central Land Council (CLC) has been particularly effective
in negotiating oil royalties for traditional owners and in confronting
the Northern Territory government on prospective changes to the
Land Rights Act. The CLC and the government have clashed seriously
on both matters of motive and of law. The Chief Minister asserts
that the CLC is trying 'to justify an all out grab for almost every
bit of unalienated Crown Land in the Northern Territory' and that
Aboriginal land ownership should be 'somewhat in proportion to the Aboriginal
population: if the present trend continues it is likely that it will
far exceed this proportion'.[10] The CLC has accused the Chief
Minister of referring to Aboriginal-run cattle stations as 'running
sores' and 'harbours of disease'. It points to that government's
contesting of the Utopia claim. It argues that that government's
submission to the Rowland inquiry is to the Aboriginal detriment,

specifically: the government wants prevention of any further

conversions of currently held Aboriginal leases to Aboriginal

freehold; a cut-off date for the lodgement of Aboriginal claims;

prevention of a second claim where one has failed; exemption from

claim of land set aside for 'public purposes'; exclusion from claim

of stock routes and watering points; mining rights on Aboriginal

land for those who held exploration licences prior to the land

becoming Aboriginal; and protection of the mining leases and

interests of Nabalco and the Jabiluka uranium project.[11]

In these important senses Aborigines are beginning to flex some

real muscle through the most powerful organizations in their

contact history. These rough legal beasts, designed by Europeans and

not really suited to Aboriginal decision-making processes, are nevertheless

asserting, demanding and adopting hard negotiating stances. The NLC has

lost out on what it really wants: no mining on traditional lands.

It has a tough haul ahead in securing protection for the outstation

groups, on the filling of mine pits at the end of exploitation, on

mitigating the inevitable social, economic and cultural impact of mining

and royalties on the traditional life of the people in the uranium province.

But the legal existence of such Councils has made them bodies of account,

organizations of men to be accommodated to, to be reckoned with.

Unlike all other European-created Aboriginal organizations before

them, they have the structure and the base to use legal processes to

protect themselves and to assert the rights of their members.

Let us now look briefly at four efforts by Aborigines to protect

sites and recover rights against the impacts of resource development.

In 1976, the Aurukun Aborigines challenged Queensland's Aurukun

Associates Agreement Act 1975 which, without consulting Aborigines,
incorporated agreements between the Director of Aboriginal and
Islander Affairs and a multinational consortium.[12]   In return for a
42-year bauxite lease, the Director would be paid royalties of
three per cent, for dispersal into the Aborigines Welfare Fund
for Aborigines in general.   The Supreme Court ruled for the Aurukun
people against such general dispersal.   However the Director then
appealed successfully to the Privy Council.[13] Substantial legal issues
were involved in this dispute, not all of which have been finally
resolved.   In August 1978, the Aurukun Council obtained an interim
injunction against their being dismissed by Russell Hinze, Minister for
Local Government.   Mr Justice Campbell recommended priority trial of
the matter, but political events overtook legal recourse.   These
actions may have led the Queensland government to tread a fraction
more warily as it bludgeons all Aboriginal opposition.

At this time a major legal battle is being fought by the
Winychanam (or Winchinam) Aborigines who live near Aurukun.[14]   In
January 1977, their complaint to the Commissioner for Community
Relations was that the federal government purchase of land at
Archer River -- under the Aboriginal Land Fund Act 1974 -- was
negated by the Queensland government's refusal to transfer title to
them.   Queensland Ministers and officials refused to attend two
compulsory conferences to which they had been summoned under the
Racial Discrimination Act 1975.   The Commissioner then issued his first
(and only) certificate entitling the complainants to bring court
proceedings under the Act.   On 10 April 1981, the writ in
Koowarta v Bjelke-Petersen and Others was issued from the Supreme Court.
It does not ask for transfer of title.   Rather it seeks a declaration

that the refusal to permit transfer and Cabinet's general policy against
such transfers are unlawful under the Act; it also seeks an injunction
against similar future action -- and damages. The Queensland
government has filed a demurrer: a plea that there is no basis for
action because of the invalidity of the Racial Discrimination Act
and the Aboriginal Land Fund Act. The federal Attorney-General has
sought transfer of the whole matter to the High Court's jurisdiction.[15]
[On 11 May 1982, four judges of the High Court upheld the
validity of the Racial Discrimination Act, which had been challenged
by Victoria, Queensland and Western Australia. Koowarta's right to
use the Act against the Queensland Premier has been upheld. This is
one of the most significant decisions in the history of state-federal
relations.]

In September 1978, two Aboriginal members of the Northern
Land Council obtained an interim injunction against the NLC's signing
of the Ranger Uranium Agreement. They claimed there had been
insufficient compliance with the legal requirements to consult with the
traditional owners.[16] The NLC did concede the strength of their
claim and, rather than contest the matter by trial of the issue, they
engaged in more elaborate explanation and consultation procedures.
This was the first action by Aborigines against Aborigines. It
achieved speedily what weeks of political noise -- mainly by European
supporters of pro- and anti-uranium factions -- could not achieve.

Beginning in 1980, two Victorian Aborigines, Lorraine Sandra Onus
and Christina Frankland, sought an injunction to stop Alcoa of
Australia Ltd. from interfering with relics on the site of the company's
$1000 million smelter at Portland. The matter went before the Supreme Court,

then on appeal to the Full Court of the Supreme Court. The applicants

then sought an injunction from the High Court per Mr Justice Aickin.

He dismissed their application in that they had not identified specific

sites for relics and that the Archaeological and Aboriginal Relics

Preservation Act 1972 gave no right of access to the descendants of the

prehistoric occupiers of the land. The applicants were given leave to

appeal by three judges of the High Court.[17] In March 1981, the matter

went before the full High Court and in September all seven Justices

ruled the two appellants had standing in law to challenge the Alcoa

construction.[18] The matter has been remitted to the Victorian

Supreme Court. Whatever the final outcome, these court actions have

enabled Victorian Aborigines to bring to public notice the notion of

Aboriginal descendants attempting to reclaim custodianship of their

culture, law and customs.

Action to give to Aborigines or action to subtract from them now

needs law for its legitimacy. The sheet assertion of 'whiteness' over

'blackness' is no longer sufficient to sustain that authority. In law

used against them or for them, there is as much male fides as there is

bona fides. Aborigines then don't need to recover legal procedure so

much as to discover it. Bereft by law, often beset by legal constraint

and restraint, they need to find its uses and processes, to use the

instruments of their depression as their convivial tools for their

social and political change.

NOTES

1. Draft memorandum 'Notes for a Research Agenda on Aboriginal

    Political Development', 18 October 1981, addressed to Christine

    Jennett, Peter Loveday, Hilary Rumley, Colin Tatz and

    Myrna Tonkinson. It is likely this memo will be expanded and

    published.

2. Hyacinth Tungutalum for the Country-Liberal Party coalition from 1974 to 1977; Neville Perkins for the Australian Labor Party in August 1977 and again in June 1980; Eric Deeral for the National-Country Party from 1974 to 1977; Ernie Bridge for the Australian Labor Party in 1980; and Senator Bonner, elected in 1972 to represent the Liberal Party in Queensland.

3. The significant early body was the Aborigines Advancement League (AAL) in Victoria, the state with the fewest Aborigines and the most vociferous criticism. The AAL urged the creation of the Federal Council for the Advancement of Aborigines and Torres Strait Islanders (FCAATSI), born in 1957. In 1978 FCAATSI became the National Aboriginal and Islander Liberation Movement. Lamentably there has been no serious study of the origins, aims, personnel, functions, tactics, successes and failures of these organizations.

4. Gillespie and Others v Ford and Commonwealth of Australia [1978] 19 ALR 102.

5. Councillor Paul Mosaka's epitaph to the Natives' Representative Council on its voluntary demise, quoted in C. Tatz (1962: 116).

6. The National Aboriginal Conference's 1980 delegation to the UN in Geneva to explain to the world the Western Australian government's treatment of Aborigines, especially at Noonkanbah; the 1981 attempts by the Foundation for Aboriginal and Islander Research Action to inform (Commonwealth) Third World countries about Aboriginal conditions in Queensland as a reason for boycotting the 1982 Commonwealth Games in Brisbane; the opening of offices in Europe by Aboriginal groups seeking to spread

information about their treatment, led by Gary Foley;
Aboriginal representations to black Commonwealth Heads of
Government in Melbourne in September-October 1981; the
investigatory visit of the World Council of Churches in 1981;
all are important first beginnings in an attempt to
'internationalize' the Aboriginal situation.

7. Only recently has this subject become the matter of serious
scholarly analysis: see, for example, the journal Aboriginal
History, edited by Diane Barwick and T. Stannage; some of the
work of G.C. Bolton, P. Biskup, C. Rowley; H. Reynolds (1981)
and A.T. (Sandy) Yarwood (1982).

8. The Sydney Morning Herald, 19 September 1981.

9. The Age, 2 October 1981.

10. 'Statement by the Chief Minister of the Northern Territory on the
Central Land Council Document Background to Review of Aboriginal
Land Rights (Northern Territory) Act 1976'. This bound and
roneod document is undated, but from internal evidence it must be
September 1981. It contains a 16-page statement by Paul Everingham,
with 12 attachments. The quotations here are from p. 2 and p. 4.

11. Ibid. The CLC document is included, and it refers to one of the
attachments entitled (as Attachment 'D') 'Examination of Land
Rights Legislation: Submission by the Northern Territory Government'.
The material quoted here is from that attachment, at pp. 1 - 32.

12. Peinkinna and Others v Corporation of the Director of Aboriginal
and Islander Advancement, W. No. 553 of 1976, 5 October 1976.

13. The Corporation of the Director of Aboriginal and Islanders Advancement v Peinkinna and Others [1978] 52 ALR 286.

14. Reference on this case should be made to the second, third and fourth Annual Reports of the Commissioner for Community Relations and to the Aboriginal Law Bulletin, No. 1, August 1981: 8.

15. The Sydney Morning Herald, 17 September 1981. [See also The Sydney Morning Herald, 12 May 1982, for the High Court decision.]

16. Dick Mulwagu and Johnny Marali No. 1 v Northern Land Council, NT Supreme Court, No. 703/1978, 19 September 1978.

17. See The Canberra Times, 23 January and 14 February 1981; the Age, 15 and 23 January 1981 and The Sydney Morning Herald, 4 March 1981.

18. The Sydney Morning Herald, 19 September 1981.

REFERENCES

Berki, R.N.   1977 The History of Political Thought. Dent, London.

Dahl, R.   1970 Modern Political Analysis. Prentice-Hall, New Jersey.

Marx, E.   1976 The Social Context of Violent Behaviour: a social anthropological study in an Israeli immigrant town. Routledge and Kegan Paul, London.

Metcalf, H.C. and L. Urwick eds 1940 Dynamic Administration: the collected papers of Mary Parker Follett. Harper, New York.

Reynolds, H.   1981 The Other Side of the Frontier. James Cook University, Queensland.

Schall, J.V.   1978 The best form of government: a perspective on the continuity of political theory, The Review of Politics, Vol. 40, No. 1.

Tatz, C.   1962 Shadow and Substance in South Africa. Natal
                       University Press, Pietermaritzburg.

Tatz, C.   1979 Race Politics in Australia: Aborigines, politics
                       and law. University of New England Publishing Unit,
                       Armidale.

Tatz, C.   1982 Aborigines and Uranium and other essays. Heinemann
                       Educational Australia, Melbourne.

Yarwood, A.T. 1982 A History of Australian Race Relations. Cassell,
                       Sydney.

ON THE QUESTION OF GOVERNMENT

H.C. COOMBS

There are two predominant issues which arise from the land rights movement and government responses to it. The first and critical issue is where within our federal constitutional structure responsibility for government action lies. The second is what effect has the movement had upon Aboriginal institutions for the conduct of their own affairs, and for giving effect to the acknowledged policy of self-management of self-determination.

The seminal event for both these issues was the Woodward Report to the Whitlam government on Aboriginal land rights. This Report recommended, in brief:

1. That Aborigines should be able to obtain land in one of three ways:

   (a) By grant of freehold title to all lands which had been reserved for their use and benefit;

   (b) By claims to unalienated crown lands to which the relevant Aboriginal group could demonstrate title in Aboriginal law and custom; and

   (c) By claims to land necessary for their economic and social purposes -- such land to be purchased for them.

2. That, subject only to the emergency right of the government to proclaim that the national interest required otherwise, Aborigines were to have a right of veto on mineral and similar exploitative enterprises and the right to negotiate about the terms on which such enterprises would be allowed.

3. That, in negotiations with governments, with mining companies etc., Aborigines would be represented by regional, Land Councils of their own leaders chosen by their own methods who would have statutory responsibilities and resources adequate to these.

While the Woodward Report referred specifically to the recognition of Aboriginal land rights in the Northern Territory, it was clear to those involved at the time that the Report contemplated:

1.   That the principles underlying the recommendations were capable of quite general application in the various states and regions; but

2.   that there were significant differences in the historical and social circumstances of Aborigines in the various parts of Australia which would require consideration of the way in which those principles were applied in different contexts.

The government of the day, rightly I believe, interpreted the Report's recommendations as a guide to the various legislatures which would require adaptation to meet the differing needs and circumstances of Aborigines. Obvious examples of this need arose, for example, from the facts that:

(a)   In New South Wales, Victoria, Tasmania and large parts of other states, little land remained unalienated; and

(b)   in Queensland, Western Australia, and to a lesser extent in other states, it had been deliberate policy to move Aborigines away from their own traditional territory and consciously to seek to break their identification with those territories.

At the least, these considerations would have made necessary a shift of emphasis between the various means by which Aborigines could obtain land, giving greater weight to claims based on need and on the purchase of land in states where most land was alienated and where the links between Aborigines and the lands of their ancestors had been broken or seriously impaired.   The government, I believe, therefore expected the Woodward principles to be applied differently by the various legislatures but none-the-less expected them to be applied.   It was widely accepted at that time that the Referendum of 1967 had clearly placed responsibility for Aboriginal issues with the Commonwealth parliament while not precluding state influence necessary to ensure flexibility and local relevance of decisions made.

In the event, however, this deference to the right of the states
to achieve these purposes has been used to justify an acquiescence in
the rejection of the Woodward Report and the non-partisan acceptance of
it by all parties in the Commonwealth parliament. Again and again -- at
Aurukun and Mornington Island; at Archer River, where a state government
refused to transfer a pastoral lease purchased for them to an Aboriginal
community; at Noonkanbah, where a state government used the ultimate
coercive power of the state to over-rule the rights of Aborigines to protect
land they held sacred in the interests of foreign mining companies -- the
states concerned have openly and deliberately set at nought the policies
of the Commonwealth government.

Yet even today, the then Minister for Aboriginal Affairs (Senator Baume),
at a recent seminar in Sydney, asserted that, if it became necessary, the
Commonwealth would exercise its constitutional powers to legislate for
land rights for Aborigines. He argued that it was wise, however, for this
action to be delayed to enable it to be reached by consensus and with
concern for local circumstances. It is now almost eight years since the
Woodward Report was presented and endorsed in principle. What chance is
there of reaching a consensus if every defiance of those principles and
of Commonwealth authority during that time has been met by an abject
withdrawal by the Commonwealth? Yet I agree, local initiative is
preferable, as the South Australia Pitjantjatjara Land Rights legislation,
the outcome of patient and sympathetic negotiation with the Aborigines
concerned, demonstrates. But it must be initiative within the ambit
of a general set of principles which it is the responsibility of the
Commonwealth to determine.

May I offer a suggestion to the Minister concerned with Aboriginal
Affairs? I suggest that he write to the Premiers of all states other than

South Australia, drawing attention to ultimate Commonwealth authority

in this matter, to the principles of the Woodward Report and the Commonwealth

government's commitment to them, and inviting those Premiers to legislate

in accordance with those principles and in the light of local circumstances

before the end of next year. He could go on to inform them that, unless this

invitation is accepted, the Commonwealth government would present

legislation to its parliament to achieve these ends for application

throughout the Commonwealth, indicating that preparation of the necessary

legislation had been set in train. He might finally commend the

negotiating procedure adopted by the South Australian government in

reaching an understanding with the Pitjantjatjara peoples.

The recommendation that Aboriginal communities in various parts of

the Northern Territory would be represented in their dealings with

governments, mining companies and others by Councils of their own

leaders chosen by their own processes is an interesting and important

example of the recent emergence of Aboriginal political institutions.

Those institutions have their roots, to varying degrees, in the traditions

and practices of their own people, enabling them to deal with the tasks

and problems which confront them. Gatherings of clan and other group

leaders to deal with common organizational problems, and with the

resolution of conflicts, have long been an aspect of Aboriginal life,

however informal and unstructured their processes may appear to us.

Land Councils composed of leaders deriving their authority from the

traditional land owners have 'caught on'. Even where there has been

criticism and dissension within those councils, the essential rightness

of the institutional form seems widely accepted. Other land councils,

lacking perhaps the 'blessing of white authority', but deriving their

'political clout' from Aboriginal acceptance, have emerged and are emerging in all parts of Australia where significant Aboriginal populations exist, and there is increasing demand that greater authority, and resources, be entrusted to them.

But the land councils are examples only of an increasing class of political institutions concerned to express the political will and to exercise the administrative and executive capacity of Aboriginal people. From earlier years there were community councils which, despite difficulties from the conflicts arising from authority deriving on the one hand from government, and from traditional sources on the other, appear gradually to have resolved these and to function completely in the conduct of community business and administrative affairs. There are too, councils with wider geographical bases such as the Pitjantjatjara Council, the Central Australia Aboriginal Council, and more recently the Gagadju, Yolngu and Tiwi councils, with increasing competence and authority.

All of these are expressions in different contexts of demands by Aborigines to be able to manage their own affairs, and to share in political power. These demands range from those of the Torres Strait Islanders who seek a kind of 'Commonwealth territory' status independent of Queensland and with the right to secede to join a Pacific Island confederation in due course, to others which are less comprehensive but equally positive in their search for significant autonomy. Among these are the demands of local communities to be able to control their own schools, their curricula, their staffing and the emphasis on Aboriginal purposes rather than on those of Australia-European society. There is at the moment a proposal for the Pitjantjatjara Council to control all the schools in its territory for these purposes. In Yirrkala the local elders have submitted to the Australian Law Reform Commission plans for the recognition of Aboriginal customary law, for the establishment of

Aboriginal community courts whose procedures would be based upon a modified form of their traditional dispute-settling practices.

Clearly Aboriginal political life is in a ferment -- a ferment in which institutions deriving their authority from Australian-European governments and their agencies are suspect and where innovation and controversy provide the prevailing tone. This ferment is healthy. Inherent in its various forms is the persistent intention of Aborigines to maintain continuity with their past and to preserve the essence of their Aboriginality and the values it expresses. We would be wise to trust their political ingenuity and the wisdom which has enabled them to survive more than 40,000 years on this continent. The world may well have need of both.

MINING VENTURES: ALLIANCES AND OPPOSITIONS

RONALD M. BERNDT

The Australian experience of mining in recent years has been mixed. It has been subject to considerable protest. On one hand, the nation is said to be irretrievably harmed through large-scale mining; on the other, its very life is said to depend on the exploitation of natural resources. Somewhere in between these two extremes lies a kind of social no-man's land, where opinions are just as strongly expressed but are not always heard; and if they are heard, are often misunderstood. I do not propose to look at these wider issues, except to say that in a sense mining companies are often caught in between the cross-fire of differing views and actions. In spite of the power they wield, they are inevitably targets in this respect.

Where mining takes place in areas occupied by Aborigines, or in country in which they have traditional interests, whether or not Aboriginal land rights are recognized, it is Aborigines who are caught 'in between' — in between governments (state or federal) and their agents and agencies, and the mining companies and their operations. No such Aboriginal community has escaped socially unscathed, or has not emerged from such an experience markedly different from what it was before the advent of mining. There are enough examples from various parts of the country to substantiate such a statement: from Weipa to Nhulunbuy, from Jabiru to Lake Argyle, from Noonkanbah to any other area where Aborigines are or have been involved. However enlightened a mining company may be in its consideration for Aborigines within its sphere of interest, a basic assumption must be that, in such circumstances, the effects of the impact are far-reaching. At least, it will lead to considerable changes — changes which are not reversible, and will surely cause some hardship and upset. (See R. and C. Berndt 1980:38-49; R. Berndt 1981a:3-15.)

It is not simply that mining is changing the face of the Australian countryside. It is seriously affecting people. Whether mining is or is not desirable, in general terms, is beyond the frame of my discussion. What is relevant, is what is taking place in areas strategically important to Aborigines. There are three components to this: the social effects of mining; the attitudes of Aborigines who are on the receiving end; and the degree to which a social science like Anthropology can serve as an ameliorating intermediary. The last point involves a further issue. This is the extent to which Anthropology can directly help Aborigines to counteract perceived wrongs emerging from such mining and, within the context of changing situations, can aid them in planning for the future, helping to ensure that their community life is sustained.

Alliances:

Such a relationship between Aborigines and anthropologists as I imply here, suggests a special kind of alignment. An anthropologist's fieldwork within a particular area, with a particular people, ideally means that both parties meet on common ground — on some common ground — even though their separate expectations may differ, and indeed often do. Essentially, every field experience is based on a cooperative undertaking in which Aborigines are teachers, anthropologists are learners. This is the only satisfactory way of achieving understanding and explanation. (See R. and C. Berndt 1981:524-5.) In the process, ties of varying strength are built up, some extending far beyond the initial field period, and some involving strong emotional attachment. In other words, although greater understanding of socio-personal problems may engender mixed feelings from time to time, more often than not it may lead to an alliance which implies some identification of interests. I don't think this necessarily blinds an anthropologist to disciplinary aims of relative objectivity. What I am saying is that anthropologists find themselves in a special position where they can be of direct help to Aborigines who for one reason or another are unable to help themselves. And in mining situations this is often the case. The fact that an anthropologist has come into an Aboriginal community (traditional or otherwise), is accepted there, and eventually reaches some degree of familiarity and understanding, must mean a measure of commitment to the people involved. It is not easy, or proper, to push such a commitment aside.

This relationship between particular Aborigines and particular anthropologists is qualitatively different from that which exists between Aborigines and most other intermediaries and agents. There are undoubtedly some notable exceptions. The point is that a positive alliance is usually found between Aborigines and an anthropologist who has experienced with them, over a sustained period of time, a series of events which concern them crucially.

There are of course many other non-Aboriginal persons, with or without direct contact with Aborigines, who align themselves in this way for particular purposes. In gross terms, such persons could be thought of as 'the great unnumbered supporters' of Aborigines; and, in being so, they are none the less important. But because they are not necessarily uniformly committed to Aboriginal interests, or not consistently so, they could also be thought of as being nominally neutral.

As intermediaries go, there are a number of other persons who do have varying alignments with Aborigines — for instance, those who stand in relation to Aborigines as employees: as advisers, managers, liaison officers, consultants, legal personnel and so on, some professionally trained, others not. Irrespective of where the money to employ them comes from, by the nature of their employment they are either nominally

neutral, or positively allied to Aborigines in a specific or general way.

This category really requires a great deal more consideration, because it

includes non-Aboriginal welfare and social workers, missionaries, health

and educational officers and so forth, whose commitments vis-à-vis

Aborigines vary quite considerably. A school teacher working under

Aboriginal auspices in an all-Aboriginal school is obviously in a special

position. One point that is important in determining the nature of an

alliance is 'working for', in contrast to 'working with'. 'Working for'

implies an employer-employee relationship, with lines of direction

relatively well-defined: that is, in connection with organizations and

community councils which may be managed or run by Aborigines, and where

'loyalty' on the part of those persons employed is assumed, or is part

of the obligation of employment.

The situation, however, is by no means as simple as this, especially

with regard to legal personnel. (See R. Berndt 1981b: 15). It is more

clear-cut in the case of government employees appointed to administer

Aboriginal affairs. Rules, regulations and ministerial directions,

whether state or federal, loom large in all forms of social practice and

action connected with them. The same thing applies also where majority

Aboriginal control is involved, as in the Aboriginal Development

Commission, the National Aboriginal Conference, the National Aboriginal

Education Congress, etc.: obviously, Aboriginal interests predominate

in such contexts, but are limited by governmental control. Nevertheless,

broadly speaking, within this whole category under the rubric of

'government', there is nominally a positive alliance, although one that

is liable to considerable fluctuation, depending on a range of factors.

A particular crisis involving Aboriginal interests, resulting in government

action being taken or not taken in relation to it, can change the tenor
of the alliance overnight: it can easily become negative, or at best
a neutral one, on the basis of Aboriginal evaluation; or it can change
to opposition, where neutrality is not easily recoverable.

Where it comes to mining, vested interests are more obvious, and
any alliance that may exist is one of mutual convenience, essentially
transitory, and likely to shift to and fro along the positive-negative
continuum. Opposition on the part of mining-affected members of an
Aboriginal community may be latent, but sometimes quite strong, or
potentially so, within a context of assumed cooperation. Clearly, it
would be impossible to lump together all companies involved in mining
and speak of them in either wholly positive or wholly negative terms.
Much depends on the individual companies, and on the degree to which
they have 'prepared the way', or prepared a way, that could lead to
their getting what they want. But equally important is the extent to
which a government recognizes Aboriginal land rights, protects Aboriginal
sites of significance, and provides safeguards against community upset,
as well as opportunities for Aborigines to negotiate with a mining
company that seeks to operate on their land (whichever way Aboriginal
rights to that land are defined). Outside the Northern Territory and
north-west South Australia, no other state provides officially for
royalties accruing from mining or for compensation to be paid directly
to Aborigines. But the economic aspect is important to Aborigines, as
it is to the mining companies and also, not least, to the governments
concerned.

The situation in Western Australia:

I turn now to Western Australia. The state's involvement in mining
is fairly well-known. Although the recent boom has been slightly

modified owing to the Australia-wide economic depression, mining as such gives little appearance of contracting in the immediate future. In the Pilbara, despite some difficulties in employee-employer relations, it is now at full operational level. In the Kimberleys, however, it is just beginning. I shall concentrate on that region, plus the Western Desert, with Balgo at its most northerly point, and mining interests expanding southward into the Great Sandy Desert.

These areas have the greatest concentration of Aborigines, many still living in or near their traditional territories. (See R. and C. Berndt eds 1979/1980.) Past events have contributed to this. The whole region was traditionally divided among a number of more or less distinctive socio-cultural, linguistic and territorially-based groupings. Religious and trading ties linked them together in varying degrees of closeness, on the basis of common interests. This patterning was maintained, up to a point, during the period when Aborigines were caught up in the pastoral industry. They were able to keep something of their traditional culture, including beliefs about land ownership. As they saw it, the land was being only temporarily used by outsiders: it had not been alienated from its real owners. With the implementation of the Pastoral Award in 1968, large numbers of Aborigines who had been living on their 'own' land within various pastoral runs were forced to move out. They settled in such centres as Fitzroy Crossing, Halls Creek and Kununurra and northwest coastal towns. (See R. Berndt 1979:18-19.) This exodus raised both immediate and long-term problems, specifically about their employment, and more generally about sources of livelihood for themselves and their families. Also, it raised for Aborigines, many of whom were still traditionally-oriented, new questions about their rights in and to land they had always considered to be their own. These questions were highlighted by what they heard about developments in the Northern

Territory in regard to land rights: state boundaries are almost
irrelevant in social communication between them. It was in this context
that the Kimberley Land Council later came into being. The Council is
seen primarily as a unifying organization, concerned with Aboriginal
land and all matters resulting from Aboriginal-European contact; but
it has not yet succeeded in achieving official state government
recognition. Another series of episodes early in 1981 had a fair amount
of publicity in what were often confused and conflicting news reports.
Aborigines were expelled when Gordon Downs pastoral station, one of the
last Vestey properties, changed hands. Eventually a temporary reserve was
set up, later transformed into a permanent one, at Ringer's Soak (on
Gordon Downs property).

Several other things of importance to Aborigines were happening
too. Through federal government support, some Aboriginal groups were
able to obtain pastoral leaseholds; one such was Noonkanbah. These
enabled them to set up small communities under their own management.
Such leases are approved under the same conditions as set down for
non-Aborigines. The Aboriginal Lands Trust, which holds these leases,
also holds all Aboriginal reserve land 'for the benefit and usage of
Aborigines'. In 1977, this made up 8.07 per cent of the total area of
Western Australia. The greater part of it is in the Western Central
Reserve, but an appreciable area of reserve land is located in the
Kimberleys: mostly small holdings, but at least nine of reasonably
large size. Royalties from mining on Aboriginal reserve land, in varying
proportions, can be paid into the funds of the Aboriginal Lands Trust,
which is made up of Aboriginal members who are under the direction of
the relevant minister: but only a small amount of money has yet found
its way to the Trust. Officially, no royalties or compensation are
payable directly to Aboriginal communities or to persons associated with

specific land, and none to Aborigines on non-reserve land or occupying leasehold properties.

I should add that mission control of particular settlements is being wound down — at Lombadina, Kalumburu and, recently, Balgo — and being transferred to Aboriginal councils. That means, in practice, the intrusion of non-Aboriginal advisers and managers. In the Balgo area also, Aborigines, worried about the expansion of mining activities, have petitioned the Aboriginal Lands Trust for an extension of the Balwina Reserve.

The Aboriginal Cultural Material Committee was downgraded (through amendments to the relevant Act) following the Noonkanbah crisis. It is now merely advisory and, in effect, subordinated to the Trustees of the Western Australian Museum, who are responsible for its administration under the direction of the minister. This Committee is a strategic government-sponsored body which despite its current shortcomings can, or could, play a useful role. Its function is to record, preserve and protect Aboriginal sites of significance, whether they are archaeological or of immediate concern to living Aborigines. Such reserves, and land recommended to and approved by the minister, are vested in the Museum on behalf of Aborigines (or sometimes interpreted as on behalf of the wider community), and are not included in the land held by the Trust. Without going into details here, I note two points. One is the degree to which Aborigines can manage their own sites. The other is the limitations imposed on the Committee in regard to ministerial and other political control; and, more importantly, the extent to which recommendations can take into account socio-political issues. In order to reach a decision about the protection of sites from mining or other activities, survey research is needed, and some provision is made for

this. It has two facets, archaeological and anthropological, usually
handled by different people.

Depending on the area, the social anthropological type of survey
involves working directly with Aborigines. The archaeological type of
survey also usually takes into account the views of interested Aborigines.
The anthropological task is, basically, to make an ethnographic study
focusing on people-land relationships: to see the sites in their socio-
cultural context, and to document Aboriginal attitudes and wishes
regarding them. Many of the surveys are being carried out by staff of
the Museum's Department of Sites; but the expansion of mining operations
is so rapid and so extensive that archaeological and social anthropological
contractors have been sought. These are nominated by the Registrar of
Sites, and work as consultants to the mining company concerned. Reports
arising from this arrangement come to the Registrar and the Sites
Committee for evaluation. It is important to remember that there is no
direct government injunction or legal force which can compel a mining
company to accept or sponsor such surveys. Whether or not they do so,
depends on 'goodwill' on their part, and their interest in visibly
maintaining good public relations (specifically, vis-à-vis Aborigines).

One major issue is that a survey of this kind is usually funded by
the particular company. Another is that usually a limited period of
time is stipulated. This is not necessarily conducive to maintaining
high research standards: a detailed survey is not possible in a few
days or even in a few weeks. As well, not enough social anthropologists
are available, and some who do take on the task may find themselves
operating only a few paces away from the oncoming bulldozers. For a
variety of reasons, of procedure or substance or both, conflicting views
and aims can surface between anthropologists and mining companies.

As far as I know, most anthropological consultants are motivated by high professional standards, and believe they are doing a job which is in the direct interests of Aborigines — and indirectly, in broad perspective, in the interests of the wider Australian society. They are also concerned that Aboriginal views and attitudes will be conveyed in their reports. The fact remains, that they are paid by a specific company. But if no money is available from other sources, do we simply shrug our shoulders and do nothing about the urgent tasks in hand? If anthropologists won't become involved, who will be? And shouldn't mining companies, or anyone else who wants to use a situation for commercial gain, or potential gain, have obligations, including financial obligations, in that situation? Personally, I see money as merely a means to an end. What really matters is the conditions which may or may not be attached to it.

The question of morality in this respect is inescapable. In these circumstances, it is not surprising that one social anthropologist, questioning the timing and the appropriateness or otherwise of commencing seismic work in an area that had not been sufficiently surveyed, was recently told 'You are a company man, now!'. 'Loyalty' to an employer is one theme here, professional ethical issues are another, and together they underline the presence of conflicting alliances. In a sense, such conflicts are apparent in the deliberations of the Aboriginal Cultural Material Advisory Committee (in W.A.), which aims, ideally, to be as objective as possible in considering the cases before it. Yet objectivity is only part of the issue where a people's struggle for rights, and for justice is concerned. Objectivity can work either way, for or against, and not necessarily in regard to how a people feel about a particular problem which faces them.

Obviously, alliances in this context are not straightforward; and oppositions, potential or otherwise, are inherent in it but can take different forms. Aboriginal opinion also varies, as one would expect it to do — but more in terms of how to approach particular problems, than in regard to basic issues: on land and sites, or community welfare, Aboriginal heritage, and identity, there is striking unanimity. One of the major difficulties, as I see it, relates to what have been called 'cultural brokers', or active intermediaries. Aside from individual persons, in the situation I am outlining there are three primary ones: the Aboriginal Lands Trust, the Aboriginal Cultural Material Advisory Committee, and the officially still unrecognized Kimberley Land Council. Although the first and the third have Aboriginal membership, the second has only minor Aboriginal representation (although it has been trying to extend this). The Trust is concerned with acquiring, holding and managing land for the benefit of Aborigines, the Cultural Material Committee with the preservation and protection of sites, and the Council with Aboriginal land and everything related to that. Each in its own way deals with issues relevant to mining. Only two can, in present circumstances, advise the relevant state minister, who has the legal right to make a final decision. The Department of Sites of the Western Australian Museum, which, with its Committee, 'administers' the Aboriginal Heritage Act (i.e., regarding sites), has trained anthropological and archaeological personnel; and an anthropologist (with Australian Institute of Aboriginal Studies funding) is attached to the Kimberley Land Council. But there is no committee or executive body especially concerned with the broader issues of Aboriginal land or with problems which may arise (for instance) from mining; no recognized body to mediate in negotiations between Aborigines and the companies involved;

none to discuss compensation and royalties, or the effects mining may have on Aboriginal communities; nor to cope with crises as they arise. The Department of Aboriginal Affairs, in its federal and state contexts, is directly involved, as is the Aboriginal Legal Service, and the National Aboriginal Conference, through its state-elected members. But the hands of the state Aboriginal advisory committees are tied, and the state Department of Community Welfare is, officially, only peripherally concerned. In general, however, as a result of the Noonkanbah crisis, the wings of 'the cultural brokers' have been severely clipped, and many avenues which could have been available to deal with the issues relevant to mining have been virtually closed.

Noonkanbah and after:

The 1980 Noonkanbah controversy achieved nothing positive for Aborigines, but it was cathartic, and had repercussions both within and outside Australia. It hardened governmental opinion and action in various ways. Moreover, from a rather different angle, it made mining companies wary, and obliquely critical, of a state government which was so slow to articulate a fair and reasonable policy on Aboriginal land, and Aboriginal options in regard to mining activities and relations with the companies involved.

The Noonkanbah crisis, clumsily handled, was allowed to escalate beyond the point where negotiations could have ameliorated ill-feeling and obvious injustice. All that Aborigines wanted in this case was to retain the integrity of their community life, to safeguard the material representations of their religion (in the shape of sacred sites and areas surrounding them), and to carry on with their work on a leasehold that had been specifically granted to them for pastoral purposes. Initially, Aborigines did not oppose mining per se; but they did resist the way in which mining took precedence over their own urgent needs, without consultation. They, and a very wide assortment of other people, were

incredulous and shocked by the culminating sequence of events in this
drama: when the Western Australian government arranged for a convoy of
trucks under police protection to convey drilling equipment to
Noonkanbah — actually, against the wishes of the mining company and of
the company controlling the drilling rigs. The subterfuge surrounding
the actual drilling made it very clear to Aborigines where they stood
in the opinion of the government. As it turned out, the drilling proved
unsuccessful. In general, this confrontation activated the alliances
and oppositions already present in the situation. The various news
media supported a public outcry, which had continent-wide and also
overseas repercussions. Mining companies avoided making statements for
or against, at least at the public level. The state government resented
and opposed federal ministerial attempts at negotiation (by Senator
F. Chaney). The Aboriginal Cultural Material Committee, which had
arranged for surveys in the area and had recommended the protection of
the sites in question, was dampened down by the relevant state minister's
imposition of 'a direction' to the Museum's Trustees to reverse the
Committee's recommendations.

Conditions have not really changed much since the Noonkanbah affair,
except that the reputation of Western Australia in regard to Aboriginal
rights has appreciably deteriorated. The lessons which could have been
learnt from that débacle were not, even though they were spelt out in
considerable detail. Mining and drilling have continued elsewhere in
the Kimberleys, with the Kimberley Land Council, among others,
increasingly disturbed about the ways in which this has been taking
place.

I will mention briefly three examples, each different, and each
likely to have differing results for the Aborigines involved. By far

the most complex involves at least three principal companies with interests in oil, although mixed-resource investigation rights are, so I understand, included. This relates to Balgo-Malan (Lake Gregory)-Billiluna, and southern areas extending to the Stansmore Range and farther south, south-west and south-east. We can think of this whole region as being 'wide open'. By this I mean that Aborigines who continue to have close ties with this country (although some are also resident outside it) are extremely vulnerable. The second area relates to Lake Argyle-Turkey Creek, near the Ord River. We can call this project one of 'profit and loss': 'profit' because public statements have indicated that its diamond deposits are especially rich; and 'loss' because of the destruction of sacred sites. The third is the Mitchell Plateau on the Admiralty Gulf, currently unoccupied by Aborigines, but containing many sites which are the concern of members of the Mowanjum (Derby) and Kalumburu (north-east of the Plateau) communities. I call this 'a private affair' because, although it is being run by the same company as the Lake Argyle venture (C.R.A.), and is concerned with bauxite mining, the Aborigines are clearly cooperative and wish to deal with the company directly themselves.

The Mitchell Plateau example is interesting. As in all these areas, anthropological and archaeological surveys are being or have been carried out. With the Plateau, reports have not yet been completed and no recommendations have been made. The people who originally belonged to the region (and vice versa) now live elsewhere. The focus of interest is on places which are significant to them, and on previous habitation sites: direct impact is, therefore, less relevant. However, they still see it as their own land, and have expectations of establishing a settlement there, with full facilities, under the auspices of the company. This means that negotiations have taken place between Aborigines and mining representatives, but the nature of these has not been made public. Moreover, there has been no willingness on their part to have Kimberley Land Council intervention.

As far as the Lake Argyle region is concerned, the major mining area is on the Blatchford escarpment, and directly affects Aborigines of the Warmun community (Turkey Creek) as well as those at the Mandangala out-station and some at Kununurra. Several fairly detailed anthropological and archaeological surveys have been made, and each includes recommendations, the most recent (1981) by an anthropologist who is a consultant to the C.R.A. The C.R.A. made no contact with interested Aborigines prior to the commencement of its programme of exploration. Aborigines, on discovering that such activity was taking place, approached the C.R.A. and asked for a Western Australian Museum survey. In the process, it was found that some sites had been damaged, including one of considerable importance. After a series of events, an agreement was eventually signed (in 1980) with members of the Mandangala community, who constituted only a proportion of the traditional owners of the area, without initial benefit of legal advice. This agreement was held to be to the detriment of traditional owners residing in the Warmun community. Recommendations were made in one of the survey reports (on behalf of the Australian Institute of Aboriginal Studies, the Western Australian Museum, and the Aborigines involved), but not all were accepted by the government. The Warmun community is at present seeking an on-going social-impact study in order to monitor operations at Argyle, since full-scale mining in the area is likely to commence in 1985.

The Balgo situation is complex and covers a very large area of land. Two companies are involved (Mobil and Ranger Oil), with a third (Shell) preparing to operate in the south. The three major communities (Balgo, Malan, and Billiluna) are virtually surrounded and in some respects permeated; the impact of mining activities is immediate and direct. The first two companies sought anthropological advice prior to their initial investigations; and anthropological and archaeological surveys are either completed, or in the process of being so. Fortunately, too, part of the exploration is on Aboriginal reserve land which the people are attempting to have extended; but much of it is not. Because of the fairly detailed knowledge we have of this area, it is likely that major sites will be protected. However, seismic work and developmental plans are so pressing that insufficient time is permitted for additional anthropological investigation. While there are potential dangers to the local environment, as mining activities get under way with large quantities of equipment and personnel, the real dangers (in both short- and long-range terms) lie in the direction of community disruption. The Aborigines in this area are still traditionally-oriented, they see the country as indisputably theirs, and their religious sites are of particular importance to them. As with our other two examples, negotiations have already taken place between the Aboriginal Councils and the mining companies; but the terms of these are not officially known, and they operate primarily at the level of 'goodwill' gestures.

From the Aborigines' point of view, each situation is quite unprecedented, something which they never contemplated could happen to them. Consequently, they have no available precedents which might help them to manage or mitigate the resultant impact. Expectations on their part vary; but in the circumstances, there is no surety about any of these. In their experience, the government has been mainly negative in its mining policy — negative for them. It is true that reserves, where

they exist, do provide some protection — as the Aboriginal Cultural
Material Committee does, or tries to do, for specific sites. But there
is little supporting structure for them to call upon. When Aborigines
express willingness to cooperate with mining companies, they do not,
and cannot, really understand the social and personal implications for
themselves. In fact, the only alternative to cooperation is outright
opposition, which they do realize could rebound on them.

On the other hand, mining companies recognize the need to collaborate
with Aborigines within their areas of operation, as a necessary component
of resource development. To put it baldly, an 'alliance' must take
place if the work is to proceed smoothly, and if the aims of the project
are to be realized. (To quote: 'We don't want another Noonkanbah!'.)
This is primarily a commercial alliance, phrased in terms of financial
gain. This point, and the fact that a government demands its pound of
flesh in so far as mining revenues are concerned, are not lost on
Aborigines. Contrary to public opinion, Aborigines are not lost in a
haze of mystical or spiritual, non-materialistic belief. They are, have
to be, vitally aware of their own material welfare — because few others
are. It is, therefore, not incongruous to find that, other things being
equal (as they never really are), Aborigines look upon mining in their
own areas with mixed feelings. While they see mining companies as being
essentially unpredictable, they nevertheless see also that these
companies potentially represent — at least during the period of the actual
operations — a resource which should be exploited. In this respect,
their aims and those of the mining companies coincide. But, and this
is where there are crucial differences, the stakes vary markedly.

Toward a more balanced approach:

Aborigines are not, or should not be, simply pawns in a rather abstract game of deadly seriousness, being played out in our midst: a game which is often one-sided and phrased almost entirely in terms of wealth, as well as in the guise of being in the national interest — and in the interest of Australia's national prosperity. A question we must ask is, what are participants in that game getting out of it, and how will the game itself affect the players. As in all games, there are losers. For Aborigines, the stakes are high, much higher than for mining companies and government, but of a different order, possessed of a quality which is not always recognized and cannot necessarily be translated into negotiable forms.

As we have seen, in Western Australia negotiations are taking place, unofficially, on the initiative of mining companies because social conditions demand that they should; and because, if they were not taking place, disruption to mining programmes could easily occur. There are no positive official procedures to deal with such circumstances, no official delineation of compensation payable to Aborigines in affected areas, and no enforceable rule to ensure that anthropological and archaeological surveys are set in train before mining exploration begins. So much depends on the 'goodwill' of mining companies and on the assumed acquiescence of Aborigines. The only legal requirements are that sites of significance be protected, provided archaeological and/or anthropological justification is forthcoming and recommendations are acceptable to the government; and that the mining regulations be adhered to. There are obvious incongruities here. As I have noted, 8.07 per cent of the whole of Western Australia is held in trust by the government 'for the benefit of Aborigines'. What that 'benefit' means is not clear.

Real benefit can accrue to Aborigines only if they are able to have some officially recognized, more or less permanent rights in and to and over that land.

The time has clearly come when the government should transfer its rights of trust in reserve land held in the name of Aborigines to the Aborigines themselves — in the names of community councils, traditional owners, organizations, etc. Suggestions have been made from time to time, most recently by one government department, that all Aboriginal reserves should be closed. This would be a retrogressive step. Too much Aboriginal reserve land has already been transferred to other, non-Aboriginal usage. Reserve land should serve as a basis for Aboriginal land rights claims. The passing over of land that is already earmarked for Aboriginal benefit is not likely to inconvenience either the government, or other members of the wider non-Aboriginal society.

One matter needs immediate attention. That is, the long-overdue official provisions in regard to mining on land occupied by or otherwise associated with Aborigines. These provisions should cover several points. (a) Protecting and safeguarding sites of significance to Aborigines — not, as now, as isolated entities but as sites within their environmental contexts. (b) Formalization of discussions with Aboriginal communities before, not merely after, any mining exploration is planned. (c) Sufficient time for archaeological and anthropological surveys to be completed and reported on before any decision is made that mining should take place. (d) Anthropological reports at present do not go beyond discussion of living sites and what they mean to contemporary Aborigines. There are no official social impact studies which take into account the likely effects of mining on specific communities, and their implications for Aborigines. (e) Simultaneously, there should be opportunities for official negotiations to take place between Aborigines, the government (through its representatives), and the mining companies concerned. (f) Such negotiations would need to take into account the attitudes of Aborigines — whether or not they wanted mining to take place in their area of influence; and, if so, under what conditions and in relation to what compensation and/or royalty payments, community safeguards and so forth. These are minimal and essential prerequisites.

I made my first official submissions in these terms to the Western Australian government in April 1980, at the height of the Noonkanbah crisis. My most recent attempt was in September 1981; and other persons and organizations have done likewise. The situation has not appreciably changed — except in a hardening of views on the part of Aborigines, and the continued evidence that mining companies require governmental guidelines which take into account the interests of Aborigines as well as their own. Alliances between Aborigines and non-Aborigines continue to exist, along with oppositions. But the real point I am making is that oppositions, instead of hardening as they have been since the Noonkanbah crisis, could just as easily be considerably modified to the advantage of the main protagonists — in what is, for Aborigines, a drama of considerable importance. In one sense, it is for them a drama of life and partial death — spiritual and social, if not physical death. For mining companies, it is a commercial undertaking. For governments, it is largely a matter of administration and the acquisition of revenue. The only losers in this game, to date, have been Aborigines — and yet, however important other kinds of involvement may be, or seem to be, their stakes are higher than anyone else's.

REFERENCES

Berndt, R.M. 1979 Aboriginal Australians: contrasts in involvement.
In European Impact on the West Australian Environment,
1829-1979 (B. de Garis ed.). The University of Western
Australia, Perth.

Berndt, R.M. 1981a The Australian Aboriginal experience, Optima,
Vol. 30, No. 1.

Berndt, R.M. 1981b A long view: some personal comments on land rights,
Australian Institute of Aboriginal Studies, Newsletter,
No. 16.

Berndt, R.M. and C.H. eds. 1979/1980 Aborigines of the West: their
past and their present. University of Western Australia
Press for the Education Committee of the 150th Anniversary
Celebrations, Perth. (See Chapter 1 by R. Berndt.)

Berndt, R.M. and C.H. 1980 Oenpelli, then and now: a brief overview.
Australian Institute of Aboriginal Studies Newsletter,
No. 14.

Berndt, R.M. and C.H. 1981 The World of the First Australians.
Lansdowne Press, Sydney. (Revised ed.)